The **MIDI** files

The **MIDI** files

ROB YOUNG

PRENTICE HALL

LONDON   NEW YORK   TORONTO   SYDNEY   TOKYO
SINGAPORE   MADRID   MEXICO CITY   MUNICH

First published 1996 by
Prentice Hall Europe
Campus 400, Maylands Avenue
Hemel Hempstead
Hertfordshire HP2 7EZ
A division of
Simon & Schuster International Group

Typeset in 11/13pt Melior
by PPS, London Road, Amesbury, Wilts.

Printed and bound in Great Britain by
T. J. Press (Padstow) Ltd

Library of Congress Cataloguing-in-Publication Data

Young, Rob.
   The MIDI files / Rob Young.
      p. cm.
   Includes indexes.
   ISBN 0–13–262403–6 (pb)
      1. MIDI (Standard)   2. Computer sound processing.   I. Title.
MT723.Y66   1996
784.19'0285'46–dc20   96–24950
                                                                  CIP
                                                                   MN

British Library Cataloguing in Publication Data

A catalogue record for this book is available from
the British Library

ISBN 0–13–262403–6 (pbk)

---

 3 4 5   00 99 98 97

Trademarks

All product and company names are ™ or ® trademarks of their owners.

Cadenza is a trademark of Big Noise Software Inc.
Cakewalk is a trademark of Twelve Tone Systems.
Cubase is a trademark of Steinberg Soft- und Hardware GmbH.
Apple-Macintosh is a registered trademark of Apple Computers Inc.
Atari, ST, STe, TT & Falcon are registered trademarks of Atari
     Corporation
Microsoft, MS-DOS and Windows are registered trademarks of
     Microsoft Corporation.
Roland & GS are registered trademarks of Roland Corporation.
Yamaha is a registered trademark of Yamaha Corporation.

This is dedicated with love to
Mum, Dad and Graham

Contents

2: MIDI Protocols

3:   Programming Techniques

4: Tricks and Effects 124

10: Appendices 278

Acknowledgements

For their inspiration, input and support, a few people should take a bow.

Thanks especially to . . .

. . . Leighton & Chris and all the great folk at *MidiMagic International*

. . . Karen & the guys of *Silhouette*

. . . Graeme, for asking the kind of question that makes you think

. . . Jan, for starting the whole thing

. . . family & friends for prof-readnig the orignial draught

Get in touch – we'd like to hear from you!

Your opinion counts

If you have any comments about this book – positive or negative, long or short – please send them in. We want to refine our books according to the needs of our readers, so do tell us if there is something that you would like to see in future editions of this book. Your input could well appear in print! We genuinely appreciate it when people take the time to contact us, so every month we give away a free Prentice Hall computer book for the most helpful and comprehensive comments.

Please feel free to email me personally with your comments:

feedback@prenhall.co.uk

Or you can write to me:

Jason Dunne
Prentice Hall
Campus 400
Maylands Avenue
Hemel Hempstead
Herts.
HP2 7EZ
United Kingdom

Please note that Prentice Hall cannot serve as a technical resource for questions about hardware or software problems.

We would also love to hear your ideas for new books, whether it is just for a book that you want to see in print or one you intend writing yourself. Our guide for new authors can be found in the back of this book.

Thanks for choosing Prentice Hall.

Jason Dunne
Acquisition Editor, Prentice Hall

jdunne@prenhall.co.uk

Intro

Welcome to *The MIDI Files* – the indispensable guide to everything you ever wanted to know about MIDI and programming!

The Book . . .

From the moment you first consider grounding your ship on the iceberg we call MIDI, you need information. Choosing the basic elements of your MIDI setup, hooking them all up so they'll 'speak' to one another, and making your first faltering steps into programming a piece of music can be a frustratingly hit-and-miss affair. Then there are the various types of MIDI message, file-format and protocol: which to use, and why, and how? Finally you want to hone your programming skills, to get a more realistic performance from 'real' instruments, improve your mixing techniques and try out some of the sound-manipulation effects you hear on records.

The MIDI Files covers all this and a lot more, to help you graduate from beginner to seasoned pro at your own pace. The programming sections are geared towards creating a cover-version file of an existing recording (the most popular scenario), but the same skills apply equally to programming original material. And *programming* is the name of the game here: technical data is kept to a bare minimum, and the emphasis is placed squarely on using and getting the best results from MIDI. But we don't leave you to do it alone.

The Files . . .

The accompanying floppy disk contains a collection of files illustrating many of the techniques and effects covered in the text. Being able to

I

read about it, hear it and analyse it before trying it out yourself makes the whole learning process faster and more enjoyable. You'll also find an *extra* set of MIDI compositions (prefixed with an 'x') which are not referenced to any particular topic in the book, but give a wider view of MIDI programming in general.

The files are all General MIDI-compatible, with the slight exception that they've been saved in an 'exploded' type 1 Standard MIDI File format to make it easier to study an individual channel's events. To help tie things down to a common thread, all references to patches, song-header layout and beat/tick references are given from the perspective of General MIDI which is by far the most widely used commercial programming standard. If you're not using General MIDI-compatible gear – don't worry! The programming techniques are just the same, and you've probably got a wider range of sounds and controllers than the General MIDI specification offers. Converting the GM files to suit your own setup is usually a quick and easy process, described on page 289.

How To Use *The Midi Files*

The book is divided into ten *Sections*, each containing a collection of short *Topics* to save you wading through oceans of text to find the bit you want, plus comprehensive **Glossary** and **Index** sections to make quick reference easier. The language has been kept as simple as possible throughout, but jargon can't be completely avoided: occasional bits and pieces won't make immediate sense to the beginner (like the *Files* heading on the previous page, for example) but all will become clear further down the line. Many of the topics end with a ***Detours*** area containing links to related topics.

For Newcomers . . .

If you're dipping your toe into the waters of MIDI for the first time, we suggest you work through each section in turn – particularly the tutorial section ***1: Introduction To MIDI***. You may prefer to ignore the ***Detours*** at the end of some of the topics and just reckon you'll get to 'em when you get to 'em!

The **Channel Messages Menu** contains a second tutorial to guide you through the MIDI commands you'll be using most: we'll give you a prompt to skip to that section along the way to cover all the basics in a structured progression.

You might find it useful to have your sequencer running as you read, so that you can try out some of the ideas and suggestions, and load files from the accompanying disk.

Above all, don't worry about trying to remember every bit of info being thrown at you – with the benefits of the **Glossary** and **Index** you'll find it easy to locate any explanations or definitions you need any time.

For Experienced MIDI-users . . .

It really depends what you want to know! It's all here, from the basic to the advanced. The first two sections cover MIDI-basics, studio setup and allied troubleshooting, together with data-formats and protocols.

Section *3: **Programming Techniques*** takes a more in-depth look at MIDI programming from a commercial stand-point and section *4: **Tricks & Effects*** shows you how to recreate some of the sound-manipulations used in analogue recording studios, while the **Menu** sections cover everything you could want to know about notes, controllers, pitch-bend and SysEx (to name but a few), and take a close-up look at some of the oft-used controllers.

There are also tips on how to emulate the 'live' performance of acoustic instruments and collections of hints, experimental ideas and programming tricks and shortcuts. Extensive indexing and cross-referencing make *The MIDI Files* easy to use as a reference text, or just to dip into when you're looking for a something a bit different.

But why not just start from the beginning? You may find out a few things you didn't even know you wanted to know!

We take for granted . . .

❑ that you are musically literate (no training is given in music theory other than in explaining how various instruments are played)

❑ that you'll be using a keyboard of some description to play the music into your sequencer. If you're using a MIDI- Guitar or some other MIDI controller the information given is just as relevant to you: it's merely the *method of inputting* data that will differ

❏   that you're familiar with all the functions of the sequencer and tone-generator you'll be using (or can at least find the manuals!).

Let's make a start by listening to a file. Switch on your sequencer (or run your sequencing software) and load the file **ARCANA.MID**. If you're unsure how to do this, take a look in your sequencer manual for a section on loading or *importing* MIDI files. Make sure every device in your MIDI system is properly connected and switched on, hit Play and listen.

This file contains examples of some of the techniques we'll be covering – most of the techniques have their own file associated with them to make them easier to analyse. Sometimes, though, just when you think you've got something nailed down it runs away with the hammer, so you might want to come back to **ARCANA.MID** for another look.

Here are a few of the programming effects and instrument-emulations used, together with page-references for the inquisitive:

❏   The piano part on Channel 1 has been copied to Channel 9 and double-tracked/delayed (page 129).

❏   Channel 9's piano uses panning echoes repeating the stabs played on Channel 1 from bar 20–23 (page 141).

❏   Channels 12 and 4 begin and end the piece with a gate effect (page 142) using crosspanning (page 137).

❏   Channel 11's flute trill in bar 8 ends with brief spikes of pitch-bend to imitate vibrato (pages 159–60).

❏   The flute line in bar 10 uses maximum chorus and zero reverb to bring it to the front of the mix (pages 217–21).

❏   Brass, trumpet and guitar parts all contain slides and falls using both pitch-bend and separate notes at different times (page 154).

❏   Channels 4, 7 and 8 use expression (CC11) to create crescendos in bar 19 while the trumpet fades up and down again 3 bars later.

❏   The drum-part (ch 10) contains snare-flams and has the handclaps moved off the beat for a thicker hit (page 149).

❏   Modulation (CC1) is used as a synth-effect for the flute in bar 10 and bass in bars 10 and 23 (page 208).

***And here's the low-down on how the file was created and some of the techniques
used:***

The piece was recorded section-by-section rather than by, for example,
recording the *whole* drum-part followed by the *whole* bassline, and was
edited to smooth out the joins. Drums were recorded on about 6 different
tracks and mixed down to one at the end. In each section, the drums, bass,
piano and piano-double were recorded or created first, followed by strings
and pads then melodies and fills.

There's obvious copying and pasting going on (page 98) – string, guitar and
bass parts all contain copied sections, and the brass figures in bars 8 and 23
were copied from bar 4 and varied by editing. Channel 4's string-line from
bars 13–19 was copied from channel 8 and edited to play in harmony. Phrases
containing expression-fades were recorded 'notes-only' with the fades
overdubbed afterwards, usually onto a different track.

There's some evidence of channel-planning too (page 78): General MIDI's
patch #92 is a dual-voice sound which would often need a higher channel
priority to prevent notes 'dropping out'. In this case it's been given the lowest
priority (ch. 12) since there's little else playing during these sections. The
delayed piano has been given a fairly low priority (ch. 9) – because of the job
it's doing, we don't mind too much if the occasional note is 'stolen' by one of
the more essential instruments.

1

Introduction to MIDI

Aimed at musicians with little or no knowledge of MIDI, this section addresses the basic questions 'What is it? How does it work? What does it look like? Can you smoke it? And so on.

Very often, as in most new subjects, to understand one aspect requires some understanding of another, so the learning curve can initially be a steep one. If something doesn't make immediate sense, don't be put off – it'll almost certainly be mentioned again. You'll also find definitions and explanations of the technical terms used in this section in the Glossary.

What Is MIDI?

MIDI is an acronym for **Musical Instrument Digital Interface**, a computer 'language' that allows electronic musical instruments to communicate with one another. In the world before MIDI, instrument manufacturers designed their own systems for connecting devices together, but none of these spoke the same language. MIDI arrived on the scene in 1983 to provide a standardised language with simple messages replacing the old non-compatible systems.

Ins and Outs

An example of a MIDI message is the **note message**: when you play a note on a MIDI-equipped keyboard, it's translated into binary code and sent from a socket marked MIDI OUT on your keyboard to a socket marked MIDI IN on another MIDI keyboard, via a MIDI cable. The second keyboard sorts out the code again and responds as if you were playing the same note on that keyboard too. Other messages can tell the slave synth if you change to a different sound (**program-change message**), press down the sustain pedal or apply vibrato (types of **control-change message**). And all this occurs with no noticeable delay! Indeed, you can chain several synths together and send this data to all of them by use of a third socket, MIDI THRU, which 'copies' all the data received at a keyboard's *In* socket back out to the next keyboard.

MIDI sends its data down 16 paths or **channels**. Thus, you can control each synth in your chain independently by telling a synth to respond to messages set to channel 3 (for example) and to ignore all other channels.

A single MIDI message actually contains several pieces of information. The note message, for example, will tell a device which note to play, when to play it, how loudly to play it, when to let go, and which channel to send it to.

MIDI In Use

Of course, it isn't just keyboards that can send MIDI data. A converter can be connected to almost any instrument allowing MIDI control from a guitar, a flute, a drum-kit ... even a human voice! Similarly, it's not only *music* that MIDI can control: one of its fast-growing uses is in controlling stage-lighting rigs, smoke-machines and so on.

One of the most important and hugely useful benefits of the MIDI age is the ability to *record* this data as it's being played in a similar way to recording music 'live' into a multi-track tape-recorder. Recording and editing this data is what MIDI *programming* is all about, and to do it requires a **sequencer**.

What's A Sequencer?

To continue the analogy, when recording into a multi-track *tape*-recorder you can select a different track for each instrument and gradually build up a complete arrangement. You can record 4, 8, or perhaps 16 tracks, isolate a particular track to hear on its own and, if you wish, erase it and record on that track again. If you make a mistake you may be able to 'drop-in' halfway through a track and re-record a portion of it. With a tape-recorder, this is about the limit of your editing possibilities.

A sequencer is a multi-track recorder which records *data* as opposed to actual sound, using computer memory instead of tape. So the recording methods are still very similar, but because we're dealing with *numbers* rather than *sounds* the scope for editing is immense. For example: (1) if you've recorded the verse of a song which is then repeated you can simply copy the data to the point in the song where it next occurs; (2) you can record the data first and decide later what sort of instrument should play it; (3) tracks can be mixed, bounced, edited, overdubbed and generally subjected to the most stomach-churning of surgical operations without any loss in sound quality.

The recorded data can be viewed as lists of numbers and/or as graphic blocks depending upon your choice of sequencer and personal taste.

So if you played a wrong note while recording, or mucked up the timing, it's simplicity itself to put it right by just changing a number or moving a block.

Sequencer Types

There are essentially two types of sequencer: **hardware** and **software**.

A **hardware sequencer** is a stand-alone box with a small screen and a collection of buttons. It is a good deal more restricted in data-processing and storage terms than its rival but, for this reason, it's often easier to use and has the added attraction of portability for live use. Most hardware sequencers have a built-in disk-drive so files can be loaded and saved quickly and easily. The hardware sequencer is usually restricted to 8 tracks which, because MIDI allows you to use up to *16* instruments at once, can result in a fair bit of mixing to 'free-up' tracks.

The second, and more powerful, of the two types is the **software sequencer** for computers, of which even the most basic will usually beat the hardware hands down on processing capability, speed, choice and of course memory capacity. A software sequencer will often let you record 48, 64 or even 256 tracks, and some put no limit on it at all. The seemingly endless power of the computer sequencer can at first be intimidating to newcomers, but even with a more comprehensive computer sequencer you'll soon be saying *I wish it could do so-and-so*, and upgrading to one that can!

> *For the purposes of this book we assume that you'll be using a computer-based software sequencer but, as usual, if you're using a hardware sequencer we're not ignoring you: the same information and techniques still apply, but you'll be missing a few of the sequencer facilities referred to, so you'll need to limber up your button-pushing finger!*

Sound Sources

So, you've got your sequencer, you've recorded tracks of data and you're ready to play it back. You've selected one of the 16 MIDI channels for each track of data and chosen an instrument for that channel, and there are your sixteen synthesisers lined up and waiting to play it. But surely there's a cheaper way?

There is, and it's called a polyphonic multi-timbral tone-generator. In effect, it's like having a chain of sixteen synthesisers rolled into one, each set to respond to messages for one particular MIDI channel and to ignore messages being sent to the other 15. Using program-change messages, you can select a sound (or *instrument*) for all or any of these 'synthesisers' and send different note and control-change messages to each as if they were individual devices.

Tone-generators come in various shapes, sizes and formats but contain the same essential ingredient: the sounds! The most basic is the **module** (also known as an 'expander'), usually a smallish box with a screen and a few buttons. The module contains the 'sounds', often with some scope for editing them. Similar to the module is the **soundcard**, basically a module minus the attractive casing and buttons, which slots into your PC. Next up is a larger **synthesiser**-shaped box adding, unsurprisingly, a keyboard, and greater potential for sound-editing. Finally comes the **workstation** which adds a sequencer (often of the limited variety, similar to the hardware sequencer); some of the more recent models also include basic sampling facilities (see page 28).

Master Control

Bear in mind that if you opt for the modular tone-generator or soundcard, neither of which has a built-in keyboard, you'll need some form of MIDI controller in order to play the sounds. The most common controller type is the **master-keyboard** (also oddly known as a *mother-keyboard*), a remote keyboard with no internal sounds, but with a facility to add a foot-pedal, use pitch-bend and change from one sound to another. For keyboard players the huge benefit here is that if you can find a controller with an action you like you can keep it forever, even when your module sounds old-hat and needs replacing. For non-keyboard players, **MIDI guitar** controllers and **wind synths** are now becoming increasingly common and a great deal more responsive (not to mention affordable).

Chained Up and Ready

The ability of the tone-generator to play notes for 16 instruments at once means that this one piece of musical kit and your sequencer can form your entire MIDI studio! But, in the same way that you can chain three synthesisers together, you could also chain three tone-generators together.

This won't give you 48 MIDI channels because MIDI contains only 16. However, you can direct different modules to respond to or ignore certain MIDI channels thus giving yourself roughly triple the poly-phony and a frighteningly large choice of sounds! Or add an extra output port (see page 19). Throw in a couple of external effects units (the on-board effects contained in synths and modules can be limited, though they are fast improving) and the world is your mollusc.

The next few topics take a closer look at sequencers, tone-generators and MIDI-controllers and how all these gadgets are connected together.

Detours

➡ If you're new to the world of multi-timbrality, take a look at **General MIDI Maps** on page 61 to find out what these monsters can do. Remember, you can use 16 of these sounds at the same time (including the drum-kit) and change from one sound to another on any channel faster than you can say *How*?

▦ Software Sequencers

For computer-based MIDI studios, there are basically two types of sequencer: Linear and Pattern-based. Which type you choose is largely down to your own personal taste and methods of working. In general terms, a pattern-based sequencer usually requires a little more setting up when entering record mode but the enhanced editing flexibility of the system is valuable. The linear system, on the other hand, tends toward a faster way of recording tracks, sacrificing a little of the subsequent editing flexibility.

Linear Sequencers

On any sequencer, *tracks* are an important commodity: you can't possibly have too many of them. On a linear sequencer they're the vital building-blocks of a song: every time you enter record mode an unused track is selected for you automatically and, provided you don't run out, the actual recording process is very quick and easy.

In simple terms, the system works like this: first you select a channel to record for (perhaps you want to record the piano part first, so you might set up a piano sound on channel 3 of your tone-generator and select channel 3 on the sequencer). You hit *Record*, wait for the metronome count-in, and start playing the piano part. When you've finished you hit *Stop* and, if you want to, play back the recorded part – it might be just the first verse or maybe even the whole song, it doesn't matter. If you're happy with the result, select another MIDI channel (or the same channel again), hit *Record* and start playing again – the sequencer automatically records this data to the *next* unused track.

As with any sequencer, it's possible to edit the recorded data (see **Viewing MIDI Events**, page 20), and tracks may be mixed and merged if required – this is a pretty vital facility to have due to the track-hungry nature of the linear system, allowing you to 'free up' tracks for continued recording, but you might like to merge all your piano tracks together anyway so that you can find any piano section quickly.

It can be easily seen that linear sequencing could be likened to *tape-recording* in the sense that (as long as you have enough tracks) long sections of music are recorded, a new track is selected for each instrument or 'take', and tracks are bounced or merged only when absolutely necessary.

Pattern-Based Sequencers

The pattern-based sequencer tends to be the standard, and preferred, system for data recording. It's a definite case of 'because we can!' – if it were possible to make analogue recordings this way, you can bet your boots we would, hence the rising excitement at the latest digital-audio technologies (see page 287).

From the earliest days of sequencing, drum-machines were pattern based. Multiple drum-patterns of varying lengths were created and numbered, and then strung together in a chain to create a whole song by simply typing in a list of pattern-numbers in the required order. Some hardware sequencers still operate in a similar way. In software sequencers, however, the system has moved on from a list of numbers to a clearer and more intuitive *graphic* portrayal of the patterns.

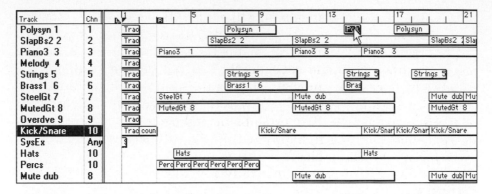

Track	Chn				5		9		13		17		21
Polysyn 1	1	Trac				Polysyn 1				Polysyn			
SlapBs2 2	2	Trac			SlapBs2 2			SlapBs2 2				SlapBs2 Sla	
Piano3 3	3	Trac	Piano3 1				Piano3 3		Piano3 3				
Melody 4	4	Trac											
Strings 5	5	Trac			Strings 5			Strings 5		Strings 5			
Brass1 6	6	Trac			Brass1 6			Bras					
SteelGt 7	7	Trac	SteelGt 7				Mute dub				Mute dub Mu		
MutedGt 8	8	Trac	MutedGt 8				MutedGt 8			MutedGt 8			
Overdve 9	9	Trac											
Kick/Snare	10	Trac coun				Kick/Snare			Kick/Snar Kick/Snar Kick/Snare				
SysEx	Any	3											
Hats	10		Hats					Hats					
Percs	10		Perc Perc Perc Perc Perc Perc										
Mute dub	8					Mute dub				Mute dub Mu			

Fig. 1 **Pattern-based sequencing, *Cubase*-style**

Once recorded, patterns are usually shown as graphic blocks on the screen (as shown in Fig. 1) and can be easily moved, deleted, split, copied and repeated, as well as being assigned names for easy recognition.

One of the immense benefits of pattern-based recording lies in the ability to see at a glance which instruments and/or channels are playing at any one time, and to see which tracks have a clear space at the position where you want to add another pattern.

Hardware Sequencers

Dedicated hardware sequencers are few and far between, though adding those included in workstations raises the total considerably. Most workstation sequencers have similar functions, operating methods and memory limitations to their stand-alone counterparts, but tend to be bought for different reasons. In simple terms, a dedicated hardware sequencer is more restricted than even a basic software program, and often more expensive than a fully-featured program, so one of the few reasons to go for this option is if you neither have nor want a computer.

Similarities

Clearly hardware and software sequencers must have a lot in common since they both record exactly the same types of MIDI data. Both record onto *tracks*, for example, and both let you view and edit the data you've recorded. Limitations in the hardware sequencer are generally due to its size: the amount of data you can see at any time is limited by the much smaller screen, usually letting you view one event at a time; the number of facilities available is restricted by the number of buttons and sliders that can be fitted into the available space; the quantity of data that can be recorded is limited by the size of the internal memory. The number of tracks is usually reduced to eight, though some devices have an extra dedicated track for recording drum-parts.

Many hardware sequencers (and obviously the workstation varieties) have a built-in disk-drive to let you save the file in one or more file formats as quickly and easily as you can with the computer, but some can only dump their data to cassette-tape which makes loading and saving files a long-winded and messy business. Hardware sequencers also fall into the same two categories, *linear* and *pattern-based*, though each works in a slightly different way from its software counterpart.

Pattern-Based Hardwares

A pattern-based hardware-sequencer works in a similar way to a drum-machine, usually having two different modes, *pattern* and *song*. In pattern mode, a length for the pattern is specified (such as four bars), and you can then record up to four bars of music onto any or all of the eight tracks. Usually you'd set each track to a particular MIDI channel and thus record data for eight different channels, but to record a ninth means that you have to first mixdown a couple of tracks to gain a free one. The need to pre-define a pattern-length requires a little careful thought about how the song can be 'broken up' into these bite-sized chunks, though two patterns can usually be linked together to create one longer one.

Once you've recorded all the patterns you need, you move into song mode and punch in a list of pattern numbers in the sequence they should be played back. This method of working means that you'll usually need to keep a running list of what each pattern contains, and doesn't make for the most musical approach to programming.

Linear Hardwares

This is the more flexible of the two types: rather than assigning a channel number to a particular track, you set your MIDI keyboard (or guitar, etc.) to *transmit* on the desired MIDI channel and then record onto any track you choose, at any position, overdubbing data already recorded onto a track if need be. In effect, you're recording one long pattern containing the whole song and gradually building the arrangement in a similar way to multi-track tape recording, giving a much clearer overview of the whole song.

Of course the pattern-based sequencer could be used in this way, provided you can specify a sufficient pattern length to contain the whole song, but since it's designed to work in shorter patterns some of the editing facilities become difficult or even impossible to use. A prime example is *Copy & Paste* – a pattern-based sequencer usually restricts you to copying either a whole pattern or one whole track from a pattern, whereas the linear version will let you select just a group of events.

Hardware Benefits

The benefits of using hardware over software are few, and they boil down to the one single advantage: *portability*. A hardware sequencer makes an ideal 'notepad' for ideas, and saves the need for a separate MIDI-file player if you use sequences in live performance. Some hardwares have a *Playlist* function which will play the files on the disk one by one in the order you choose.

To get the best of both worlds, a laptop computer will give you all the power and flexibility of the software sequencer combined with hardware portability. Compared with a desktop computer system or a hardware sequencer this seems an expensive option, but for busy 'live' performers the total cost is similar to that of adding a new synth to your setup.

Tracks and Channels

Newcomers to MIDI are often confused by the relationship between tracks and channels: What's the difference? Or are they the same thing? How do they work? In this topic we'll take a look at the fundamental differences between the two, and how they're used.

What's The Difference?

Tracks are in fact nothing to do with MIDI as such – the idea has just been carried over from multi-*track* tape recording because they're a practical and intuitive method of organising your work. Tracks are supplied by your sequencer and they're simply used as a kind of labelled storage space for MIDI events, in the same way that you might keep labelled boxes for paper-clips, drawing pins and staples for example. If you put all these in the *same* box, you've got a couple of empty boxes to put something else in, but it's now a bit harder to find a paper-clip. Similarly, there's nothing to stop you having *two* boxes with paper-clips in them.

Okay, enough stationery. The great thing with tracks is that you can use them however you like, so let's substitute these office consumables with notes, say for piano and drums. For the piano part, you might like to have one track for the left-hand part and one for the right; perhaps even another one for the sustain pedal data. With the drum-part, you might like to keep each kit-instrument on its own track so that you can easily find a particular snare-drum hit without searching through a plethora of hi-hats. The only limit to the number of tracks you can use is in the number of tracks your *sequencer* is capable of providing. On hardware sequencers, sadly, this is often only eight. On a computer-based (*software*) sequencer you might have an unlimited number.

Channels, on the other hand, *are* limited, and are provided by MIDI itself rather than by your sequencer. MIDI contains 16 channels and on each of these channels you may set up an instrument (or sound), giving you the potential to program for 16 instruments playing at the same time. So to return to the example above, you may have two or three or more *tracks* containing your various drum-kit instruments but as long as these have all been assigned to the same *channel* and you've set up a drum-kit on this channel on your tone-generator, all these tracks will play drum-sounds. If you were to merge all these drum tracks into a single track the result would still be the same *as long as this single track is still assigned to that drum-kit channel*.

It's also possible to combine notes for *different* channels on the same track. This is because all MIDI *events* contain a channel setting – a number from 1–16 to tell your tone-generator which channel should play that event.

Load the file **EVENTMIX.MID** into your sequencer, select one of the two data-tracks in the file and go into *Edit* mode so that you can see the list of MIDI events within that track (consult your sequencer's manual or the **Troubleshooting** section on page 242 if you get stuck). On both of the tracks you should see that the events for different channels have been mixed together. Keep the file open while you read the rest of this topic.

A track is usually assigned a channel number before you start to record onto it. Say for example you've already recorded your drums and bass parts using channels 10 and 2 respectively, and you now want to record a piano part. Choose a free channel, such as channel 4, and call up a piano sound on this channel on your tone-generator. Next choose (or create, depending on your sequencer) an empty track to record onto and set *its* channel to 4 as well. Now enter record mode, and as you play you'll hear your piano sound being recorded while at the same time your sequencer is playing back the bass and drums parts. If you now want to record some more piano notes, simply pick another empty track, set it to channel 4 as well, and hit *Record* again. If you take a look at Fig. 1 on page 13 you can see that three tracks have been set to channel 10 for different drum-kit sounds, and a second track has been created for channel 8 to record an overdub for the muted-guitar.

> *Note: some aspects of this basic description rely rather heavily on having made the correct settings for* **Soft MIDI Thru** *and* **Local Control**, *both of which we'll be covering soon. For the eager, these topics can be found on pages 37 and 38 respectively.*

Rechannelizing

In the example above, we set the track's channel to 4 and we could hear the piano-sound assigned to channel 4 on the tone-generator. If we'd set the track to a different channel number we would have heard whatever sound was assigned to *that* channel instead. The act of setting up a channel for a track in this way is called *rechannelizing*.

Very often, the keyboard (or MIDI controller) from which you enter your data will be transmitting on channel 1 (this is the usual factory default setting). So if we were to go into *Edit* mode and look at the piano events we recorded they would all have their channel set to 1.

The rechannelizing function overrides these event-settings and sends them off to your tone-generator on channel 4.

As well as being able to rechannelize tracks to MIDI channels 1–16, sequencers have another setting which may be termed *Any, Off, No* or something similar. This *turns off* the rechannelize function and allows all the events on the track to be transmitted on whichever channel is contained in the actual event. So another way to achieve the same result would have been to set the track's channel to *Any* (turning off the rechannelize function) and set the *keyboard's* channel to 4 and then start recording. Returning to *Edit* mode, we would now see that each recorded event has a channel setting of 4. This is really only of passing interest; in practical terms, it's quicker and easier to use the rechannelize function than to keep resetting your keyboard's transmit channel, with the added advantage that you can tell just by glancing at your computer-screen which channel a track is assigned to without having to delve into the *Edit* screens and look at individual events.

Multiple Channels On One Track

By making use of the *Mixdown* or *Merge* function on your sequencer, it's usually possible (though rarely desirable) to mix the data for several channels onto a single track. The exact method of doing this will depend on the sequencer you're using (yup, manual time again!), but usually you would select an empty track and set its channel to *Any*, mute any tracks that you don't want included in the mix, and then hit the *Mixdown* button. Since the original tracks were rechannelized, the mixdown process will re-write each event's channel-setting substituting the rechannelize setting, the final result being a single new track consisting of all the events from the old tracks, each event containing the correct channel number.

This should be a *non-destructive* process, i.e., it doesn't erase the original tracks. Once you're sure the operation was successful you can delete the originals yourself. If something went wrong, you can delete the mixed-track and try again.

 EVENTMIX.MID is a good example of this process. Each instrument was originally recorded by rechannelizing (e.g., selecting channel 2 for a track and recording the bass-line on it) and then mixed down to two tracks so that the 'rechannelize' channels were automatically inserted into each event and the resulting two tracks set to *Any/Off*.

It's usually also possible to reverse this process by a function normally called *Remix* or *Split By Channel*. This process takes a track containing data for several different channels and creates a new track for each of those channels. The new tracks will still be set to *Any* with the actual events still containing their channel settings. This should also be a non-destructive process. Remix is a useful facility to keep in mind for 'exploding' any type 0 format Standard MIDI files for easier editing.

If your sequencer has a *Remix* or *Split By Channel* function, try selecting one of the data-tracks in **EVENTMIX.MID** and hitting *Remix*. If it works, do the same thing with the other track.

Mute and Solo

These are sequencer facilities for *tracks*, and can be used during playback or recording. *Muting* a track 'silences' it (prevents it sending out its data); *Soloing* a track silences all *other* tracks so that you can just hear this one.

Going back to **EVENTMIX.MID**, try muting the two original tracks and playing the file again. Does it sound as it should? If so, erase those two muted tracks – you are now left with an 'exploded' version of the original file. Experiment with muting and soloing different tracks to isolate the various instruments.

Output Ports

MIDI, as we already know, contains 16 channels. In most cases this is enough, but what if you've got two great tone-generators and you want to use them *both* to create a sequence? One way is to connect the MIDI Thru on the first to MIDI In on the second and then mute channels on them, either manually or using System Exclusive messages (for example, mute channels 1–10 on the first and 11–16 on the second). In this way you can decide which device you want to play a certain part and choose your channel accordingly. It works, but it relies on being able to mute channels on both devices (not always possible) and it still only gives you 16 channels.

Nowadays, 32-channel sequencing is becoming the norm. How come? Well, your sequencer sends all the data from its Output port to the tone-generator. So if you have *two* output ports you can send two lots of 16 channels to two tone-generators. Provided your sequencer lets you specify different output ports for each track, it's then simply a case of selecting the port that connects to the required device. So this is just *rechannelizing* on a grander scale.

Apart from the luxury of having two tone-generators at your disposal and a pretty huge array of sounds, there are vast practical advantages in the increased polyphony and the reduced likelihood of MIDI timing glitches, not to mention the enhanced mixing possibilities of having two separate sets of on-board effects.

As well as needing sequencing software which supports multiple output ports, some additional hardware will be required to actually *provide* another port to plug into, though for most platforms this is usually cheap and simple to fit.

Detours

➡ For more information on 32-channel sequencing and its hardware requirements, take a look at pages 35–6 and **Appendix One: Interfaces & Disk Formats** on page 278.

➡ The **Recording Session** on page 63 guides you through the process of recording and editing a short MIDI file, giving you hands-on experience with tracks, channels and rechannelizing.

▨ Viewing MIDI Events

As we've already mentioned, when you connect your MIDI controller keyboard's MIDI Out to your sequencer's MIDI In and play a few notes, what you play is translated into binary code which can then be recorded into the sequencer. Binary code isn't a pretty sight (10010000 00111100 01010110 – and that's just one note). Fortunately, sequencers are able to display this code in a variety of more meaningful and user-friendly ways, all of which ultimately boil down to a choice of two: **graphic** or **numeric**.

Graphic Display

Many programmers find graphic display of MIDI data less intimidating and more intuitive to work with. The most immediately recognisable form of graphic display is the standard **musical score** (recorded sounds represented as notes on a stave). Another often-used method is to show the notes as rectangular blocks beside a piano-keyboard: the position of the block tells you the pitch of the note, and the block's length indicates how long the note is held, as shown in Fig. 2. Changes in **pitch-bend** and **controller** data are often shown as lines or bars on a graph. Data can be easily edited by moving these graphic symbols or altering their shapes. Nearly all software sequencers have a facility (or a choice of facilities) for viewing data graphically.

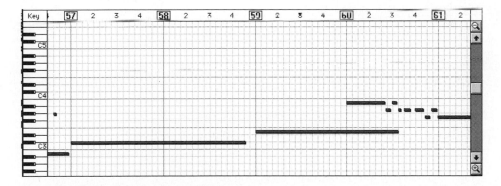

Fig. 2   **Piano-roll note display in** *Cubase*

Numeric Display

The standard type of data display, found on both soft- and hardware sequencers, is the numeric list of MIDI events. An event list could look something like this:

Position	Value 1	Value 2	Length	Channel	Type
17.3.48	C#3	67	144	3	Note
17.3.50	A3	54	94	3	Note
17.4.12	64	127	–	3	CC Sustain Ped
18.1.0	D1	80	48	3	Note
18.1.12	64	0	–	3	CC Sustain Ped

In this example *Position* refers to the point in the song where the event occurs (bar 17, beat 3, tick 48); *Value 1* is the name of the note or the number of the controller; *Value 2* is the velocity of the note or the setting of the controller; *Length* refers to the length of the note in ticks (controllers don't have a length – they simply remain at the value they were set at until another command alters them); *Channel* specifies which of the 16 MIDI channels the event will be sent to; *Type* describes the type of MIDI event: in this example controller 64 (sustain pedal) was first switched on (value 127) and then switched off a beat later (value 0).

Some higher-level sequencers also display (or give you the option to display) the *time-position* of an event in hours/minutes/sec-onds/frames. This is chiefly used in synchronising MIDI with video, for example when creating film soundtracks (hence the inclusion of *frames*).

While the visual layout of the list will obviously vary between different softwares, the information it gives will basically be the same. Figure 3 shows our example list of events above displayed on a software sequencer.

Using the numeric display allows for greater accuracy when editing an event: you can simply select any entry and change it by typing in a different number. This is the editing method adopted by hardware sequencers due to the limited size of their display.

Event List - Track 4: Piano 3							_ □ ×
Trk	Hr:Mn:Sc:Fr	Meas:Beat:Tick	Chn	Kind		Values	
4	00:00:34:16	17:3:048	3	Note	Db3	67	1:048
4	00:00:34:16	17:3:050	3	Note	A 3	54	94
4	00:00:34:29	17:4:012	3	Contrl	64-Pedal [	127	
4	00:00:35:14	18:1:000	3	Note	D 1	80	48
4	00:00:35:15	18:1:012	3	Contrl	64-Pedal [	0	

Fig. 3 **List Editor from** *Cakewalk Pro*

On the subject of numbers, zero is regarded as a legitimate number in MIDI-speak, not only as a *value* (such as specifying a reverb setting of zero on the bass guitar channel), but also as part of the numbering system for basic events such as notes, controllers and so on, and for tick-positions (as demonstrated by 18:1:000 in Fig. 3). Another number to watch out for is 127: the mathematics of the infamous binary code result in this being the largest number that MIDI can transmit – just about every MIDI event-type you'll work with will have a range of 0–127.

Basic MIDI Events

There are five basic types of MIDI event you need to know about: Notes, Controllers, Program Change, Pitch-Bend and Aftertouch. These event types are collectively known as *Channel Messages*. Each type of event will appear in your event-list as a row of values, similar to the example in Fig. 3.

Different types of value are needed for different types of event, but all events have two things in common: they'll have a *position* within the song and they'll be assigned a *channel*. Additional values contained in different event-types are as follows:

❑ **Notes** are the staple diet of sequencers. As well as channel and position, a note event contains a pitch (also referred to by a MIDI Note Number), a velocity and a length.

❑ **Program Change** is the MIDI command that tells your tone-generator which sound you want to use on a particular channel. The program change command consists of a single number.

❑ **Controllers** are a range of commands which allow you to change aspects of the sound you hear (such as volume, pan and reverb), use foot-pedals like the sustain-pedal, and access different banks of sounds in your tone-generator. Controllers are *numbered* in the same way as notes and program changes, so a controller event would contain the controller-number and the desired value for that controller.

❑ **Pitch-bend** is an effect usually controlled by a lever or wheel on the keyboard which makes a note slide upwards or downwards in pitch. Different sequencers have different ways of displaying pitch-bend data; in addition to position and channel, a pitch-bend event may consist of one or two values.

❑ **Aftertouch** is a sort of vibrato effect accessed by pressing harder on the keyboard while holding down a note or chord. There are two slightly different types of aftertouch. Not all keyboards and sequencers can transmit or respond to aftertouch, and of those that do, many will recognise only one type. (And at least one workstation-synth won't even *load* a file containing aftertouch data!) The list-display for an aftertouch event may also contain one or two values depending upon which of the two types it is.

If you've still got the 'exploded' **EVENTMIX.MID** loaded into your sequencer from the previous topic, now would be a good time to take a look at your sequencer's *Edit* screens. Start with the track containing channel 6's events. Channel 2's track contains pitch-bend data near the beginning. The track with channel 10's events is the drum-track – you can usually edit drum-events with any editor at your disposal, but try looking at these events on the dedicated *Drum-Edit* screen if your sequencer has one.

Detours

➥ For more detailed explanations of the various control events mentioned in this topic, take a look at the **Channel Messages Menu** on page 172.

➥ For information on the control events within the specific framework of the General MIDI protocol, read the **2: MIDI Protocols** topics on **General MIDI** (page 50) and **Song Header** (page 57).

Tone-Generators

What Is A Tone-Generator?

In general terms, a tone-generator is any electronic device capable of producing a sound. In more musical terms, it's a piece of hardware containing a collection of different sounds which might be tuned (such as a flute), untuned (drums) or sound effects (the ubiquitous 'helicopter'). For our purposes, it must also be *MIDI-equipped* – it must, at the very least, have a MIDI In socket to allow it to receive MIDI data from your sequencer and a MIDI Out socket to transmit data.

A Brief History Lesson

In its original humble beginnings, MIDI was used simply to make one synthesiser control another. In these early days, most synthesisers were *mono-timbral* – they could play one sound at a time. MIDI was a method to create duo-timbrality by setting up a different sound on each synthesiser and using one to control the other, creating a layered sound. Being mono-timbral, a synthesiser could respond to only one MIDI channel at a time so MIDI sequencing was an expensive affair, each channel of data requiring its own synth to play.

Gradually, as computer microchips replaced analogue components in synthesisers, digital sound-synthesis became the norm, bringing with it the potential for *multi*-timbrality and a more powerful and flexible system of communications between synthesisers. Added together, this meant that one device could effectively conduct a whole orchestra of sounds contained in the other, all at the same time.

Just as importantly, microchip technology made it possible to build these enhancements into smaller and smaller boxes, and to combine these 'boxes' into another single unit capable of a wide variety of musical applications without needing a warehouse to put it in.

The result today is that there's a huge choice of tone-generators of varying qualities, with varying features, at varying sizes, and at various prices from *Wow!* to *Eeeek!* To make any sense of it all, it helps to start with some idea of what you need.

What Do I Need?

For programming purposes there are some basic requirements you'll need from a tone-generator of any description. It must be multi-timbral to the tune of at least 16 simultaneous sounds or instruments, at least one of which should be a drum-kit; it should preferably have some form of on-board effects processor to give at least the bog-standard reverb and chorus; it should be velocity-sensitive; there should be facility to set individual pitch-bend ranges for each channel.

It should have a MIDI Thru socket, and at least one each of MIDI In and MIDI Out. (For future expandability, the more MIDI Outs you have on a synth or workstation the better.) Another consideration is: will you be buying, using or creating General MIDI files? If so, you'll need a tone-generator with GM compatibility (see page 50).

The next considerations are: Do you like the features? Do you like the sounds? Have you got the money? Each of these is important, but on the subject of the first, it's well worth checking out as many tone-generators as you can get your hands on to see what features are current. At the time of writing, the larger manufacturers are introducing 32-channel, 64-voice polyphonic devices: these are solid, practical enhancements worth stretching the budget to have.

Having sorted out the basic requirements and features you need, what sort of box do you want them in? The four types to choose between are **synths**, **workstations**, **modules** and **soundcards**.

The Synthesiser

A synthesiser (or *synth*) is the usual collection of sounds built into a keyboard. The keyboard part of the instrument is, of course, used to play and control the on-board sounds but may be used to control an external device (such as a **module**) either as well or instead. Using a synthesiser for MIDI programming will require some knowledge of **Local Control**, which is covered on page 38. Synths very often provide editing facilities for the on-board (preset) sounds and may contain a *user-bank* into which you can store your own sounds for future use.

Modern synths tend to be hugely expandable. Due to the size of the casing there's usually room to cram in a few additional features, and the most popular add-on is always more sounds. There may be a slot into which a card containing another bank of sounds can be plugged, or you might be able to add extra ROM or RAM chips containing either new sounds or extra storage space for your own creations.

The Workstation

This is a synthesiser *and* a sequencer all rolled into the one unit. It looks a lot like a **synth**, and everything we've said about the synth applies equally to the workstation. The built-in sequencer can be used to record and play back data for an external device as well as the workstation's own internal sounds, but make sure you check out the sequencer's memory capacity and its ease of use. A particular point to consider is the size and clarity of the screen since you could be spending hours at a time working with it.

Some workstations also include basic sampling facilities (see p. 28) but, like the sequencer, if sampling is your thing, it's worth doing some careful comparison between the workstation's specifications and a stand-alone sampler.

The Module

Also sometimes called an *expander*, the module is a small box containing all the sounds and internal workings of a **synth** but without the keyboard. The module may be in a rackmountable or a desktop form, usually with a screen and a much-reduced collection of front-panel buttons. It's designed to be controlled by a separate device, either a sequencer or a MIDI-controller. In a programming situation, data is recorded to the sequencer by playing the MIDI-controller, and the sequencer automatically passes this data on to the module to let you hear what you're doing. Most of the popular synths are also available as modules; some have basic sound-editing features but this tends to be the exception rather than the rule.

The card slot for additional sound-banks has been around for a while on modules, and some recent models also have facilities for adding extra ROM or RAM chips.

The Soundcard

This is simply a board which slots into your computer and, in programming terms, has very similar capabilities to the **module**, requiring a MIDI-controller and software sequencer to control it. Soundcards are usually capable of a variety of additional audio applications including CD-audio and sample playback.

Bear in mind that soundcards vary in price and quality more than the other types of tone-generator. At the cheaper end of the scale, the methods of sound-synthesis used can make the 'instruments' almost unrecognisable: these are bearable for computer games but hopeless for serious *musical* applications.

Decisions, Decisions . . .

When deciding which of these best suits your needs, remember to consider the practical stuff like how much space it'll take up, whether you want to use it for live performance and so on. If you already have a computer and software sequencing-package, the extra cost of the built-in workstation sequencer is unnecessary. Similarly, if you own a good MIDI keyboard, why pay extra for the one built into the synth when there's probably a module version?

Of course there's no reason why you couldn't use two (or more) of these linked together to give much more power and flexibility, or you could use a favourite MIDI-equipped drum-machine as a tone-generator for all your percussion sounds.

Sampling

Many recent synths and modules include a collection of basic wave-forms which can be used as a basis for creating new sounds from scratch. **Sampling** is another way of getting your hands on new sounds, but in this case the deed is done by *recording* an analogue sound into the sampler which is converted to a sequence of numbers and stored internally or to floppy disk. The digitised sound can then be edited in a variety of ways, and played back in the same way as sounds contained in the other forms of tone-generator. Samplers have the same polyphony restraints as other types of tone-generator, with 32-voices the current standard in mid-priced machines.

Despite the fact that recording and editing of samples is possible, it tends to be a job requiring skill and patience, and few people really bother. Samplers are mostly used as *playback* devices for the vast quantities of commercial samples available. For this purpose, the samplers and sample-players found on a few workstations are often quite adequate, and it's usually possible to use sampled sounds alongside tone-generator preset sounds in MIDI programming situations. For more on sampling, turn to **Appendix Three** on page 285.

> **Detours**
>
> → Take a look at **Appendix Two: MIDI Add-Ons** on page 283 for a brief look at some of the other types of MIDI hardware available.

MIDI Controllers

What Is A MIDI-Controller?

'Controller' is one of those annoying words in MIDI-speak that refers to two entirely different things: it's widest use is as an abbreviation (of sorts) for *control-change messages* – types of MIDI event that are entered into your file to change aspects of the sound such as volume or modulation (vibrato). Control-change messages are covered in the **Channel Messages Menu** on page 172.

The second use of the word 'controller' is the one we're concerned with here and usually has the word *MIDI* inserted in front of it. A MIDI-controller is a 'musical instrument' with no on-board sounds: it's mission in life is simply to play the sounds and control the effects contained in *other* devices, or to record musical data into a sequencer which will then be transmitted to a sound-generating device.

If you're using a module or a computer-soundcard (as covered in the previous topic), you'll need some form of MIDI-controller to access its sounds and control-parameters (unless you're prepared to step-record everything into the sequencer!).

There are four types of MIDI-controller in common use: the **master-keyboard** (also sometimes called a mother-keyboard), **MIDI-guitar**, **drum-pads** and **wind-controller**.

Master Keyboards

A master keyboard is identical, on the surface, to a synthesiser with the exception that it may be a bit lacking in the knobs and sliders department. The basic necessities for a master keyboard are: velocity-sensitivity, pitch-bend and modulation controls, facility to send program-change messages, and a socket to connect a sustain-pedal (control-change 64).

These are certainly not found on *all* master-keyboards, so always check 'em out carefully – in particular, the program change facility may require you to enter a different mode and use notes on the keyboard to enter a number, which can be a fiddly thing to do in 'live' performance or real-time recording.

Other features to look for (all of which add to the price!) are: extra keys (where most synthesisers traditionally have a 5-octave keyboard some controllers have 7); weighted 'piano-action' keyboard; Polyphonic or Channel Aftertouch; Zoning (the ability to 'split' the keyboard into separate sections, each transmitting on a different MIDI channel); programmability (a number of buttons allowing you to store and recall complete sound and channel setups for your entire MIDI system); extra knobs and sliders to let you control a wide range of parameters easily.

Some master keyboards are equipped with several MIDI Out sockets: these may allow you to send *all* the data to every device in your system without 'daisy-chaining' (connecting them together using the MIDI Thru or a MIDI Splitter box), or they may let you send data for particular MIDI channels to different MIDI Outs so that you can control several devices independently.

MIDI Guitars

The MIDI guitar comes in two flavours: it may be an ordinary guitar fitted with a pitch-to-MIDI converter, or it may be a dedicated MIDI device in the same way as the master-keyboard – in other words, without a tone-generator to connect it to, you'd have to call it an ornament.

Using the modified guitar gives you the option to combine 'live' guitar sounds with MIDI sound (with the added advantage that you can use the guitar you know and love). The dedicated MIDI guitar looks a little unusual but is often easier to use as a controller and encourages you to experiment with different playing techniques. It tends to demand a more precise playing style than its counterpart will let you get away with. Despite recent advances in the pitch-tracking of the add-on unit, the dedicated MIDI guitar is still the winner in the tracking stakes.

Some MIDI guitars have a built-in tone-generator resulting in the guitarist's version of a synthesiser. If you use this type of instrument, you'll need to check out your **Local Control** settings (see page 38).

One of the problems you can run into with a MIDI guitar is pitch-bend. Bending strings is an inherent technique in guitar-playing and this produces the pitch-bend messages. However, pitch-bend messages affect all notes currently sounding on a channel. For this reason, the guitarist needs each string to transmit on its own MIDI channel, so MIDI guitars are usually set to Mode 4 (see **MIDI Modes** on page 40). Of course, it's also possible to use Mode 3 and filter out pitch-bend messages, for example when playing rhythm parts.

Drum Pads

The most usual form of MIDI drum-pad setup is, once again, *dedicated* drum-pads with no internal sounds which are then hooked up to an external tone-generator. These may be in the form of a box with eight or so pads on the face of it, or may be separate boxes each containing a single, larger pad which, when set up, look like a sort of space-age drum-kit. The pads should always be velocity-sensitive, and can be programmed to trigger a particular drum-sound or MIDI note number.

A second way of achieving a similar result is to 'MIDI-up' an acoustic drum-kit. Drum-pickups are attached to the kit-instruments and connected to a trig-to-MIDI converter . This allows you to use your regular kit (though you'd need to damp the heads) and, if you choose to, combine acoustic and MIDI sound. Once again, the dedicated pads are often easier and more expressive to work with.

More advanced systems let you set an output channel for each pad individually, so you can make up a sort of 'custom' kit using drum-sounds from the different kits in your tone-generator. You may also be able to transmit program-change and controller information from the unit. Some systems will let you configure pads to transmit different MIDI note numbers according to how hard they're struck.

Wind Controllers

These fall into two categories in much the same way as MIDI guitars and drum-pads do; a dedicated MIDI device or a modification to an acoustic instrument. To use an acoustic wind instrument requires the fitting of a pitch-to-MIDI converter. The dedicated wind-controller (with no on-board sounds) often looks similar to a soprano saxophone and usually has the potential for greater expression. It will usually also have built-in controls giving access to pitch-bend and control-change parameters. The mouthpiece of a wind-controller determines the velocity of the note and controls the vibrato characteristics via aftertouch or control-change data.

Being monophonic instruments, MIDI wind-controllers may be used in the mono modes 2 or 4 (see **MIDI Modes** on page 40) if the receiving tone-generator supports them.

. . . And Finally

With all forms of MIDI controller it's worth making a distinction between live use and home-studio use. For home-studio use, particularly when coupled with a computer-based sequencer, you can often make do with less in the way of real-time control, programmable memory buttons, program change functions and so on, which could result in a substantially cheaper piece of kit.

For instruments using pitch- or trig-to-MIDI converters, you may be able to sacrifice some processing speed in favour of a reduced price, especially as your final result is always editable and you have the option to reduce the tempo when recording.

For live use however, all the features mentioned above acquire a new significance. In particular, when considering the purchase of a pitch- or trig-to-MIDI-equipped instrument (whether as a modification or as a dedicated unit), always check carefully for accuracy of pitch-tracking and the processing speed of the converter.

Detours

➞ Guitarists should take a look at the *MIDI Lead Guitar* heading in **MIDI Modes** on page 42.

■ MIDI Setup Diagrams

The following diagrams and descriptions should help you turn that jumble of cables and boxes into something useful. If you set it all up as shown and it still sounds like a Trappist monk in a library, consult the Troubleshooting section or your user-manuals for more specific instructions. If your setup is successfully connected and working, you might still like to skim this topic for extra info before continuing.

Controller devices have been noted here as 'keyboards' – of course, these could just as easily be substituted with one of the other types of MIDI controller mentioned in the previous topic.

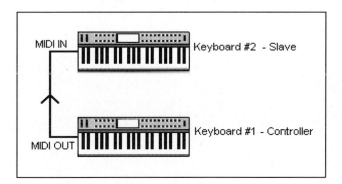

Fig. 4 **Controller to Slave**

Figure 4 is the most basic MIDI connection, letting you play one keyboard which remotely controls a second (slave) keyboard. (The slave keyboard could be replaced by a different type of tone-generator or by a sequencer to record the incoming MIDI data.) If you're using a computer with a soundcard installed this is the setup you'll use, where the slave represents your computer.

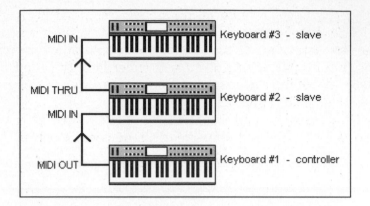

Fig. 5 **Controller to two Slaves**

Figure 5 is an extension of the two-keyboard setup, in which the data is still processed by the second keyboard but is also passed to a third.

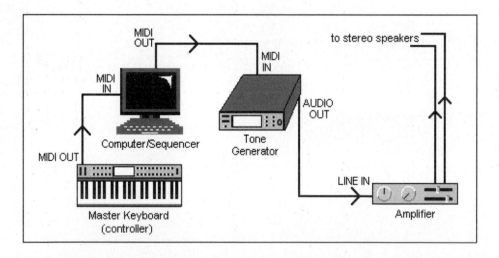

Fig. 6 **Standard studio setup**

In this setup (Fig. 6) your master-keyboard sends data directly into the sequencer to be recorded, and this data is (almost) simultaneously transmitted from sequencer to tone-generator so that you can hear what you're playing. If you've previously recorded some MIDI tracks into the sequencer these will also be sent to the tone-generator so that you can monitor the whole mix while you play. This is made possible by means of a nifty sequencer facility called *soft thru* (see page 37). If you're using a **synthesiser** setup rather than separate master-keyboard and tone-generator, the MIDI OUT of the sequencer will instead be connected to the MIDI IN of your synth. You'll also need to find out something about **Local Control**, covered on page 38.

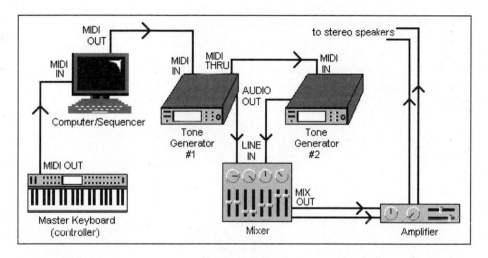

Fig. 7 **Advanced studio setup**

Figure 7 is an extension of the Standard setup, now using two tone-generators. The two data streams (recorded and live) that were sent from the sequencer to the tone-generator to be converted to an audio signal are now being passed *through* the first generator to the second which will also convert them to an audio signal. The two audio signals are then passed through a mixing-desk to merge them to a single stereo signal before being routed to the speakers. (You could of course use more than two tone-generators by linking the MIDI Thru port of number 2 to the MIDI In of number 3, and so on, but if you're planning to do this make sure you read the Appendix topic **Interfaces and Disk Formats** on page 278.) If you're really determined to impress your friends and annoy your neighbours, a possible addition to this setup could be an external effects unit (often also controllable via MIDI) to give a greater range of effects than some tone-generators provide.

Figure 8 shows the same setup, this time using two output ports from the computer to control two generators individually, effectively giving 32 MIDI channels (provided your sequencer supports multiple output ports).

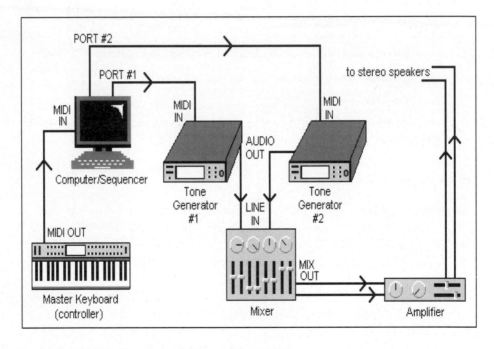

Fig. 8 **Advanced studio setup using two output ports**

NOTE: MIDI cables should never be more than 15 m in length to prevent parts of the data being delayed or degraded. If this looks like becoming a problem for you, set your studio up in a smaller room.

In Fig. 9, two output ports have been used to give a potential 32 MIDI channels as shown in the 'Output' column. Several tracks are being directed to channels 1, 2, 3 and 10 of the computer's soundcard while the remaining tracks are routed to channels 1–6 and 10

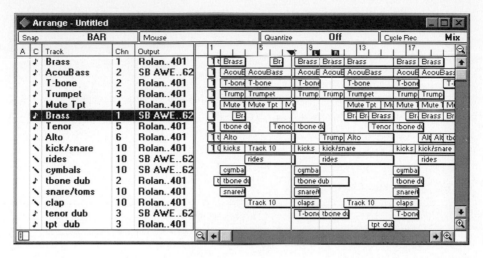

Fig. 9 **Using two output ports in** *Cubase*

of an external tone-generator via a MIDI interface (see **Appendix One: Interfaces and Disk Formats** on page 278).

'Soft' MIDI Thru

The way the three MIDI ports work has previously been explained, but many sequencers have a simple facility called *soft-thru* which reconfigures the MIDI Out to *also* work as a MIDI Thru (sometimes known as MIDI Echo). This means that data already recorded to the sequencer can be played (in usual MIDI Out fashion) while incoming data from your keyboard is processed and sent out with it (in typical MIDI Thru style). This facility allows you to rehearse a section of the music by playing along with previously recorded tracks, or to try out different sounds to see which one 'sounds right' in the mix, or to see what effect a particular controller would have on an existing track without the need to record it and play it back.

Some hardware sequencers have limited implementation of soft-thru in that it's active only *while you're recording* and not in playback mode, which of course deprives you of these rehearsal options.

The other benefit of soft-thru is in rechannelizing and applying filters to incoming data. In this way, you can set up all the parameters of the sound you want to record on a particular channel and filter out any data-types you want the sequencer to 'destroy', so that when you begin to play you can monitor the exact sound being recorded.

Some sequencers let you specify a channel that soft-thru won't transmit on – this is for programmers using a multi-timbral synth to record *and* playback the data. If you decide to use this function, you would select the channel your synth is set to transmit on (usually channel 1). Another option is to change the setting of your synth's **Local Control**.

■ Local Control

If you're using a **master-keyboard** (a keyboard with no internal sounds) and a separate tone-generator you can cheerfully regard Local Control as one of life's unanswered mysteries and skip this section. If you enter and play back all your MIDI data from a multi-timbral synthesiser however, you'll need to know something about this area of your keyboard's private life.

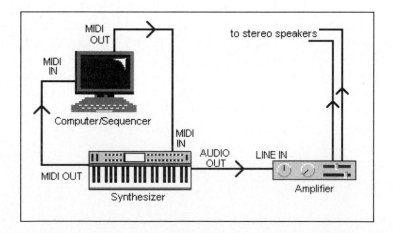

Fig. 10 Standard synthesizer setup. Data transmitted by your synth is immediately returned to it via your sequencer's *soft thru* facility, possibly causing deep grief when it gets there.

What's The Problem?

If you use a synthesiser (i.e., a combined keyboard and tone-generator) to both enter *and* play back your MIDI data you'll have a setup similar to the one shown in Fig. 10. At different times, you'll want to set your sequencer to assign incoming data to particular MIDI channels (rechannelize it) depending which sound you want to use and which channel that sound is assigned to. You can also set your synth to transmit its data on a particular channel but since it's so much easier to select the required channel at the sequencer end it isn't worth the hassle: you'll probably leave your synth to transmit data on channel 1.

Therefore, MIDI data is sent from your synth on channel 1 and on arrival at the sequencer it's converted to your chosen channel, say channel 3, to be recorded and your sequencer's soft-thru facility returns this same data to your synth to be played on channel 3 letting you monitor your performance. The problem is that as you play, your notes are being doubled: your synth, being internally connected to channel 1, is playing the notes on the sound assigned to channel 1 at the same time as the sequencer is sending the notes back to the sound assigned to channel 3. As there's no noticeable time-delay in this happening the problem isn't usually unbearable, but it *is* often undesirable for three reasons: firstly, if every note is being played twice this is gobbling up your polyphony; you could find that the hefty brass-stabs you're playing keep vanishing because channel 1 is 'stealing' their voices. This doesn't affect the recording of the data as such, but it will tend to make it more difficult for you to play well. Secondly, if you're trying to record a glockenspiel part on channel 3 and you have a brass-patch assigned to channel 1, your cute little glockenspiel is going to be blown away by force ten trumpets! Finally, if you have a brass-patch on channel 1 for which you've already recorded a track and you want to lay down a piano part on channel 3, channel 1 will try to play its own existing track plus your piano part at the same time, possibly even expecting it to play the same note twice.

These are all, of course, just monitoring problems which have no *direct* effect on the recorded data, but they can dramatically undermine the speed and effectiveness of your programming and, by extension, the quality. Fortunately, there's a solution ...

What's The Solution?

The solution (unsurprisingly, given the topic header) is **Local Control**. This is essentially an *On/Off* switch to connect or disconnect your synth's keyboard from its sound-generator. To avoid all the pitfalls of programming by synth listed above, simply switch Local Control **Off**. Data will still be sent from your synth on channel 1 and return to it on channel 3 (or whichever channel you selected) but only this return-channel has a *direct connection* to your synth's sound-source, so only one lot of MIDI data will be heard – the one you *wanted* to hear!

It should be remembered that the Local Control setting affects data *transmission* from your synth only – tracks already recorded on any of your sequencer's 16 channels will continue to play back whatever the setting. Local Control can be set using a *switch* Control Change message (see page 186) for inclusion in your MIDI files.

Pssst ...!

If you also use your synth live on gigs, don't forget to *reconnect* its keyboard and sound-source again by turning Local Control back on!

MIDI Modes

This topic is included more as a troubleshooting reference than as required knowledge. It isn't necessary to memorise these details as your tone-generator's default mode should be satisfactory, but it's worth remembering that the information *is* here if you ever need it.

The MIDI Modes define the way your tone-generator responds to incoming data. There are four modes, each containing two parameters. The two parameters are:

❑ **Omni On/Off:** The Omni (meaning 'all') parameter refers to whether the tone-generator should respond to *all* data received at its MIDI In, ignoring the channel information contained in it (Omni On), or whether the channel information should be observed (Omni Off).

❑ **Poly/Mono:** The Polyphonic setting allows an instrument or channel to play several notes at the same time. Monophonic restricts an instrument or channel to sounding one note at a time – playing a second note cuts off the first.

These two parameters are grouped together in four different ways:

❑ **Mode 1: Omni On/Poly** (known as *Omni mode*). This mode tells an instrument or MIDI channel receiving data to respond to it *whatever channel settings it contains*, and to play the notes polyphonically. For programming purposes, Mode 1 is a definite no-no. Imagine sending a 10-channel MIDI file to a tone-generator set to Omni mode: every MIDI channel would try to play every note all at the same time, resulting in a godawful din! The main use of Mode 1 is when chaining several MIDI devices together (as in Fig. 5 of **MIDI Setup Diagrams** on page 34) and you want the second and third devices to play the notes you're playing on the first. Instead of matching and re-matching the receive channels of all three synths, just set the second and third synths to Mode 1 and they'll respond to all the data they receive regardless of any channel setting changes you make on the first synth.

❑ **Mode 2: Omni On/Mono** This mode functions in the same way as Mode 1 with the exception that the synth receiving the data will respond monophonically. This mode has little practical use to anyone and can be safely ignored.

❑ **Mode 3: Omni Off/Poly** (known as *Poly mode*). This is the usual programming mode. Instruments or channels will respond only to MIDI messages that are 'addressed' to them and will ignore the rest. For example, a bunch of MIDI data set to channel 3 being received by a tone-generator in this mode will be played by channel 3 and ignored by the other 15 channels. Each channel is able to respond polyphonically.

❑ **Mode 4: Omni Off/Mono** (known as *Mono mode*). This mode functions in the same way as Mode 3 with the exception that the device receiving the data will respond to it monophonically: mono mode is chiefly used for guitar and wind instruments.

The mode settings belong to the group of Control Changes known as *Channel Mode Messages*. All four MIDI Modes can be set using **fixed**

Control Changes (see page 187) allowing settings to be programmed into your MIDI files and set automatically whenever you play back the file.

MIDI Lead Guitar

The primary use for Mode 4 is with MIDI-Guitars, particularly for lead work: each of the six strings is assigned its own channel (each usually with the same sound setup and pitch-bend range) and each channel will respond monophonically in the same way that a guitar string does. This gets around two major problems: firstly, as a guitar is capable of playing the same note twice at the same time (on two different strings), having each string on a separate channel avoids the problem of retriggering. Secondly, the guitarist can apply pitch-bend to a single string without affecting the pitch of the others.

Detours

➡ Your setup should now be running better than Linford Christie on prune-juice. If it isn't, take a look at the **Troubleshooting Menu** on page 242.

What Is A Standard MIDI File?

When you've finished programming a song into your sequencer, you want to save the data to disk as a file, in the same way that you would a document file on a word-processor. It's at this point that you have to decide what **format** you want the file saved in. File formats fall into two categories: **Sequencer Song Files** and **Standard MIDI Files** (usually abbreviated to SMF).

Song Files

Your sequencer probably gives you the option to save your data as a song file with a name like TITLE.SNG, TITLE.ALL or TITLE.WRK and the result will be a fairly large file containing all your recorded MIDI data (of course), but possibly also including information about how you like your data to be presented on the screen (colours, shapes, sizes, etc.), layout of all the tracks, layout of all the separate segments or 'patterns' on the tracks and their names and so on. All this information is very useful, especially if you later want to reload the song into your sequencer to edit it in some way. And there's the crunch: it has to be loaded back into the *same* sequencer! All that extra information saved with the file is peculiar to your sequencer – a different sequencer wouldn't have a clue how to deal with it – so if you're programming a song to give to a friend, and she hasn't got the same sequencer you have, you're nobbled! Unless . . .

Standard MIDI Files

. . . you guessed it, unless you give it to her in SMF format (usually TITLE.MID). Nearly all sequencers give you the option to load & save SMFs (sometimes termed 'import & export' for no satisfactorily explained reason). Saving as a SMF strips out all of that sequencer-specific information and concentrates on saving just the recorded data plus any tempo and time-signature settings. This obviously makes for a smaller file by comparison and that's good news for your floppy disk mountain, but the best bit is the question of compatibility. SMFs are a standardised format which can be loaded into almost any sequencer and all the data will be exactly as you recorded it (with the possible exception of the resolution) even though the sequencer's on-screen presentation of it looks different.

For computer-users, the Standard MIDI File follows the same concept as that of saving a word-processor document in plain-text (ASCII) format: the layout and presentation detail is removed, leaving a file in a universal format but still containing all the sense of the original.

Standard MIDI File Formats

The idea of SMFs being a universal standard is quite a straightforward one, but it's complicated slightly by the fact that there are actually three different types of SMF: **Type 0, Type 1** and **Type 2**. Each format saves recorded data, tempos and time-signatures, but does it in a slightly different way.

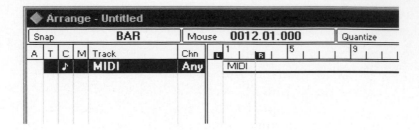

Fig. 11 **A Type 0 file in** *Cubase*

TYPE 0 (Fig. 11) was the original SMF format and remains the recommended format for General MIDI files. Type 0 takes all the tracks of data you recorded and mixes them together onto a single track (this doesn't alter the original channel settings of the data though). Some workstations and MIDI File Players will playback only a type 0 file.

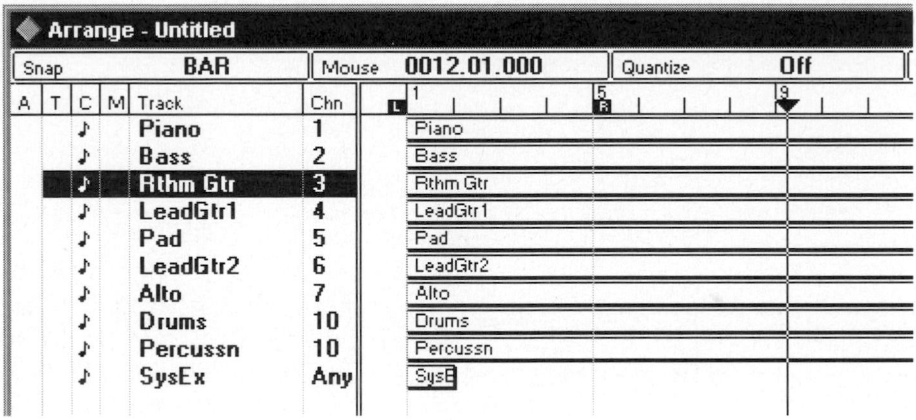

Fig. 12 **A Type 1 file in** *Cubase*

TYPE 1 (Fig. 12) is a more recent format which leaves the file very much the way it was; a collection of separate tracks, presumably with data for different channels on different tracks (depending upon your method of working). Type 1 will also save the names you gave the tracks such as Drums, Bass, etc. On some sequencers, if you had recorded your drums parts (usually on channel 10) on say four different tracks, one each for kick, snare, hats and toms, the sequencer will merge these tracks together when loading or saving the file to create just one track for that channel.

A few file-players and workstations cringe at type 1 files consisting of more than 16 tracks: in most of these cases, only the first 16 will be loaded; in the remainder, the file won't be loaded at all. If you're in the habit of creating extra empty tracks to use the track-name facility to enter your copyright or the song-name, check the number of tracks before saving (or *exporting*) as a type 1 file.

TYPE 2 format is more recent still, attempting to offer a more readily editable format than Type 1. As well as containing track information, the file saves pattern-data for each track to preserve layout when exported from a pattern-based sequencer. Type 2 has been almost universally ignored and, without this paragraph, you'd probably never be aware of its existence.

A few software sequencers offer an import-facility that produces a similar result to a type 2, often called *optimise*. This examines a type 0 or 1 file, splits each channel to a separate track (for a type 0) and removes blank sections from each track to display the file as a collection of patterns (albeit a rather arbitrary one at times).

Which One?

Most often, when you save your song as a Standard MIDI File, your sequencer will do one of two things: either ask you what type of file you want to save and then do what you tell it, mixing down to one track for type 0 if necessary, or it will simply look at whether the file consists of a single track or multiple tracks and save it accordingly. So you'll normally have full control over which *type* of file is saved.

> *For the purposes of this book, it's assumed you'll save as a Standard MIDI File (in either format), this being a necessity for most commercial programming. You might choose also to save it as a sequencer song file for your own use to make any later re-editing a bit easier. Throughout the book we refer to the finished file by the wider term* **'MIDI file'** *unless discussing a topic specific to the SMF alone.*

Are We Compatible?

So now we know that the SMF can be circulated widely for use in almost any MIDI setup (that's why the files on the accompanying disk are in SMF format). So is that all there is to this compatibility lark? No, not quite. The raw MIDI data can now be loaded into someone else's sequencer, but when she hits *Play*, and the data hits the tone-generator, what's it going to *sound* like? In **Section 2: MIDI Protocols** we'll examine this other vital aspect of compatibility.

Detours

➡ On the subject of saving and keeping your work in Standard MIDI File and other formats, take a look at the heading *The Backups* on page 91.

2

MIDI Protocols

MIDI was conceived in the early 1980s to allow all electronic musical instruments to 'speak' to each other in the same language. Up to this point, a few manufacturers had created their own communication systems for their instruments but none was 'multi-lingual'. MIDI's arrival, bringing with it standardised commands such as the Program Change, answered the communications question once and for all . . . and replaced it with a new one: if you can use this new language to record a song using one tone generator, and the standardisation of MIDI means that a different tone-generator could understand all the data and play it back, wouldn't it be nice if it could make it *sound* a little bit similar too?

The problem was that, although manufacturers included the same types of sound in their devices (organs, guitars, etc.), there was no consistency in the way these sounds were mapped to program-changes: a MIDI-file arrangement for piano and strings created on one device could easily become oboe and steel-drums when played back on another.

This section takes a closer look at the three existing protocols offering a solution to this problem, and culminates in an entirely unconnected beginners' tutorial on basic MIDI sequencing.

Data Compatibility

If you're planning to playback your completed MIDI file through a different tone-generator from the one you were using when you programmed the file, you'll probably be asking yourself '*What's it gonna sound like?*' or perhaps, if you've already tried it, '*Why did it sound like THAT?*' The question you should be asking yourself, of course, is '*Is it compatible?*'

Why Compatibility?

General MIDI and Roland's GS burst onto the scene almost simulta-neously in 1991. In the previous few years, MIDI files had started to become commercially available thanks to the standardised system of communications, but the file-producers either had to create files aimed at specific devices or include reams of text to explain how you should set up your tone-generator to make the song recognisable. While most devices included a trumpet patch, for example, in one device it might be patch #33 and in another patch #110. So while the program-change message would be received and understood, it wouldn't necessarily call up the right sound. And many devices of that era gathered their sounds into *banks* which weren't accessible via MIDI, complicating the issue still further. Hence the need for another level of compati-bility, and the 'protocols' were born.

What Are The Protocols?

The most established standard is **General MIDI** (GM), with most of the major hardware manufacturers either producing a dedicated

General MIDI tone-generator or including GM compatibility in their devices alongside their own specific sounds and features. Snapping at General MIDI's heels are Roland's **GS** and Yamaha's new baby, **XG**, both of which actually use General MIDI as their basis but include more sounds and enhanced control and editing facilities.

Data Types

The various types of data that could be included in a MIDI file can be loosely categorised under three headings: **universal**, **specific** and standard.

❏ A good example of a **universal** message is the *note* message: a file containing the note C3 (MIDI Note Number 60) will make any tone-generator play C3. It follows that notes can obviously be included in any file (well they're useful things in music, aren't they?) and never cause any compatibility problems. Certain other messages have become universal such as Control Change #7 controlling channel volume and Control Change #1 controlling modulation.

❏ **Specific** data is a function that only one tone-generator (or perhaps one manufacturer's series of tone-generators) can respond to. A good example here is System Exclusive: these messages contain a manufacturer's identification number so a message coded for a Korg device would be ignored by any *non*-Korg device that received it. Other examples along similar lines are the *Undefined* and *General Purpose* groups of controllers which individual devices may use for widely differing jobs, and the NRPN controllers (see page 190).

❏ The third type is data that conforms to a **standard** or 'protocol'. The most important example of this is in the way the patches (and/or banks) are numbered. This calls into play the earlier point that some manufacturers build General MIDI compatibility into their devices together with *extra* banks of sounds and control-parameters. Stick with the GM sounds and controllers and the file should play accurately on any GM-compatible device. Include one of the *extra* sounds and a different GM-compatible device might call up the wrong sound entirely or no sound at all. In other words, these extra sounds and features are *specific* to that tone-generator.

Do I Care?

If you're programming for your own needs (performance, recording, etc.) the question of protocols and compatibility need not arise and you're blissfully free to use any tone-generator (or combination of them) you like. For commercial MIDI file programming however, compatibility is a fundamental requirement and unless you're prepared to create different versions of your MIDI files for use with different tone-generators (unlikely), you'll want to choose a single protocol to allow your files to be used by the maximum number of people.

Detours

➟ **System Exclusive** is explained in all its glory on page 225.

➟ For more on General Purpose and Undefined Controllers, take a look at the **Controller List** on page 176.

▓ General MIDI

General MIDI (GM) was the first protocol developed to create a degree of compatibility among MIDI tone generators, and many manufacturers now produce at least one GM-compatible device. A MIDI file created using one GM sound-source may be played back on a different GM sound-source and will still call up the intended sound patches.

The GM protocol specifies a list of 128 sounds (the *sound set*) accessed by Program Change commands. So a MIDI file containing Program Change #30 (Overdrive Gtr) on a particular channel will still call up an Overdrive Gtr on that channel when the file is played back on any GM tone-generator. It's worth noting that the exact nuances of the sounds vary between manufacturers and tone-generators: a particular instrumental part that sounded great on *your* synth or module may not sound so hot on a different device. (Of course, it might sound even better!)

A GM device should have at least 24-voice polyphony with dynamic voice allocation, and give access to 16 MIDI channels. Each channel is polyphonic and can be assigned a different patch (with the exception of channel 10, the drums channel). By convention, channel

2 is made the Bass channel, channel 4 is reserved for the melody-line (in UK-produced files; other countries tend to ignore the melody) and channel 5 is becoming adopted as the vocal-harmonies channel. A single drum-kit, termed the GM or Standard Kit, is automatically called up on channel 10 by the GM Reset (see page 57) containing 47 percussion sounds mapped to MIDI Note Numbers 35 to 81. Reverb and Chorus effects are usually included as unofficial 'extras'. GM MIDI Files should be in Standard MIDI File type 0 format with a timebase of 96.

General MIDI also recognises a limited range of Control Change (CC) commands:

CC1	**Modulation**
CC6	**Data Entry MSB**
CC7	**Volume**
CC10	**Pan**
CC11	**Expression**
CC38	**Data Entry LSB**
CC64	**Sustain Pedal**
CC91	**External Effect (Reverb) Depth**
CC93	**Chorus Depth**

In addition to the above controllers, a more recent addition to the protocol is the Registered Parameter Number (RPN). RPNs are used chiefly to access the pitch-bend range of a channel. The RPNs are a collection of five controllers placed on consecutive ticks:

101:0
100:0
6:7
101:127
100:127

The first two controllers 'point' to the pitch-bend range parameter (number 0), the CC6 value sets the range (7 semitones in this case), and the final two controllers close the message (always with the value 127).

RPNs can also be used to control the tuning of a channel: assigning a value of 1 to CC100 allows control of Fine Tuning (this also requires the addition of CC38 following CC6); a value of 2 will control Coarse Tuning.

A more complete list of widely recognised control changes, including RPNs, can be found in the **Channel Messages Menu** (page 172), together with explanations and tips on use.

It should be pointed out that General MIDI compatibility is often included in a MIDI tone-generator as a *minimum standard*. Many tone-generators contain additional banks of sounds and on-board effects and will recognise a wider range of Control Change commands. Use of these extra features can provide a far greater potential for musical expression but will rather knock the concept of compatibility into a cocked hat. For example, if you use a non-GM patch or controller in your file you can't be sure how another tone-generator will interpret the command, or even if it'll recognise it at all!

Consult the MIDI Implementation Chart at the back of your User Manual to find any other features provided by your tone-generator.

> Note: General MIDI is still in its first incarnation, **Level One**. At the time of writing, the vague whispers about the long-awaited **Level Two** are becoming louder (though no less vague). Popular opinion suggests that the specification release for **GM Level Two** will occur roughly a fortnight after the author of this book thought he'd finished.

Detours

➡ If you want to know more about the glamorous world of General MIDI, take a look ahead at the **Song Header** topic (page 57) and at the **General MIDI Maps** on page 61.

Roland GS

What's GS?

Roland's GS Standard is an extension of the General MIDI protocol providing additional sound-banks, drum-kits and control-change implementation. (Contrary to popular belief, GS isn't an abbreviation for *General Standard* but is actually the name of a microchip used in Roland tone-generators.) First introduced in Roland equipment in the early 1990s, the steadily evolving GS specification has been included in a large proportion of Roland tone-generators ever since.

The Compatibility Question

General MIDI files are fully compatible with GS tone-generators, but won't use them to their fullest potential. Like General MIDI, GS offers a degree of compatibility between tone-generators and, as usual, this compatibility has its pros and cons. On the positive side, the additional features allow for more programming flexibility and the quality and timbre of the sounds remains consistent across the range of GS equipment. On the negative side, this compatibility is (at the time of writing) limited to Roland tone-generators only, thus restricting the commercial viability of a GS MIDI file.

GS Reset

The GS Reset is a System Exclusive command which resets GS-compatible tone-generators to GS defaults. The SysEx string is F0,41,10,42,12,40,00,7F,00,41,F7. Roland's implementation of the *GM* Reset has changed over the last few years: early GS tone-generators would interpret the GM Reset in the same way as the GS Reset, still allowing full control of all GS features. More recent equipment recognises the GM Reset more specifically, effectively 'locking' the tone-generator into General MIDI mode. GS files should therefore contain the GS Reset on the first tick of the file to ensure full recognition of GS control.

GS Sound Sets

GS sound sets are contained in separate banks accessible by **Bank Select** control changes 0 and 32. The General MIDI sound set is the primary bank, referred to as the *Capital* set. Many of these 128 Capital patches have one or more *Variations*, for example the Capital sound *Jazz Gtr* has a variation called *Hawaiian Gtr*. Variations are called up by placing CC0 and CC32 with the required values before the Program Change command. The value for CC0 is the number of the bank containing the required Variation; the value for CC32 is zero.

GS implementation of Bank Select messages has changed since the initial release. Originally, GS required only CC0; CC32 could be used, but was ignored. More recent releases definitely *do* require CC32, but always with a value of 0. This is still not quite in line with MIDI specifications, covered in **Variable Controllers** (page 182).

GS Percussion Sets

GS contains a number of different percussion and sound-effect 'kits', used by default on Channel 10. Each kit is accessed by its own Program Change command where the default *Standard Kit* is the General MIDI kit. Many of the kits, including the Standard Kit, contain extra sounds assigned to a wider range of MIDI note-numbers. A useful feature of GS is that you can set up more than one channel with a drum-kit, letting you use two different kits at the same time if you need to.

Non-Registered Parameter Numbers

As well as those required by General MIDI, GS recognises an increased range of controllers including MIDI's new toddler, the Non-Registered Parameter Number (NRPN), a method of providing easy user-access via control-changes to patch-editing parameters previously reachable only by System Exclusive. NRPNs, and their counterparts RPNs, are covered in more detail in their own topic on pages 188–9.

And Finally . . .

As a last word on GS, it should be remembered that its features and capabilities tend to expand with each new GS hardware release, in the same way that every manufacturer tries to use and improve on the latest technologies. Taken as a point on its own, this is just dandy. Realistically for programmers however, this means that there are a lot of people out there using GS equipment of various ages conforming to various points along the evolutionary path of the standard.

Detours

➡ For an explanation of the System Exclusive message in terms of the GS Reset skip ahead to the topic **System Exclusive: Analysis** on page 233.

▓ Yamaha XG

With the announcement of **XG** in late 1994, Yamaha threw their hat into the protocols ring. As with Roland's GS, the intention was to provide a more advanced alternative to General MIDI, particularly as the discussions over GM Level Two drag on, but Yamaha have had the additional challenge of having to compete with an already established GS.

Cross-Compatibility

One of the most basic, yet extremely important, advantages of XG is in the compatibility stakes. XG devices can play back a General MIDI file as faithfully as a GS or a dedicated GM unit. But Yamaha's master-stroke has been to include a degree of GS compatibility as well, with similar controller and NRPN mapping, plus some recognition of GS System Exclusive messages. An XG device should therefore replay a GS file almost as successfully as a Roland device. In effect, for users intending to program to an established protocol, the basic choice has come full-circle to what it was in the pre-protocol days: *whose sounds do you like best?*

The inter-compatibility consideration also means that XG files can be played back on a GM or GS device. Clearly some of the XG features will be lost in this instance (on a dedicated GM device, in fact, a *lot* will be lost), but you will still get the closest instrument approximation for each channel and the devices will react to any control data they recognise and simply ignore any they don't. Of course, XG has a few extra features to make it a protocol in its own right.

What's It Got?

Clearly most of the features of GS mentioned in the previous topic are implemented by XG. Here are a few of the major differences:

❑ Use of up to three simultaneous drumkits, on any MIDI channels (though the default is still a single kit on channel 10 for compatibility with both GM and GS).

❑ Three simultaneous effects: in keeping with GM and GS, two of these are Reverb and Chorus (CC91 and 93 respectively). The third is a bank of switchable effects, responding to CC94, containing effect-types such as distortion, wah, echo, autopan and EQ. Only one effect from this bank can be selected at a time and, as in other devices, the effect types chosen are global for all channels.

❑ 32-voice polyphony. This is the minimum polyphony specification: there are both GS and XG devices on the market offering 64-voice polyphony.

❑ All editable parameters are accessible via System Exclusive, and many are more easily reached using the NRPN controllers (see page 190). SysEx codes for chosen settings can be displayed on the device's screen and copied into your sequencer, which saves some delving into the back of the user-manual.

Bank Balance

XG includes full implementation of the Bank Select command (CC0 and 32) as contained in MIDI specification, which means that, in conjunction with the Program Change message, there are over 2 million possible voice locations (i.e., 128 cubed). Not that the devices actually *contain* 2 million voices, of course . . . and if they did, would you ever actually *choose* one?

The banks are constructed in the same way as the GS method. The 128 sounds of the General MIDI sound-set form the basis, with each of these sounds having a potential 16,383 *variations*. For example, variations on the GM Tenor Sax (patch number 67) might be a bright tenor, a mellow tenor, a breathy tenor and so on.

Open Format

A curiosity of the System Exclusive form used is that all the codes specify 'an XG device' rather than 'a Yamaha device'. The reason for this is simple: as an aid to establishing XG as a force to be reckoned with, it was conceived as an *open format*. In other words, Yamaha are encouraging other manufacturers to produce their own XG devices, in much the same way that most of the major manufacturers are now producing General MIDI instruments.

A further point worth mentioning about XG System Exclusive messages, which should appeal to anyone having previous SysEx experience: XG SysEx messages don't require use of a checksum, which means that the data-portion of the message can be entered or changed with very little mathematical exertion.

■ Song Header

What Is The Song Header?

The song header of a MIDI file is the first bar of the file, containing Program Change and Controller data which sets up your tone-generator to play the song body (i.e., the note-data). This topic describes the header layout for a **General MIDI** file but the header concept holds true for any file you program, though the data it contains may vary.

The header may actually be longer than just a single bar if a lot of data is required to make the correct settings or if you're working in a time-signature containing fewer than four quarter-note beats, but General MIDI recognises so few commands that the GM header should never really need to exceed the single bar.

Load **HEADER.MID** into your sequencer to see an example of a General MIDI header-bar. The file is in type 1 format which splits the data for each channel onto a different track (usually with an extra track containing the GM Reset, depending upon how your sequencer handles System Exclusive). If you'd prefer the data all on the same track, you can use your sequencer's *mixdown* or *merge* functions to do this.

GM Reset

The first event of the header bar is the GM Reset, a System Exclusive command that resets a General MIDI-compatible tone-generator to GM defaults. The GM Reset should always occur on the first tick of any GM file. Since System Exclusive data takes longer to process than channel data, it's usual to allow the whole of the first beat for this to take place. The SysEx string is F0,7E,7F,09,01,F7. The default settings called up by the reset for each channel are:

CC7 Main Volume	:100
CC10 Pan	:64 (Centre)
CC11 Expression	:127
CC91 Reverb	:40
CC93 Chorus	:0
Pitch-Bend Range	:$\pm$2 semitones

The GM Reset also sets each channel to Acoustic Piano (General MIDI patch #1), returns pitch-bend to zero (centre-point) and sends an All Notes Off message to all channels.

Header Layout

You'll see that each event is carefully placed so that no more than three events will occur on any one tick. Notice also that the events for channel 1 start on 1.2.2. The first two ticks of the beat (1.2.0 and 1.2.1) are reserved for Bank Select commands (in preparation for their future inclusion in the GM spec) and there are two 'empty' ticks before each channel's events for the same purpose, so channel 2's data starts on 1.2.7, channel 3's on 1.2.12 and so on.

The control-changes for all channels range from lowest to highest numbered with CC7, 10 and 11 occurring on the same tick and CC91 and 93 on the next tick.

The drums channel (channel 10) is slightly different: in General MIDI, as there's only one drumkit, no program change is used, and panning of the drums isn't part of the specification so CC10 is left out.

The RPN #0 controllers begin on 1.3.0 thru 1.3.4 for channel 1; 1.3.5 thru 1.3.9 for channel 2 and so on. These should always be on separate ticks to make sure they arrive at the tone-generator in the correct order.

RPN Time-Saver

HEADER.MID contains RPN #0s for every channel (except 10) set to ±2 semitones. These have been included in the file to save you the laborious task of entering all these controllers when you need them: you can just set the pitch-bend range you need (by changing the value of CC6) and get on with the business of recording. Since the GM Reset automatically sets each channel to the same range however, you should delete any RPNs in the song-header *still* remaining at ±2 when you've finished programming – the only effect they're having is to clutter up your file.

The following is a quick run-down on the events found in the General MIDI song-header and their functions. Each of these has a topic of its own containing more detailed information on the given page-numbers.

Program Change

The Program Change command selects the required instrument for a particular channel from the GM sound set. Program Change commands can be numbered in two ways, depending on the sequencer you're using. One method numbers the patches from 0–127, the other 1–128. By the first method, #30 would call up the Distortion Gtr patch whereas the second system would call up the *true* patch, Overdrive Gtr. (Bear in mind that these are simply differences in the *display* of data – the data itself when saved and/or transferred to a different sequencer is unaffected.) Channel 10 doesn't contain a Program Change because the GM Reset automatically sets up the default (only) drum-kit. (See page 197.)

CC7 – Volume

CC7 sets the main volume for the channel. It should only ever be used in the header-bar: during the course of the song all changes in volume should be made by CC11 Expression. (See page 208.)

CC10 – Pan

CC10 adjusts the panoramic position of the sound within the stereo field, ranging 0–127 (left to right) with 64 representing 'Centre'. Note that there's no CC10 event for Channel 10: GM doesn't allow for panning of the drum-kit. (See page 210.)

CC11 – Expression

Another method of controlling the volume of a sound; within the *body* of a song (i.e., after the header-bar) CC11 should be used for all adjustments to volume. (See page 213.)

CC91 – Reverb*

Adjusts the reverb depth, an effect which imitates the way sound 'bounces around' in a concert hall or a room. (See page 217.)

CC93 – Chorus*

Adjusts the chorus depth, a 'thickening' effect created by delaying and detuning elements of the sound. (See page 219.)

CCI0I and 100 – RPNs

Chiefly used to set or alter the pitch-bend range, but GM also recognises the RPN commands to change the fine or coarse pitch-tuning of a sound. (See page 188.) These are used in conjunction with CC6 and 38 (Data Entry) which are mentioned on page 184.

* Check the footnote to the table 'GM Recognised Commands' (p. 63) regarding the implementation of effects in General MIDI.

To save time when starting to program a file, why not use **HEADER.MID** as your start-off point? Just enter the required values for each event and get on with making the music!

Detours

→ At this point, MIDI newcomers who are diligently working through the book to learn all the basics in a structured way should skip to the **Channel Messages Menu** on page 172 and read the *Overview* section to learn about the finer points of notes, controllers, pitch-bend, etc., before continuing (we'll give you a shout when it's time to come back!).

→ The most frequently used control-changes (including those listed in this topic) are covered in more depth with topics of their own from pages 206–23.

→ To find out more about how GM, GS and XG System Exclusive reset messages can be used in combination, turn to page 236.

→ More detailed information on System Exclusive can be found in the **System Messages Menu** on page 224, including a SysEx alternative to the Song Header.

General MIDI Maps

GM Patch Map (Sound Set)

1 Acoustic Piano	43 Cello	85 Charang Lead
2 Bright Acoustic Piano	44 Contrabass	86 Voice Lead
3 Electric Grand Piano	45 Tremolo Strings	87 Fifths Lead
4 Honky-Tonk Piano	46 Pizzicato	88 Bass & Lead
5 Electric Piano 1	47 Harp	89 New-Age Pad
6 Electric Piano 2	48 Timpani	90 Warm Pad
7 Harpsichord	49 Marcato Strings	91 Polysynth Pad
8 Clavinet	50 Slow Strings	92 Choir Pad
9 Celesta	51 Synth Strings 1	93 Bowed Pad
10 Glockenspiel	52 Synth Strings 2	94 Metal Pad
11 Music Box	53 Choir Aahs	95 Halo Pad
12 Vibraphone	54 Voice Oohs	96 Sweep Pad
13 Marimba	55 Synth Voice	97 Synth FX Rain
14 Xylophone	56 Orchestra Hit	98 Synth FX Soundtrack
15 Tubular Bells	57 Trumpet	99 Synth FX Crystal
16 Dulcimer	58 Trombone	100 Synth FX Atmosphere
17 Drawbar Organ	59 Tuba	101 Synth FX Brightness
18 Percussive Organ	60 Muted Trumpet	102 Synth FX Goblins
19 Rock Organ	61 French Horn	103 Synth FX Echoes
20 Church Organ	62 Brass Section	104 Synth FX Sci-Fi
21 Reed Organ	63 Synth Brass 1	105 Sitar
22 Accordion	64 Synth Brass 2	106 Banjo
23 Harmonica	65 Soprano Sax	107 Shamisen
24 Bandoneon	66 Alto Sax	108 Koto
25 Nylon Acoustic Guitar	67 Tenor Sax	109 Kalimba
26 Steel Acoustic Guitar	68 Baritone Sax	110 Bagpipes
27 Jazz Electric Guitar	69 Oboe	111 Fiddle
28 Clean Electric Guitar	70 English Horn	112 Shannai
29 Muted Electric Guitar	71 Bassoon	113 Tinkle Bell
30 Overdrive Guitar	72 Clarinet	114 Agogo
31 Distortion Guitar	73 Piccolo	115 Steel Drums
32 Guitar Harmonics	74 Flute	116 Woodblock
33 Acoustic Bass	75 Recorder	117 Taiko Drum
34 Fingered Elec Bass	76 Pan Flute	118 Melodic Drum
35 Picked Elec Bass	77 Bottle Blow	119 Synth Drum
36 Fretless Bass	78 Shakuhachi	120 Reverse Cymbal
37 Slap Bass 1	79 Whistle	121 Guitar Fret Noise
38 Slap Bass 2	80 Ocarina	122 Breath Noise
39 Synth Bass 1	81 Square Wave Lead	123 Seashore
40 Synth Bass 2	82 Saw Wave Lead	124 Bird Tweet

41	Violin	83	Calliope Lead	125	Telephone
42	Viola	84	Chiffer Lead	126	Helicopter
				127	Applause
				128	Gunshot

GM Percussion Map (Standard Kit on Channel 10)

Note	MNN	Instrument	Note	MNN	Instrument
B0	35	Acoustic Kick	B2	59	Ride Cymbal 2
C1	36	Rock Kick	C3	60	High Bongo
C#1	37	Side Stick	C#3	61	Low Bongo
D1	38	Acoustic Snare	D3	62	Mute High Conga
D#1	39	Handclap	D#3	63	Open High Conga
E1	40	Electric Snare	E3	64	Low Conga
F1	41	Low Floor Tom	F3	65	High Timbale
F#1	42	Closed Hi-Hat	F#3	66	Low Timbale
G1	43	High Floor Tom	G3	67	High Agogo
G#1	44	Pedal Hi-Hat	G#3	68	Low Agogo
A1	45	Low Tom	A3	69	Cabasa
A#1	46	Open Hi-Hat	A#3	70	Maracas
B1	47	Low Mid-Tom	B3	71	Short Whistle
C2	48	High Mid-Tom	C4	72	Long Whistle
C#2	49	Crash Cymbal 1	C#4	73	Short Guiro
D2	50	High Tom	D4	74	Long Guiro
D#2	51	Ride Cymbal 1	D#4	75	Claves
E2	52	Chinese Cymbal	E4	76	High Woodblock
F2	53	Ride Bell	F4	77	Low Woodblock
F#2	54	Tambourine	F#4	78	Mute Cuica
G2	55	Splash Cymbal	G4	79	Open Cuica
G#2	56	Cowbell	G#4	80	Mute Triangle
A2	57	Crash Cymbal 2	A4	81	Open Triangle
A#2	58	Vibraslap			

GM Recognised Commands

Command	Range or Value	Function
Program Change	0–127 *or* 1–128	Selects patch #1–128
Pitch-Bend	0:0–127:127	Bend pitch of note (0:64 = no bend)
Note-On	0–127	——
Control Change 1	0–127	Modulation
Control Change 6	0–127	Data Entry MSB for RPNs
Control Change 7	0–127	Main Volume

Control Change 10	0–127	Pan
Control Change 11	0–127	Expression
Control Change 38	0–127	Data Entry LSB (RPN Fine Tuning)
Control Change 64	0 or 127	Sustain Pedal
Control Change 91*	0–127	Reverb Depth*
Control Change 93*	0–127	Chorus Depth*
Control Change 101	0	RPN MSB
Control Change 100	0	RPN LSB – Pitch-bend range
Control Change 100	1	RPN LSB – Fine Tuning
Control Change 100	2	RPN LSB - Coarse Tuning
System Exclusive		
F0,7E,7F,09,01,F7	—	GM Reset (Turn GM mode On)

* Despite being listed here and elsewhere in this book, there is actually no provision in the General MIDI Level One specification for Reverb and Chorus. However, since most of the hardware companies producing GM equipment recognise the fundamental nature of these effects and include them anyway, they've become a sort of 'unofficial' feature of the protocol.

Recording Session

The following is a short tutorial to introduce the basics of MIDI programming in step-by-step fashion, and to encourage you to use some of the basic programming techniques and sequencer functions. As exact sequencer facilities vary between models and software packages, make sure you keep that manual handy to help you find your way around your specific sequencer.

As usual, all the tick references in this topic assume a sequencer timebase of 96, so if your sequencer uses a different timebase, a bit of arithmetic will be needed (e.g., for a timebase of 192, multiply all the given tick-numbers by 2).

Before you begin, make sure you have a clean formatted floppy-disk ready (if you're not using a hard-disk system). The tutorial is split into three sessions and we'll prompt you to save your file at the end of each one (under three different names) so that you can later compare them with our examples.

Session One – Record and Quantize

 Load the file **HEADER.MID** into your sequencer (for more details about this file, skip back to **Song Header** on page 57).

Setting up

Edit your sequencer's tempo-track (which may be called the *Conductor* or *Mastertrack*) to read 116 beats-per-minute and check the time-signature is set at 4/4. If your sequencer has a *Record Quantize* function (to automatically correct the timing of the notes as you record), turn this off.

Now select the header for channel 1 and open it in your list-editor so that you can see the program-change and controller events displayed. Alter the program-change number to a patch-number corresponding to a pad sound (for General MIDI devices, use patch #94 – Metal Pad). Close the editor, making sure this alteration will be kept. Now select channel 2's header to edit and set a program-change for a synth-bass sound (GM patch #40) in the same way. Next, set a piano sound for channel 3 (GM patch #3) and a strings sound for channel 4 (GM patch #49).

If you're not using a GM tone-generator, you might need to call up a drum-kit on channel 10: this is usually done in *List Edit* by manually inserting a program-change event (one tick before the first control-change event) and setting it to the required patch number and channel. GM devices will automatically call up the kit.

Now play the header portion of the file from the beginning so that all these events are sent to your tone-generator to reset it and call up the chosen sounds for each channel.

TASK #1 – Record a 1-bar drum count-in

Select the drums track (or a new track rechannelized to 10) and set it up to record from 2.1.0 to 3.1.0. Make sure the metronome is activated so that you can keep in time when recording, and is set to give you a 4-beat countdown.

Hit the *Record* button, and after the metronome countdown play a 4 quarter-note count-in using the hi-hat or something similar. Now quantize these notes fully (100% if your sequencer has a partial quantize) so that they play on 2.1.0, 2.2.0, 2.3.0, 2.4.0 – you could easily do this manually by moving them but now's a good time to get those quantize functions sorted out!

The count-in bar we've just recorded isn't important in this file, but in any file intended for live use a count-in is vital.

TASK #2 – Record a basic 4-bar drum pattern
Now set up the same drum-track to record from 3.1.0 to 7.1.0 and after the metronome countdown record a simple kick & snare pattern. Set the quantize value to eighth-notes and once again quantize 100%. Next select a new track and set its channel to 10. After the metronome countdown record a simple hi-hat pattern with an 8th-note feel (you should be able to hear the kick/snare track playing while you do this). Now quantize the hats in the same way.

TASK #3 – Editing Note Velocities
By quantizing these drum tracks we've eliminated any chance of human feel creeping in (which isn't something we want to make a habit of!), but we're going to try to recreate at least *some* of that feel by changing the velocities of the notes. How you do it is up to you, but a useful tip is that wide velocity differences can be very effective – usually the *in-between* eighth-notes will be a good deal quieter than the others. You might choose to use the *Drum Edit* screen to do this if your sequencer has one.

TASK #4 - Recording a pad track
At this point you can turn off the metronome - it should still give you a 1-bar countdown but you can now use your drum-part to guide you which will give you a decidedly better feel. This is a good reason to record and edit the drum-tracks first.

Recording the pad-track next has a similar role: it can help give you *harmonic* feel for later parts as the drums give *rhythmic* feel. It's worth getting a pad down at least roughly in the early stages even if you want to re-record it or delete it later.

Select channel 1 which has already been set up for the pad sound and make sure you're still set to record from bars 3 to 7. After the countdown record the pad part:

Quantize the part fully to a value of 1 (whole-note) so that each note occurs on the first tick of a bar, and then adjust the note lengths to make every note *finish* about 10 ticks before the end of the bar (a length of roughly 374 ticks).

TASK #5 – Recording the bass-line
Now switch to channel 2's track and record the bass line below for the same 4-bar section.

Quantize this to quarter-notes (a value of 4) and fix the *length* of each note at an eighth-note (48 ticks).

TASK #6 – Recording a rhythmic part
Now we move to the track set up for channel 3 to record an ad lib rhythmic part (but obviously following the same chord-chart as in Task #4). If you're using a MIDI guitar to enter data you might prefer to change the header's program-change to a guitar sound rather than the piano we set earlier. What type of pattern you play is up to you, but as our other rhythmic parts (bass and drums) are fairly 'straight' a slightly syncopated rhythm would help to loosen things up.

Quantize this to eighth or sixteenth notes, depending on whether the shortest notes you played were eighth-notes or sixteenth-notes. (Check the result carefully – the quantize function moves the notes to the nearest division of the beat you specified, so if your timing was a bit dodgy some of the notes might actually move to the *wrong* sixteenth-note division!)

TASK #7 – Recording a solo-line

Now we'll record a string-line on channel 4, once again for the same 4-bar section:

We're not going to quantize this because sounds with a slow attack tend to sound late when quantized – the note-ons should usually occur 'early'. If the timing seems a bit ragged, set the quantize value to sixteenth-notes and either use a lower percentage (50–75%) to just pull the notes *towards* the beat or select an *Intelligent, Analytic* or *Iterative* quantize option if you have one – any of these should do a similar job. If you don't like the result, you should be able to undo the quantize, or at least exit the edit-screen without saving the change and try again.

If the line sounds as if it's late or dragging slightly, try moving the notes manually so that they all start earlier (or, in a pattern-based sequencer, pull the whole pattern forwards a few ticks).

Now that the basic recording of this section is complete, the final task is to play the sequence through a couple of times and manually correct any velocity or timing errors, or indeed anything you think could be better!

Now save the song to disk as a Standard MIDI File (your sequencer might term this 'Export MIDI' or 'Save as MIDI') giving it the name SESSION1.MID.

Session Two – Editing

Now we're going to perform some surgery on the file we've just saved as SESSION1.MID, and later save it again under a different name.

TASK #1 – Copy/repeat the 4-bar arrangement

Next we want to copy all the recorded sections (except the count-in) to start on 7.1.0 so that we'll end up with an 8-bar phrase consisting of two identical 4-bar phrases. In a pattern-based sequencer, this should be as easy as drawing a box around all the patterns and selecting the *Repeat* function. On a linear sequencer, it might be the *Copy/Paste* menu-option you go to within an *Edit* screen, but the process should be just as straightforward.

TASK #2 – Create a new kit-instrument part

Create a new track rechannelized to 10, and *copy* the kick/snare pattern to this track, positioning it to begin at 6.4.94 (in other words all the events contained in this copy are shifted forward two ticks). Now delete all the kick notes, and transpose the remaining snares to handclaps – you may be able to do this by changing one note into a handclap and selecting a *Fix All Notes* function; otherwise select the transpose function and enter the direction and number of semitones you want the notes transposed. Offsetting the claps from the snares in this way gives a 'thicker' hit and goes some way towards *pushing* the tempo as the beat now starts earlier.

TASK #3 – Add crash cymbals and fill

Select the first hi-hat pattern to edit, select the first note (on 3.1.0) and manually change it to a crash cymbal; you might also want to alter the velocity of the note. If you have a note on 3.1.48 delete it – the drummer isn't likely to rush back to the hi-hat quite so quickly. Do the same thing in the repeated section (7.1.0).

Now we want to add a drum-fill at the end of the first kick/snare pattern leading into the repeat. There are three possible options here, firstly, go into edit and insert extra note-events manually. Secondly, if your sequencer has an *Overdub* facility, cue up to record over the kick/snare track from 6.1.0 to 7.1.0 and play it in real-time, using *Undo* if it goes wrong. The third option is to create another channel 10 track and record bar 6's drum-fill on it. The last two options need some care (and possibly editing) to avoid *retriggering* – trying to make the channel play the same note twice at the same time; you might find it easier to manually delete all the kick/snare events in bar 6 and just record a whole *new* bar 6.

Depending upon the complexity of the fill, you might want to edit the hi-hat part at bar 6 to remove any hits a drummer with fewer than three hands couldn't play.

TASK #4 – Another bit of copying

Now we need channel 5 set up with a muted-guitar sound, so edit its header to insert the correct patch number (General MIDI patch #29). Now select the second bass pattern and copy it to channel 5's track, but position it to start at 7.1.48, in other words to make the guitar play the same bass notes an eighth-note later. Finally transpose this new muted-guitar pattern up an octave.

TASK #5 – Basic mixing

At the moment the file is *dry* (no effects) and everything is still panned to centre, so we need to set reverb/chorus levels (CC91 and 93 respectively) and possibly change the panning on some of the sounds (CC10). These controllers are in the headers of each track, so it's back to *List Edit* again!

As you get more familiar with the sounds and the controllers you'll start to have a pretty good idea of the settings you need in particular cases before you start recording and you might want to enter them then. For now it's a case of experimentation and the easiest way to do this is to set up your sequencer to *Loop* or *Cycle* continuously between bars 7 and 11 while you make changes to the channels from the front panel of your synth or module (but if you have a *Chase* facility on your sequencer, make sure it's switched off or it'll keep resetting the controls every time it loops!). You might also want to adjust the volume of various channels using CC7. When you've got the sound as you want it, just 'copy' the settings manually from your tone-generator's screen into the appropriate headers.

Alternatively your sequencer might have a built-in facility allowing you to mix the sound in real-time on the screen. If you use this, make sure you know how these changes are inserted into the file – if *new* events are created you would need to delete the *unused* events in the headers.

Now save the file to disk as SESSION2.MID.

Session Three – Controller Remap and Ending

Now a last bit of editing to the file we just saved and a final spring-clean.

TASK #1 – Use remap to create a pan-sweep

This relies on either your sequencer having a Controller Remap facility (which might be buried in a *Filters* or *MIDI Setup* menu), or your keyboard allowing you to assign a particular controller-number to a wheel or fader. We need to access the pan-controller (CC10), so if your keyboard has a volume fader (transmitting CC7) reset it to CC10 on your keyboard, or use your sequencer's facility to remap CC7 to CC10.

Now create a new track rechannelized to 3 and cue up to record from 3.1.0 to 11.1.0. Start recording and use the remapped fader to enter gradual pan-sweeps across the stereo field as the channel 3 rhythm part plays.

A point worth mentioning here is that this process will always record unnecessary data – controller events being recorded while no notes are sounding and therefore having no effect. It's good practice to remove these events, as described in the **Clean Up**! section of the **Pitch Bend** topic (page 203), but we won't hang around doing that now!

TASK #2 – Create an ending

This is a very quick, unimaginative and lazy way to end and it's just included here to add a sense of completeness to the file!

Start by repeating/copying the recorded patterns to the end of the song as we did at the top of Session Two, but don't include the handclaps, pan-sweep or muted guitar parts. Now work through the new patterns deleting all the events occurring after 11.1.0 so that we're left with only the first 'chord' of this new section – you might be able to do this quickly by highlighting all the events and hitting *Delete*.

Now stretch the lengths of all except the drum notes in this 'new' section to last a bar or so. Finally, select the tempo track and enter a tempo of 43 at 11.1.4 (which will make this chord last the equivalent of almost three bars at our original tempo).

TASK #3 – Clean Up !

As always, listen to the song a few times hunting for anything that could be improved, such as timing, volume or velocities, the mix, clashing notes and so on. Finally, delete the headers for any unused channels (in this case 6–9 and 11–16), and delete any unnecessary RPN controllers from the remaining headers (in this case, *all* the RPNs are unwanted).

Save this completed file to disk with the name SESSION3.MID.

What Now?

The point of this exercise was of course to provide you with something to record and to give you the opportunity to find the basic sequencing tools and use the basic techniques – hopefully you've learned something from all this and are ready to embark on a full-length song-file. But what of the files you've just created?

For the sake of interest, and the possibility of learning a little more, try comparing your SESSION?.MID files with our example files, named **COMPARE?.MID**. Try to look for *programming* differences as opposed to *musical* differences and try to decide which result is the more effective and why.

> ### Detours
>
> ➨ Having created these files, you might also like to use them to try out other sequencer facilities, add some extra instruments or apply some of the ideas from **Tricks and Effects**, starting on page 124.

3

Programming Techniques

In this section we take a look at some of the basic considerations, techniques and skills involved in programming a MIDI file. Most of the following topics are slanted towards programming a cover-version file for commercial or 'live' use (you'll see references to *the original record* and so on) – nevertheless, all the points covered apply universally.

Keep in mind over the next few pages that we're not trying to tell you what to do or how to do it – *everybody's working methods are different and equally legitimate* – but these topics should provide a start-off point for the beginner and hopefully give the old hand a few new ideas!

Preparation

Once all the elements of your studio are up and running, you need to optimise your working conditions to make the creative process as constructive as you can. Here are a few points worth considering.

Environment

It's very important to make sure that your working environment is comfortable: once you're involved in working on a file and buzzing with ideas about what to do and how to do it, you want immediate access to everything. So make sure that you can easily reach all the pieces of equipment in your system, and see their front-panel displays, without too many physical contortions.

Sound

Make sure your speakers are well positioned to give you a good representative mix: above all this means that they shouldn't be too close to you, but how far *apart* they are is important too. If they're too close together you won't be able to gauge the changes in pan-position of sounds as easily, but if they're too far apart you might find that a well-spread mix seems to have a 'hole' in the middle. This last situation can be countered (to some degree) by turning the speakers slightly towards each other.

If you use headphones, it's worth investing in a quality set with a good frequency response – cheaper headphones are particularly lacking at the bass end which could result in your files all having kick and bass volumes sky-high!

Forward Planning

If you're using a floppy-disk system, make sure you've got a few formatted floppies ready – if your computer isn't multi-tasking you'd have to shut down your sequencer (song and all) to format the disk! Keep a supply of pencils, paper and manuscript handy.

If this is your first cover-file or full-length MIDI file, choose a fairly short, simple and repetitive song, one that gives plenty of opportunities to repeat, copy and paste sections – in your early days of MIDI programming you can still learn a vast amount by doing the simplest things, and finishing a song (however simple it was) is one of the best motivators there is to start another one!

Preferences

Most computer-based sequencers have some form of Preferences File (possibly also called an *Autoload, Default* or *Setup* file) which loads into your sequencer automatically every time you run the program. As the name suggests, this file can be customised, saving you the hassle of manually setting everything up the way you like it each time you want to program something new. Now is the time to set up your Preferences file and resave it, and here are a few things worth including if you can:

❑ Include HEADER.MID with a one-bar count-in on channel 10 so that you can just enter the necessary channel settings and start programming.

❑ Set the *Controller Remapping* function to remap CC7 (Volume) to CC11 (Expression). The reasons for this are explained in detail on pages 208–9.

❑ Ensure that MIDI Thru (or MIDI Echo) is On.

❑ Set any *Record Quantize* functions to Off (you can always quantize later if you need to, but you want to keep your options open!)

❑ Check metronome settings are as you'd like them, including whether MIDI metronome is on or off and which drum-note it will play – setting it to Claves (GM note number 75) is usually a good idea as this sound isn't frequently used in a file and is easily audible.

❑ Turn Chase or Update Events on.

❑ Set any aesthetically pleasing factors, which may include such things as colour-schemes, sizes and positions of edit-screens and menus, etc.

❑ Turn on the *Autosave* function if one exists, and specify how often to save (try setting it to 10 minutes and see how you get on).

There are bound to be other options included in the Preferences file, and they may be listed in your sequencer's manual. If not, try to set *everything* up the way you like it (including options only available within edit-modes, etc.). To save the file once all the settings have been made, you would usually select a menu option such as *Save Preferences* or *Save Setup*. You might even be able to save several different Preferences files to suit different working methods or musical styles.

No Preferences Facility?

All is not lost. Set up all your preferences as above, and simply save the song with an obvious name like *Setup* or *Default* in your sequencer's own song-file format (you may have several generic formats, so check which one saves all the user-preferences with the song-data). You may not be able to convince it to load automatically but even loading the file yourself is still a lot quicker than setting up the sequencer every time!

Remember – once you load this file and then start programming, it takes only one punch of the *Save* button (or the *Autosave* kicks in) and this file has been overwritten. So, firstly make sure that you keep a copy of the file somewhere else and, secondly, as soon as you've recorded or entered the first few events of a new song, use the *Save As...* file function and save it under a different name to prevent this happening any more often than it has to!

Autosave Or Not?

On first sight, the *Autosave* facility found on some sequencers seems a positive Godsend – at last you can just get on with programming and not have to remember to save regularly. The interval between saves can usually be set to suit your speed of working (see Fig. 13), but intervals of 10–15 minutes are usually best however slowly you work – the worst it can do is to resave an unchanged file. And if you experience the dreaded software-crash, at least the *scale* of the disaster has been minimised.

Fig. 13 **Autosave in** *Cakewalk Pro*

But *Autosave* has its negative side too. It's a long shot, but it happens: you've just accidentally erased the entire drum-track, the *Autosave* suddenly kicks in and saves your newly drum-less file and it's bye-bye bongos. Unless the *Autosave* creates an automatic backup of the previous save, or you recently saved manually under a different filename, you have to start your drum-programming over again. Without *Autosave*, it would have been a simple case of just reloading your last save.

Hint

➡ If your Autosave doesn't create backups, it's probably best to regard it as merely a time-saver, meaning that you don't need to save quite as often as you usually would. To cover all bases you should still aim to save manually under a different filename regularly, and preferably alternate between three or four filenames or floppy-disks for total security.

You might also find that the *Autosave* temporarily 'steals' your control over the sequencer while it saves – it seems a minor point but when it happens every 10 minutes it can be frustrating.

Detours

➥ For more on the vital questions of saving files and keeping backups, take a look at the *Save And Prosper* heading on page 82, and *The Final Save* and *The Backups* in **Finishing Touches** (pages 89 and 91).

▓ Organisation

An important part of serious MIDI programming is to establish a working method which suits you and try to stick with it. Making a **skeleton plan** for a song and trying to foresee likely pitfalls in advance can mean the difference between a good file and an unfinished file!

Skeleton Plan

The first job is to listen to the recording several times, concentrating on different aspects each time. Try to understand the **structure** of the song (verse/chorus, etc.) and notice sections that could be copied and pasted from an earlier part of the song. Try to gauge the **number of instruments** used, especially near the end when arrangements tend to get busier.

It's often useful to sketch out the song's chord-sequence bar-by-bar (without repeat-signs), leaving alternate lines blank to scribble down ideas or belated discoveries. Don't try to put too much detail on paper as over-analysis can often dampen your enthusiasm for a song (just as a joke stops being funny as soon as you think about it).

Finally, and most importantly, make written notes of the instruments you hear and/or the patches you can use to emulate them. It's well worth playing the song a few times to do this: it's very easy to miss an instrument because you weren't *tuned in* to that area of the mix.

General MIDI Programming

For General MIDI programming, be aware of the polyphony limitations: 24 voices get used a great deal quicker if your song relies on synth sounds which often require more than one voice per note: be prepared either to change a sound or thin-out the note data on certain channels.

Remember that General MIDI is a limited specification and anyone using GM files *knows* it is – it's not always possible to find a good match for the sound on the original recording so choose the best working compromise and accept that it's GM's failing, not yours!

Channel Planning

Next try to determine which patch should be assigned to which MIDI channel, bearing in mind the voice allocation system your tone-generator uses. Excluding drums (channel 10), channel 1 often has maximum priority over voice allocation and channel 16 has least. A monophonic (solo) instrument such as a trumpet can usually be given a lower channel priority than a piano or a string section for example. Similarly, it's pointless to 'waste' a high-priority channel on an instrument which occurs only during sparser sections of the song.

Advance planning of this kind can save you from a whole host of nasty surprises, not least of which is having to deal with lack of polyphony. Technically your GM file should not require more than 24 voices. In practice however, unless you can actually *hear* notes 'dropping-out', you can't tell that you've exceeded the maximum polyphony. The bottom line in this situation must be: if it sounds okay stick with it! Careful choice of MIDI channels will make it more likely to sound okay.

Dictation

Some parts of this section are geared towards programming a *cover-version* of an existing record, which almost always involves 'lifting' the arrangement from CD or tape by dictation.

Dictation is one of those areas of music that doesn't particularly require talent, but takes perseverance and practical experience – slowly but surely you get better at it, and start to develop your own tricks and methods to work out chord progressions, bass-lines and so on.

If you're programming original material instead, the position is very similar to working with covers, except that you're getting around the dictation problem quite neatly.

Working Method

Whether working on covers or original material you need to decide how to construct your file. There are two equally legitimate ways to go about it: either record each instrumental part in turn for the whole song (for example, the whole drum-track, then the whole bass-track and so on), or pick a section of the music (the intro is the obvious place to start) and record all the instruments in that section, then move on to the first verse, etc.

Whichever of these methods you choose, there's one golden rule that can't be over-emphasised: *EDIT AS YOU GO!* Every time you record something, mix it, balance it, check it for unnecessary data and listen for timing errors or polyphony problems before you start work on the next area of the arrangement.

Creation

Okay, so you're prepared, you're organised, you're itching to actually *do* something. So let's go...

Set 'Em Up

Fire up the trusty sequencer and your Preferences file if you have one, or HEADER.MID if you don't, and copy as many of the settings as you can from your skeleton plan into the header (particularly the patches). Try to put something in, even if you think it's not *quite* the right sound – you can always change it later. Now is a good time to name the tracks (e.g., Bass, Pad, etc.) for quick reference.

Volume Setting

Volume (CC7) has been intentionally set at 100 for all parts in the header – this is to give you some headroom while programming to turn up any sound that needs it. This headroom is valuable, so as you work through a file make full use of note velocities first to balance the ingredients, and only raise CC7's value as a last resort. If it *all* seems too quiet while you're working, turn up the global master-volume control on your synth/amp/mixer.

Speed Tweak

Call up your sequencer's tempo track (or *Conductor/Mastertrack*) and enter the basic song-tempo. Some records, especially older ones, were recorded without a click-track so the tempo can fluctuate wildly according to how excited the band was getting – in cases like this, either try to pick a comfortable average or be prepared to enter a few extra tempo-events during the song.

If you wrote out a chord-chart for the song, you'll know if there are any changes of time-signature – enter these before you start recording (remembering also to enter an event to *return* the signature to its previous setting after each change).

Clicks and Bleeps

When setting up the *Metronome*, use the options available to adjust the sound and relative volumes of the beats (and sub-beats if possible). If you opt to use a MIDI click as well as (or instead of) internal click, choose a drum-note with a short, sharp hit (vibraslap, for example, would be a bad move). At most tempi, a countdown of a single bar is enough, but you might find that at a faster tempo you need a 2-bar countdown. Figure 14 shows the metronome options in Steinberg's *Cubase*.

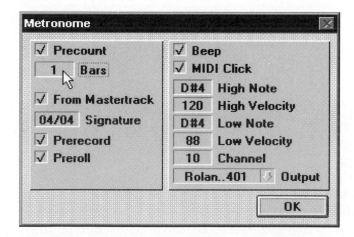

Fig. 14 **Setting up *Cubase's* metronome**

Count-In

Create a one-bar count-in on the second bar, using whichever drum-kit instrument takes your fancy, but make sure it's a tight and easily audible one such as hi-hat, sidestick or claves. Alternatively, you might want to start with a drum-fill instead of just a plain 4-count. If the record you're working from has an instrumental pickup, the count-in should still be included over the top of it, or covering the beats before it. (If the record starts with a *vocal* pickup, read **Cover Version Problems** on page 118.)

Hit The Kit

Generally it's wise to record the drum-part for the section you're working on first, for two reasons: firstly, it gives you a groove and a feel to play from as you record the subsequent parts and, secondly, it means that you can then turn off that lousy metronome! Depending on the tempo of the song, and complexity of the drum/percussion pattern, try to get at least the first four bars down. Then spend as long as it takes getting this drum-part 'perfect' in terms of timing, velocities and feel. As soon as you have, pick a name for the song and save it.

Hints

➡ Use separate tracks for kick/snare, hi-hats/crash cymbals, latin-percussion, etc.

➡ However dull the original drum-part, don't settle for four identical bars: make subtle changes to timing and velocities, add occasional extra 'hits', open hi-hats, different conga rhythms.

Bomb The Bass

Along with the drums, the bass-part is a vital thing to get down early on – as well as accentuating the rhythm, it underpins the harmonic structure of the section you're working on. The combination of drums and bass gives you the best possible chance to get maximum feel into all the subsequent parts.

Hints

➡ Without fully quantizing either, try to keep the bass moving in time with the kick (or a couple of ticks before it): letting the bass-end get too loose can give a muddled sound and 'drag' the beat.

➡ Bass is nearly always recorded 'dry' (no reverb). Use of chorus can add extra punch just as effectively as hiking up the velocities if the bottom-end is lacking that certain something.

Grab A Pad

Not all songs have a pad sound, but if yours does it's a useful thing to get down next. It's usually easy to record and edit, and it gives you a harmonic basis to work from in the same way that the drum part gives you a rhythmic one. Once again, tidy it up as much as possible before moving on.

Hints

➡ Watch out for 'overlapping' notes and chords, especially in dual-voice synth pads, and shorten them to save some polyphony.

➡ Some pads have a long 'release' phase — they may not be visibly overlapping in your graphic-editor, but that slow release could still be using polyphony as the next chord is played.

Go For The Gut

Where you go from here is up to you and, of course, depends upon what parts there are to be recorded, but the best move is usually to get all the *major* elements of the backing recorded first such as rhythm-guitar or piano, and work your way up to the solo-lines and incidental fills that might occur.

Save And Prosper

Make sure you save your work frequently, and especially if you've just accomplished something useful or tricky. If you're using a hardware sequencer with *Dump-to-tape* instead of a disk-drive this can be a time-consuming exercise and an inspiration-killer. Try to weigh up the consequences of losing your work against losing a few minutes' programming-time: there usually comes a point at which you suddenly feel you're in high-risk territory – when this happens, stop and save! Occupy your mind by making written notes on what to do next.

Hints

➡ Watch out for the small changes you make to a file. It's easy to think that none of the changes by itself is worth bothering to save for, but before you know it you've spent half-an-hour making small improvements and the sequencer crashes!

➡ If your sequencer has a facility to make a backup of the previous version each time you save, use it!

➡ Consider saving successive versions manually as *FILE01*, *FILE02*, etc., particularly if you're of a nervous disposition or experimenting with different ideas. As you progress you can gradually delete earlier versions.

Tough Stuff

Once in a while we all come across the fabled 'tricky bit' – it might be that actually *playing* the notes is technically demanding, or that the line needs pitch-bend *and* modulation, or that the pitch-bend *range* has to change halfway through – how do you deal with it?

The easiest way to deal with **technical playing** is to record at a slower tempo, but the result won't always have the feel you'd like. If you use this method, decrease the tempo as *little* as you can and be prepared to muck it up a few times first – when you *do* get it right it'll usually sound far more natural.

A second way to deal with the same problem is to use the *overdub* facility – mentally split the line into manageable sections of a few notes each and gradually build up the line by adding each section onto the end of the last. If you play a section badly, the *Undo* function should take care of it. (A similar method is to set several tracks to the same channel, record each little section onto a different track and mixdown to a single track when you're done.)

You can use the same method to add **continuous controller data** – record the notes first and then either *overdub* or select a new track to add the pitch-bend or modulation afterwards. Don't try recording pitch-bend at a slower tempo – the result rarely sounds natural and a large amount of unnecessary data is often recorded.

Hint

➡ However unlikely it seems that it'll work, try to record everything 'live' and at the correct tempo at least once – you may be surprised! And if it does go as badly as expected, you might still be able to salvage something from it.

What if you need a change of **pitch-bend range** halfway through a line? Using a similar approach, step-enter the necessary controllers in the right position *first*, and then overdub the part. In situations where you can't do this (for example, if the pb wheel is in almost constant use), play the part as accurately as you can, ignoring the way those painful 'wrong' bends sound, and step-insert the RPN #0 controllers afterwards.

Hints

➡ Make sure you position the RPNs between pitch-bend curves so that the last pb event to occur was zero/centre. Changing the range halfway through a bend could sound very odd!

Multiple Takes

You may be trying to record one of the aforementioned 'tricky bits', or perhaps just experimenting with ideas – either way, try to keep every 'take' that had some merit in case you can steal from it later. If you use a pattern-based sequencer, give each attempt-pattern a name and gather them together on one *muted* track. By the same token, don't rehearse a tricky operation by just *playing along* with the sequence, record it – what have you got to lose?

Recording Whole Tracks

If you like to construct your file by recording each instrumental part all the way through, try recording a rough melody-line early on to guide your position in the song. If you don't usually record the drum-track first (or the song doesn't have a drum-part), create a simple two-bar drum-rhythm that fits the basic style and copy it for the length of the song: it makes a far more user-friendly 'metronome' than the MIDI click.

Note Velocities

For every musical phrase you record, you are of course going to edit, tidy and generally perfect it before recording another. Part of this editing involves *balancing* the volume of this new phrase by changing the note-on velocities. Think of balancing as two separate operations: firstly, and paradoxically, you need to balance this phrase with itself; secondly, you need to mix it into the arrangement as a whole.

Start by making sure the *relative volumes* of the notes are correct by soloing the track – does the phrase sound good even when you hear it by itself? If (or when) it does, listen to it within the existing arrangement to check the balance. You can then use a simple sequencer command to raise or lower the velocities of each note by the same amount, knowing that its own *internal* balance will still be right.

Hint

➡ When globally raising the velocities of a phrase, always check the headroom first: if the loudest note of the phrase is 120 you can raise the velocities by only 7 – any more will alter the internal balance.

Name It !

If you're using a pattern-based sequencer, make the most of the pattern-name facility to help you find your way around the arrangement: you might use a descriptive name (*Drum-fill, Bass-slide*), or a chord sequence (*D, Bm, A7*) or a snippet of lyric (*Oh Baby, Yeah*), etc.

Hint

➡ Make Track 1 a guide track, as shown in Fig.15. Create empty patterns called 'Verse 1', 'Gtr Solo' and so on in a chain so that as you move around the arrangement you can see at a glance where you are.

Ghosts

Some software sequencers have a Ghost Pattern facility. In simple terms, ghosts are empty patterns which act as repeat-markers for a chain of identical patterns. For example, to create a two-bar hi-hat pattern that plays repeatedly for 16 bars, you simply record the first pattern and add 7 ghost copies on the end. This has two huge advantages: firstly, the 'ghosts' take up a lot less memory than 7 *real* copies would and, secondly, any change you make to the original pattern will automatically update the 'ghosts' in the same way.

Used in the manner mentioned above, this second advantage is a somewhat dubious one: are you really sure you want 8 *identical* patterns in a row? However, apart from the actual note and controller data they 'contain', ghosts can be assigned different playback parameters from the original. These may include time-delays, different MIDI channels and output ports, transpose settings and so on. When you export or save in MIDI file format, the ghost-patterns should be automatically converted to 'normal' data, but any playback- or track-parameters set for them (and, indeed, for any other part of the file) might require you to confirm that they should be applied before you save.

Like so many facilities found in software sequencers, used badly ghost patterns can make your music sound repetitive and stilted, but with a little imagination and some experimentation they can become incredibly powerful and musical programming tools.

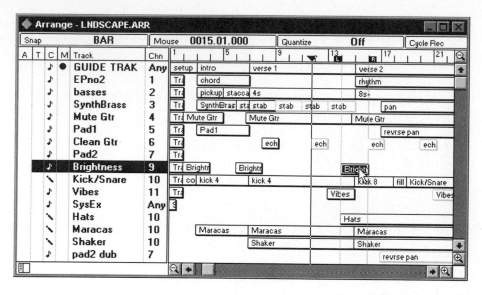

Fig. 15 **Guide track and 'ghost' patterns in** *Cubase*

Figure 15 above shows ghost patterns in use in Steinberg's *Cubase* on channels 3 and 6 (among others) – most sequencers display them with either a grey or a dotted outline.

Stop Rodent Abuse!

Many of the oft-used software-sequencer facilities have keyboard shortcuts to save constant mouse excursions to the menu-bar. These are excellent time and sanity savers, so it's well worth spending some time learning them. If your user-manual has long lists of these hot-key combinations, try to learn a few new ones every week.

Hint

➡ Try using a mouse-accelerator – PC and Apple Mac computers have mouse utilities in the main Control Panel. Some Atari MIDI software comes with a built-in accelerator – if yours doesn't, there are plenty available as Accessory modules from Public Domain libraries.

Remote Control

Along similar lines, you may be able to assign hot-keys to your synth or master-keyboard to save swivelling back and forth between computer and synth when recording. Pick these hot-keys with care: they need to be keys that you won't be trying to play and on a 5-octave keyboard there's no such thing! If in doubt, disable this feature.

Finishing Touches

'Right, it's done, complete, it's brilliant, it'll win awards! I'm gonna do another one ...' BONG – big mistake! At this point 95% of the work is probably done and that was the enjoyable, creative stuff. But if you don't do that last 5% now, when *are* you going to do it? Once you've started on a new file, the last thing you'll want to do is to come back to this one again. This is the final finishing-off; not remotely creative, but quick, fairly easy, and always gratifying to know it's done.

Tidy The Song Header

First, delete the song-header data for any unused channels. If you're using the GM, GS or XG Reset at the start of the file, next delete any RPN #0 controllers setting pitch-bend range at ± 2 semitones – they're not being used.

Raise The Volumes

Now maximise the volume of the overall file: look at the CC7 settings in the header or on your tone-generator's screen (if you've followed the 'rules', this is the only place in your file that CC7s will occur). Raise each volume so that the highest is set to 127 while keeping the *balance* the same (for example, if the highest CC7 setting is 118 you can add 9 to all the settings).

Tidy The Ending

Now check the end of each channel's data for controller resets. The controllers we're most interested in are CC64 (sustain pedal), CC11 (expression) and pitch-bend: make sure the last occurrence of each of these was the *reset* value (i.e., 64:000, 11:127, or pitch bend zero/centre). You can probably remember which channels you used pitch-bend on, for example, so this should be a quick job.

While you're looking at the ending, make sure all the notes for all the channels finish at the same time. When you're recording the parts, you probably hold the chord and try to guess when to let go of it: do that for maybe 8 channels and you've got a very ragged finish.

Shorten The Drum Notes

If you didn't do this as you were programming, set the lengths of all the notes on your drums-channel to around 4 ticks at 96 tpq – this reduces the chance of any retriggering occurring and looks neater for any re-editing later. You might be able to specify a note-length in ticks for the whole channel, but if you have to select a length in quantize units choose the shortest (usually 64th-note-triplets).

Listen!

Now listen to the file all the way through a couple of times to check for any timing 'glitches' or mistakes, wrong or clashing notes and so on. It sounds like typical musician-speak, but try to listen to it LOUD at least once to show up any flaws.

If you're going to use the files 'live', try to get the use of a local hall for a few hours to play the files at gigging level. And make sure you've got a pen and paper – you'll learn more about producing MIDI files for live performance in half-an-hour than you'll *ever* learn in a home-studio.

The Final Save

When you're sure the file is finished, it's time to make the final save. The bottom line for this is to save in every file-format you could possibly need, and keep backups. First, save the file as you see it on the screen, in your sequencer's own song-format to make any re-editing easier. Next, save it as a Standard MIDI File; if your sequencer gives the option of Type 0 or Type 1, either make the choice or (better still) save as both (but remember to include a '0' or '1' in the filename so that the second save doesn't overwrite the first).

Hints

➡ If you're working on a computer-based sequencer and saving to floppy-disk, remember that most workstation and file-player disk-drives can't read files in directories – make sure you save the file to the root section of the disk if you'll be using one of these for playback.

➡ Consider the filename carefully, particularly with cover-versions – DONTWANT.MID could be an abbreviation of dozens of different song-titles, some of which you might program later. Try using a 5-letter + 3-number naming system.

If you're saving as **Type 1** and you've used several tracks to record different sections for the same channel, first mix these down to a single new track. Then mute the original tracks and play the file to make sure the mixdown track is okay. Finally delete the original tracks. You might choose to *keep* your drum-instruments on separate tracks, but try to make sure that the total number of tracks in the file doesn't exceed 16 (some sequencers will load only 16 tracks and ignore track 17 up).

The Final Check

On occasions, the conversion process that your sequencer carries out to create a SMF brings to light some quirks and glitches in the file, retriggering being a prime example. After saving in Standard MIDI File format (and making sure you've *also* saved in sequencer song format) always *reload* the SMF and play it through to check that everything is in order.

If everything *isn't* in order, it's easier and more practical to make the necessary changes in the sequencer song-file and then carry out all the saves again. This ensures that all copies of the song are identical and tidy, but it can also be a lot quicker: if the same problem occurred several times in a single track it was probably a copied and pasted section, in which case you could simply debug one copy and use it to replace all the others.

The Backups

How you organise copies of finished files is a matter of personal taste and paranoia, so the following is only a suggestion. Save the file in every useful format to a floppy-disk and then make a copy of this disk. Put the name of the song on the disk-labels and write-protect them. These are your master-copies, for use only in emergencies or when you need the file in one of those formats.

Next, save the file to a third floppy disk as a SMF – this is for regular use (or any time you want to just have a listen to it). Keep saving finished files to this disk in the same way until it's full and start another one, gradually building up a library. (With a hard-drive system, you may choose to keep the library in a hard-drive directory instead.) Keep all three disks containing this song in *different places* – if they all go into the same box you've just wasted two disks!

Don't forget to check the backup copies are all okay before storing them. This is the mind-numbingly tedious task of listening to the same song several times, but if you need backups, you need to know you can rely on them.

If you're using a hardware sequencer with *Dump-to-tape* instead of a disk-drive, it's worth saving the data to at least two cassette tapes despite the time it takes (it's still quicker than re-programming the file!). Floppy disks have their flaws, but they're a lot more reliable and durable than tape. Don't forget to use the *Verify* procedure if your sequencer has one.

Written Notes?

Don't forget to keep written notes of anything that can't be stored within the file itself (such as which equipment you used or outboard mixer or effect-unit settings). You might also want to note such things as the tempo, key and time-length of the song, any changes you made to the arrangement or chords, which patches you used on each channel, the date you programmed it and so on. If you can, save this as a text-file on your 'emergency' disks. It's also handy to keep a file-copy of the lyrics here too.

The Future . . .

Every now and then programmers like to have a furtive listen to their files and perhaps give themselves a little pat on the back. This is actually a very constructive thing to do for two reasons: firstly, as a measure of how your technique has improved over a period of time and, secondly, as an opportunity to put anything right that seems wrong in the light of further experience. Make sure you take this opportunity – it helps to ensure that your older files don't become an embarrassment to you!

Quantization

Quantize was one of the first editing facilities to be included on sequencers. Sometimes called *Auto-correct*, its original function was to move all the notes you played onto the nearest beat or sub-beat selected (i.e., the nearest quarter-note, sixteenth-note, etc.) resulting in '*perfect*' timing with an obviously computerised feel. Musicians usually *aim* to play on the beat, but human error and natural musical feel prevent this happening; to the human ear therefore, *perfect* timing in this sense often sounds unnatural and uncomfortable.

This is known nowadays as *full, Note-On* or *100%* quantization; the original basic function has gained new features over the years and nearly all sequencers now offer a far wider range of quantize options allowing you to make automatic timing-corrections while still retaining some of the human characteristics.

The Golden Rule

Use your ears, not your eyes! Bear in mind that we're creating *music* here – don't use quantize just because it's there or because the notes *look* badly timed on the screen; use it for effect or to tidy large quantities of poor timing. If you've always used quantize as a reflex-action after recording something you might be surprised how far from the 'target' you can move notes before they sound wrong.

Americanisms

The musical language used in the UK is unusual in that we've invented words like minim and quaver to represent note-lengths. Throughout Europe and America, a much more sensible 'mathematical' system is used: a semibreve is a 'whole note' and all the other notes are expressed as fractions of this, so a minim is a 'half-note', a crotchet is a 'quarter-note' and so on. The system has been adopted by MIDI software and is the one we'll use here.

To use the quantize functions, you need first to specify the type of beat you want the notes placed on (or moved towards). If you recorded a melody-line consisting of sixteenth-notes which you wanted to quantize fully, you'd need to set the quantize value to sixteenth-notes. If you set it to quarter-notes, for example, the notes would all be moved onto their nearest quarter-note beat giving four *chords* per bar and nothing in between. If your melody-line consisted of both eighth- and sixteenth-notes, you should still set the quantize value to sixteenth-notes; in other words, pick the value of the shortest note you played.

No Getting Away From It . . .

Everything you record is quantized to some degree, due to the nature of the sequencer. It has to place every incoming event on a tick, so the 'strength' of this mandatory quantize is determined by the sequencer's resolution. For example, a timebase of 24 tpq means that sixteenth-notes will be only 6 ticks apart – the chances of retaining natural human feel are clearly going to be severely limited, and quite noticeably so at slow tempi. A timebase of 720 tpq, on the other hand, is still obligatory quantization of a sort but even at a very slow tempo you'd never spot it!

Record Quantize

The quantize function is usually used *after* a section of music has been recorded, but some sequencers have a *Record Quantize* (or Auto Quantize) facility to correct the timing of notes automatically to the value specified as they're recorded. It's usually a good idea to override this – give yourself the opportunity to hear the phrase as you played it first and *then* quantize if you have to, using *Undo* if you don't like the result.

Where's It Gone?

Always remember that quantize moves a note onto or towards the *nearest* of the beat divisions you selected. If you quantize a phrase to sixteenth-notes and your original timing was a bit dodgy, a note that occurred more than 12 ticks late will take a hop towards the *next* sixteenth-note division. To prevent this happening, you'd need to go into *Edit* and move the note a few ticks closer to the target before quantizing. And if you're going to do that . . .

Manual Quantize

The best type of quantize there is! Listen to what you recorded, identify the notes that are 'bad timing' as opposed to 'human feel' and move them yourself in *Edit*.

Okay, so those are the basic issues of quantization. Now let's take a look at some of the other quantize options available, typified by Cubase in Fig. 16, and a few ways you can use them to good effect.

Partial Quantize

Under various names, this has become an almost universal type of quantize. As always you need to choose a quantize *value* (such as eighth-notes), but the *strength* of the quantize is selected by entering a percentage figure. 100% is full-quantize – the notes will move *onto* the chosen beat; 0% is no quantize at all; 50% means that the notes will move *halfway* towards the beat (i.e., if a note was off by 10 ticks it'll move 5 ticks closer).

Hints

➡ Try selecting a small percentage (such as 20%) and quantize several times if you need to, listening to the result after each, to keep the maximum human feel.

➡ For modern dance music such as rave, where a more 'computerised' feel is needed, use 100% quantize for rhythm parts, but try choosing a lower percentage (such as 75%) for dubs and solos.

➡ Remember that fast tempi need to be 'looser' (i.e., a lower percentage) than slower tempi to avoid an unwanted mechanical feel because the ticks pass that much quicker.

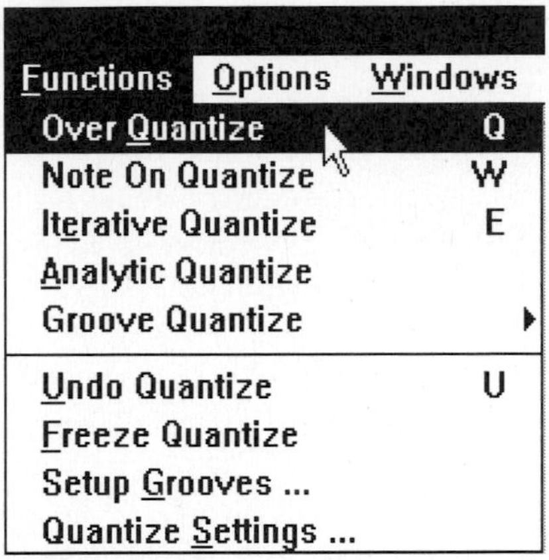

Fig. 16 *Cubase's* quantize options menu

Intelligent Quantize

Also known as *Analytic*. This quantize option analyses your playing using the quantize value only as a guide, and can identify intentional 'bad' timing such as grace-notes, triplets and glissandi.

Hint

➡ Use intelligent quantize on lead-lines and solos – it can be very effective on even the most complex line – but make sure you choose a representative value.

Groove Quantize

This is a slightly different option being included in more and more software sequencers, to the intense pleasure of the groove-pattern creators, **DNA**. A groove pattern is selected and applied to a (usually fully quantized) phrase, giving it a humanised feel by moving notes forward or back to push or drag the beat in different ways according to the groove-pattern chosen. Groove patterns can usually be edited, or new ones created from scratch.

Match Quantize

A similar effect to **Groove** above, but in this instance you record/edit a phrase with the feel you want and *copy* this feel to other phrases whose note-positions will then move to *match* this template. You may also have the option of matching the dynamic variations (velocities) of the original phrase.

Humanise

A slightly rarer form of quantize which is almost the opposite of the classic quantize function: it specialises in creating an approximation of human feel by moving notes *off* the beat. An interesting function to play with, but the best human feel still comes from humans.

Randomise

If there's one thing a computer is good at it's generating random numbers, so many software-writers can't resist popping in the *randomise* options. These may apply to velocities, pitches, note-lengths or positions. Bear in mind that 'random' means just that though – carefully applied for *effect* it might be useful, but over-used it'll start to sound like the infinite number of monkeys who, having written *Hamlet*, are now working on the score.

Swing

This is usually an *add-on* option used in conjunction with quantize and also set as a percentage (see Fig. 17). As the name suggests, this is used to create a swing (or *dotted*) feel to a phrase: as the percentage is raised from 50%, a pair of eighth-notes will gradually move towards a tripletised rhythm. A setting off 66% gives an exact triplet feel.

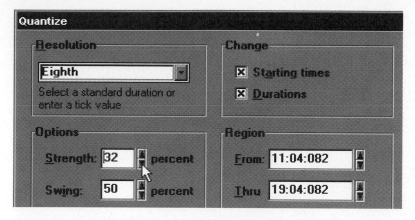

Fig. 17 **Section from *Cakewalk Pro*'s quantize-settings menu**

Length Quantize

Some sequencers offer options relating to the *length* of notes either as stand-alone functions or in combination with the usual *time-shifting* quantize. For example, you may be able to quantize a note-length to quarter-notes so that each note would be stretched or shortened to end on the closest quarter-note beat.

Some standard quantize functions also play tricks with note-lengths: you may find that you've got two *full-quantize* options which seem to do the same thing. If so, check the note-off point: the odds are that one function grabs the whole note and moves it onto the beat (keeping the length intact) while the other just moves the *note-on*, thus changing the length.

Hint

➡ Quantize can be a cause of retriggering notes: since notes are being moved it's quite possible for notes that weren't overlapping before to overlap after the operation, and some of these may be of the same pitch. Nip into *Edit* and have a look around afterwards if you think there's a chance of this happening!

Compare

An extremely useful function is *Compare* or *Return To Original*, allowing you to experiment with different types of quantize or, indeed, combinations of them, without committing yourself to the changes you've made. Your sequencer might instead have an unlimited *Undo* facility which works for any type of editing procedure you've carried out.

Don't Quantize

Another handy one for keeping some semblance of human feel: select a range (such as 'any notes within 7 ticks of the target beat') to be ignored by the quantize operation – only notes outside this range will be moved.

Hint

➡ Don't Quantize is probably the most valuable add-on option there is: make maximum use of it and start with a fairly wide range: for example a range of 8 ticks will capture any really embarrassing goofs while still keeping the whole feel fairly loose.

Detours

➡ More pros and cons of quantization are covered in **Feel** (page 102) and **Polyphony Problems** (page 112).

Cut, Copy and Paste

These are the three 'bread-and-butter' editing functions – unless you're an instrumental whizz-kid with the enviable ability to record each track top-to-tail in one take, you'll be spending a lot of happy hours with these guys. For computer-sequencer users, check out their hot-key combinations and use them! Because they're so frequently needed, they tend to be the simplest sequencer functions to use and very well documented in user-manuals. Computer users will know these functions without any explanation – they're found on almost any kind of software you care to mention – but let's start with a brief description for the uninitiated.

Cut

When you select a group of events and choose *Cut*, the events are removed from the track(s), but held in a memory store (usually called the *clipboard*) in case you want to place them somewhere else – you could think of this combination as a *move* function, which is its primary use. *Cut* is similar therefore to *Delete* with the exception that deleted events can only be salvaged using an *Undo* function, and unless your sequencer has *unlimited undo* you have to be pretty quick off the mark to retrieve them.

Copy

This is identical to *Cut*, with the sole exception that the events aren't removed (so you're storing a *copy* of the events to the clipboard).

Paste

This function places the events currently held in the clipboard (after using *Cut* or *Copy*) in whatever position you specify. Once a selection is held in the clipboard, it will remain there until you cut or copy something else. This means that you can paste the selection as many times, and to as many different positions, as you want to.

Using Cut/Copy/Paste

To cut or copy in *Edit* mode is usually a simple case of highlighting (or dragging a box around) the desired events and selecting the appropriate command or hot-key. You can then move to a different point in the track, or select a different track, and hit *Paste* – the same bunch of highlighted events should appear. Whether you're using a list, drum or graphic editor, or a combination of these, the functions usually work in exactly the same way.

In **pattern-based sequencers**, where each recorded pattern is shown as a rectangular block on the screen, whole patterns may be cut/copied/pasted in a similar fashion making song construction a very easy affair. To create a simple '12-Bar Blues' for example, record a 12-bar section of guitar, bass and drums, copy the lot, paste as many times as you have verses, and Bob's your auntie's live-in lover. Just add an ending and put the kettle on.

Copying Sections

When you start work on a new file, you can usually tell in advance whether there'll be a lot of copying and pasting involved and, in fact, it's a good idea to try to take note of any sections of a cover-version that are obvious candidates for a simple copy-job.

Knowing this, however, you tend to structure your recording so as to make the copying and pasting easier: everything starts on the beginning of the first bar and stops at the end of bar 8 so that you can just copy it all and paste it to start again on bar 9. This can result in a glitch as every channel pumps out note-on data on the first tick of bar 9, causing a tiny, but noticeable, delay.

The solution is simple and vital to the *feel* of the song: spread these events out! (On a pattern-based sequencer this will involve joining the two patterns together first.) Go into *List Edit* and move the bass and drum notes forward a tick or two. Select any tracks containing slow-attack sounds (pads, strings, etc.) and move these forward perhaps half-a-dozen ticks, shortening any previous notes if necessary to prevent overlaps. Spread out the notes of any keyboard chords slightly the way a 'live' keyboard player naturally would (even if she were trying not to!).

On the subject of keyboards, watch out for the dreaded sustain pedal 'off' event occurring at the end of a section. In normal piano-playing the CC64:0 will occur a few ticks *after* the first chord of the bar, but when recording in sections your last pedal-off of the section will either be early or may be missing entirely if the sequencer stopped recording before you released the pedal. After copying the section and spreading the first chord, move this offending controller a few ticks into the next bar (or insert the event manually if it wasn't recorded).

The function of all the foregoing suggestions is to create a *seamless* join between copied and pasted sections; for more tips on how to accomplish this, take a look at the topic on **Feel** on page 102.

Copying Short Patterns

Another common copy/paste scenario is to create a short pattern, such as a one-bar hi-hat part, and then chain seven more copies together to make an eight-bar phrase. And it works, technically speaking. *Musically* speaking, however, not so good. It's hardly a credible 'live' sound is it? By spending just a little more time, you can use copy/paste for a far more effective result. Try one of these:

❑ **Random Variation:** Take four copied one-bar hi-hat patterns and edit them to change the velocities of different notes, insert an occasional extra sixteenth-note or open-hat, make subtle changes to the timing and so on. Then paste these four patterns randomly throughout the section you're filling (see Fig. 18). Couple this with a similar treatment to the kick/snare part(s) and no single bar of drums should sound the same as the last.

Track	Chn	1				5				9			
kick/snare	10	3	2	3	1	4	2	1	4	3	1	2	4
hi-hats	10	1	4	3	4	2	3	1	4	2	3	1	3

Fig. 18 **Random Variation**

❑ **Uneven Phrases:** Record a three-bar hi-hat pattern and a five-bar kick/snare pattern. As above, edit each bar of each pattern to add variation, then chain the patterns together as required (you'll obviously be using more copies of the hi-hats than the kick/snare). Because of the different lengths, the relative start positions of the two patterns will keep changing, giving effectively a 15-bar drum-part as shown in Fig. 19.

Hint

➡ You can obviously use this idea with any single pattern you want to chain, but because music is usually written in natural-sounding 4-bar phrases, always use an odd number of bars to prevent it ever sounding like a repeating pattern.

Though we've taken drums as a widely-used example, there's no reason not to apply these techniques to any instrument.

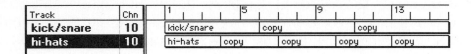

Fig. 19 **Uneven Phrase Lengths**

Split

Some pattern-based sequencers have a *split* facility – a pattern can be split into two at a selected point. This feature allows you to carry out a particular operation on one section of a pattern without affecting the other, and one of the primary operations is going to be cut/copy/paste.

If you intend to split the pattern and then use *cut* on part of it, choose the split-point carefully – this is one of the biggest causes of glitching in a file. Make sure you're not splitting any notes 'in half' – some sequencers react very badly to this (they regard it as removal of the *note-off* message and leave the note hanging). Also, check that you're not removing any continuous controller reset events – if the pattern contains a pitch-bend curve and the 'zero' event is in the section you're cutting, all subsequent notes on that channel will be out of tune. Another old enemy is the sustain pedal's zero event for similar reasons.

> ### Detours
>
> → When chaining together identical patterns that you want to *keep* identical, try using the *Ghost* facility found on many software sequencers. This is covered on page 86.

▧ Feel

MIDI programming, by definition, is music created on a computer. From this basis, anyone can make the finished result *sound* like computer-generated music very easily; all the tools are there – whack all the velocities up to 127, quantize the lot and hey presto, it's ... a bunch of notes in a sequencer.

Of course, it's readily accepted that some musical styles don't generically contain human feel; similarly, some of the most emotive music may still contain obviously synthesised effects. But the true art of MIDI programming, for most styles of music, lies in *disguising* the fact that it was created on a computer, and this ought to be easy (after all, most of it was at least played by a human-being!). Sadly it often isn't.

There could be several reasons why not. The problem could be performance-related: perhaps you're a drummer having to use a keyboard to enter the note-data? Or maybe you find it hard to resist all those editing tools and gadgets? Perhaps the data *looks* out of time in the editor if it's not sitting on a beat, so you move it? Or your copy and paste practices leave something to be desired? Here are a few ideas to help you keep or recreate some feel in your programming.

Thought Control!

If it ain't broke, don't fix it! In other words, if it *sounds* okay, it *is* okay. Avoid using global tools such as *100% Quantize* or *Fix Velocities* – it's unlikely that *every* note in a phrase needs changing, so try to limit your editing to the notes that do.

Remember that the whole basis of human feel is *imperfection*! Even when they try to, even the greatest musicians can't play every note exactly in time. And in the same way, they can't play every note at the same velocity (although in this case they usually don't want to).

Performance

The primary objective here, of course, is: try to *play* the part with the feel you want it to have. If you can do that often enough, you've got it licked! Create a repeating drum-pattern to use as a metronome instead of the infernal bleep. Regard dropping the tempo when recording as a last resort.

Feel depends very little on which notes you play: if you're up against a technically-challenging phrase, try simplifying the notes to make it easier to play with the correct feel and edit the notes themselves afterwards. (See the *Tough Stuff* heading on page 83 for more on the technical question.)

Velocities

Note velocities are as much an important part of feel as timing. Accent the wrong notes and the beat starts to 'drag'. Think in terms of *significance* – the note on the quarter-note beat is more significant than the note on the 'in-between' eighth-note beat which, in turn, is more significant than the note on the sixteenth-note beat. As a rough guide, assign higher velocity values to the most significant notes.

Exaggerate velocity differences according to the suggestion above: there can be quite a vast difference between accented and incidental notes. Take a look at the hi-hat line in **VELOCITY.MID** for an example.

With some instruments in some tone-generators, high note velocities affect the tonal characteristics of the sound as well (this is often the case with guitar and piano sounds). To give a rhythm guitar part more 'bite', try maximising the note-velocities and then balance the track by reducing the CC7 value in the song-header.

Construction

Try to record longer 'live' phrases to get a feel going – constantly recording two bars then stopping prevents you 'getting into it'. If you have a Cycle or Loop and Replace facility, try using it: assume that the first take is to get the feel and that the second 'pass' is the one you'll keep.

Do you record, then copy and paste, very short phrases? If the copies aren't varied in any way, this can give an effect similar to quantizing. A long section consisting of identical one- or two-bar phrases can still sound mechanical however 'human' the playing.

If you like to construct a file in 'sections' (i.e., intro, then verse 1, then verse 2, etc.), think of each of these as a mini-song – get the first section perfectly balanced and cleaned up before starting on the next.

Once the second section is up to scratch, spend some time creating a seamless join between the two sections to disguise the fact that they weren't recorded as a continuous whole. This could involve *time-shifting* (see below) or adjusting note velocities. Track back regularly to the previous section (or the beginning of the song) to listen to your results so far: Can you hear the section joins? Is there enough dynamic colour (*light and shade*)? Try to deal with any flaws straight away.

Time-Shifting

When creating seamless joins between sections, you usually need to shift notes forward a tick or so manually, onto the end of the previous section. Good candidates for this are the first drum-notes and the bass note. This is often enough to prevent the slight 'hiccuping' in sound that sometimes occurs, but try moving any sounds with a slow attack forward several ticks (shortening previous notes if necessary), starting keyboard chords earlier and spreading them a little, and perhaps moving a solid lead-instrument (such as a trumpet) *back* a couple of ticks. This can go a very long way to keeping a feel going, and take out MIDI delays caused by a dozen channels all playing notes on the same tick.

Do your drum-parts tend to sound a bit quantized? Well, maybe they are. Kick and snare parts can usually survive this if you time shift some of the other kit-instrument parts around them. Take your hi-hat, ride-cymbal and latin-percussion parts and apply different types of time-shifting to each so that the hits don't all come on the same tick. Coupled with velocity variations this can help to disguise even the most heavy-handed quantizing.

Step Recording

Try to avoid step-recording long phrases. Sometimes it's necessary, or just a lot less bother than recording in real-time: in these cases, enter the events where you think they'll sound effective and then spend some time listening and editing. (If your sequencer quantizes or *snaps* step-entered notes to a beat-division, turn off this facility.) When step-entering notes, the three parameters to pay attention to for the purpose of *feel* are position, velocity and length. The last of these particularly tends to get forgotten.

Light and Shade

Dynamic colour is a vital part of most musical styles: building up to a chorus or a change of key, dropping back after the chorus into another verse, and general 'rolling' dynamics throughout the song. It's largely a case of using note velocities again, perhaps coupled with judicious use of Expression (CC11).

You might have an automatic facility for scaling velocities: set the start and finish velocities for a group of notes and the sequencer will automatically create a crescendo or diminuendo. Like any tool it's worth experimenting with, but remember (once again!) you're subjecting the music to *computer* rather than *human* control.

Practical Points

If your sequencer has a *pre-roll* metronome option it's well worth using. It plays the bar before your record-point instead of giving a one-bar countdown (you might be able to set it to two or more bars if you wish). It's a much better way to 'get the feel' of the music than a cold countdown.

Better still, if there's room on the track, cue up to record from a bar or so earlier than you need to. This has two benefits: firstly, you get to *hear* those bars (as in the point above); secondly, it'll usually diminish the need to **time-shift** the first note or chord you play. For example, you'll probably automatically play a slow-attack sound before the beat: with the cue-point in the usual place, the notes would be recorded okay but they'd be placed on the first tick of the new section; in this case they'd stay just where you played them.

Try to set up the sound on your tone-generator with a fair guess at correct volume and effect settings so that you're hearing the new part in at least a *roughly* mixed context as you play it.

Detours

→ As *Feel* is such a vital part of music, whole sections of the book could have been shoe-horned into this topic. Take a look at the **Drive** and **Fades and Sweeps** topics on pages 125 and 134 respectively. You could also check out the ***Close-Ups*** view of **CC11:Expression** on page 213.

▓ Rallentando/Accelerando

A stylish Italian topic title, because *Tempo Changes* lacks that certain air of mystery. And tempo changes in MIDI programming are mysterious things – there are no MIDI-event messages for tempo, but you can still enter them. This is because most sequencers provide a tempo-message of their own invention to let you work with tempo events as easily as you do with notes, controllers and so on.

How's It Done?

The tempo facility is usually provided in one of three ways:

1. A menu option containing a list of the tempo events at various positions in the file, which looks very similar to the *List Editor* for the usual MIDI events and allows you to input tempo events by a simple step method. This is often called a *Conductor* or *Mastertrack* (see Fig. 20).

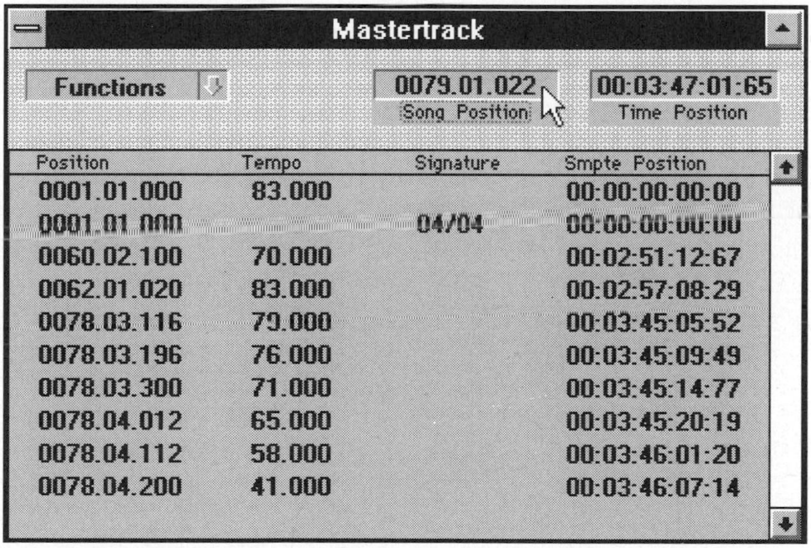

Fig. 20 **List display of tempo events in *Cubase*'s Mastertrack at 384 tpq**

2. Similar to the one above, but a graphic display, not unlike the displays used for controller data (shown in Fig. 21). It should be possible to *override* both the list and the graphic types of tempo display so that you can play back your file at one tempo if you choose to.

3 An actual tempo *event* which you can enter into a track at the correct position and specify a value for, just as you would any other type of event. It's usually possible to enter these events on any track you choose, but try to keep a track specifically for tempo events alone; this way you can override the tempo-changes (as mentioned above) by muting the track without cutting out performance data too.

Do I Have To?

In most cases, tempo-changes are used at the end of a file to create a *rallentando* finish. Of course, you could just try to play slower as you normally would when playing live. But it's not quite as easy as it seems: you've got the old problem of the metronome ticking away! There are ways round this – the easiest is to turn off the metronome, set the record cue-point so that you can hear the last few bars you recorded, and play the 'manual' rallentando on a separate track as soon as they come to a stop. Easy really. Now ... say that was the piano part. Somehow you've got to record drums, bass and any number of other instruments the same way *all slowing down by the same degree*! One of those moments when you realise the light at the end of the tunnel is attached to a train.

The other argument against this course of action is that the actual *editing* of these events is going to be a real pig – there'll be no relationship at all between the notes and the bar/beat/tick positions – and there'll be *plenty* of editing needed, guaranteed.

Okay, What Then?

The way a *rall* finish is traditionally handled flies in the face of all the aforementioned ideas on human feel: keep the metronome on (or your drum-template pattern playing) and record the ending at normal song-tempo. You have to try to forget any ideas about slowing down, but try to include any other attributes of feel such as a diminuendo.

The tempo-events are usually then entered in step-time. Some sequencers have options for real-time 'tempo recording' which can work in various ways, such as remapping a controller to tempo events, or dragging the mouse across a graph as the music plays.

Hints

➡ If you're programming a song containing changes of time-signature make sure you enter these first. Putting them in afterwards can send your carefully planned tempo positions straight out the window.

Your sequencer may have a *Scale Tempos* facility. This is similar to Scale Velocities mentioned in the **Light and Shade** heading on page 106. You simply pick a start-position and tempo and an end-position and tempo, and leave the sequencer to insert the necessary tempo-events and create a smooth transition.

If you have neither real-time Tempo Recording nor Scale Tempos, you have to enter the tempo events by hand. It usually doesn't take long, but it's almost always a trial and error process.

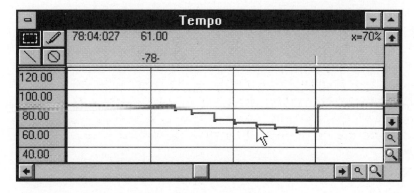

Fig. 21 **Graphic representation of tempo-changes**

Manual Tempo Changes

A practical approach is to record the main rhythm instrument (guitar or keyboards), bass and drums all at song-tempo. Then input the tempo-events, and finally record the rest of the backing. Most of these last instruments will often involve less *rhythmic* playing than the first three, so follow the rallentando as best you can each time and then edit any notes with screamingly bad timing – there shouldn't be many. This way, you get to keep the majority of the live feel in the ending.

Questions such as how many events, which tempos and where the events should go will always depend on the particular song, which is what makes it such a hit-and-miss process. The following are a few tips to try:

❑ Try to follow a pattern for each bar or beat, such as entering an event four ticks after every eighth-note beat. This way you could copy and paste one bar repeatedly, then just edit the tempos, thus saving some step-writing time.

❑ Gradually increase the *rate* of deceleration: for the first couple of events decrease by 1 each time, for the next couple by 2 and so on. Your tempo list could look some thing like this: 112, 111, 110, 108, 106. 103, 100, 96 . . .

❑ How many events per bar to use will depend a lot on the main tempo of the song and the effect you want to create. For a driving rock at 160bpm you could probably get away with a tempo event for each beat (or possibly even two beats), whereas a slow ballad tempo will require a good few more (perhaps as many as one per sixteenth-note beat). The reasoning is simple: a fast rock number will be based on a strong four-feel. As long as each quarter-note beat lasts a little longer than the previous one, you're slowing down. With a ballad the eighth- notes are a lot stronger and the feel may well contain sixteenth-notes too. If four sixteenth-notes pass and each lasts exactly the same length of time the result may be a rather stop-start jerky finish.

❑ Bear in mind that any spread keyboard chords or guitar-strums will have their notes further spread by a slower tempo – a little editing may be needed to bring the notes closer together again.

❑ Following on from the previous point, make sure the data for any continuous controllers already recorded is smooth at the point where the rall occurs – slowing down the tempo will highlight any glitches in it. Preferably record these afterwards with the tempo-track active.

❑ Use a single tempo change immediately after the last chord to vary how long it's being held – it's a lot quicker than continually editing all the note-lengths until you get it right!

But What About . . . ?

Despite the topic-heading, we've been talking exclusively about *Rallentando* and its little buddy has been ignored. *Accelerandos* are used comparatively rarely, hence the slight bias, but let's try to square things up a bit.

❑ The same rules apply as in the first four points made on the previous page except of course that the notes of spread-chords and guitar-strums will move closer together and begin to sound very mechanical.

❑ As accelerandos usually take place *within* the song rather than at the end, the playing *must* be done at normal song-tempo – you couldn't really hope to achieve a natural human accelerando and still end up on the first beat of a bar ready to resume again at the new tempo! However, if you insist on creating the accelerando by playing, you might just be able to get away with it by entering different time-signatures afterwards. For example, to speed up over the course of one bar you might be able to enter a time-signature of something like 11/16 or 23/32 to *create* a bar of the right length. But it's probably one to save for a wet afternoon.

❑ Once again, it's best to record continuous controller data (especially pitch-bend) *after* creating the accelerando, making sure the tempo-track is active when you do it.

Tempo and Time-Signature Suggestions

❑ Try putting in a large tempo-drop before the very last chord to heighten the drama. But remember – don't put it *immediately* before the last chord: slowing down massively for a grand total of three ticks or so will make no difference at all! If there was a note on the eighth-note beat before the last chord, for example, place the tempo-change on the tick after it to get maximum effect (see the final event in Fig. 20.)

❑ Try inputting a faster tempo to make the song-header pass more quickly. This is rather frowned upon in commercial programming, but dead useful when you're using files 'live'. It can be a particular time-saver in situations where your header contains a lot of System Exclusive messages, but make certain that the messages are always being implemented correctly by the tone-generator at the new tempo before committing yourself.

❑ On the subject of the song-header, if you can't cram all the data into a single bar and have to run into the next beat, rather than waiting out the bar before starting the count-in, enter a time-signature of 5/4 for example so that you can start the count-in on the beat immediately following the header data.

❑ If you use a tone-generator System Exclusive bulk dump containing all the necessary settings instead of the usual header-bar collection of channel messages, try recording the dump at a slower tempo than the main song-tempo – this way they'll play back a lot faster when you re-activate the tempo-track, but always check that the rise in tempo isn't causing messages to become muddled or missed in playback: some tone-generators are a lot more forgiving than others in these situations. For more details on the System Exclusive bulk dump, take a look at the *Replacement Song Header* sub-heading on page 228. To record the dump, you'll obviously need to connect a MIDI cable from your tone-generator's MIDI Out to your sequencer's MIDI In. The exact details for your device should be outlined in the *User Manual*.

❑ When inputting a change of time-signature for a single bar, remember that a *return* event will be needed at the start of the next bar (just as in written music). For example, to make bar ten a 2/4 bar you'd need to insert a 2/4 event at 10.1.0 and a 4/4 (or whatever) event at 11.1.0.

Polyphony Problems

Why polyphony *problems*? Simple – one of the few times a programmer thinks of polyphony is when there's a problem with it; when you've got stacks of the stuff and everything's running smoothly it'll hardly cross your mind! Here are a few pointers to get you out of trouble when notes start dropping out. (Keep in mind, though, that like any problem it's better *avoided* than solved!)

Forward Planning

As already mentioned in the *Channel Planning* heading on page 78, check out your tone-generator's system of voice allocation and make the best use of channel priority when matching your instruments to channels. Keep an eye on how many dual- or multi-voice sounds you've chosen to use. If there's not much difference between, for example, the single-voice brass and the dual-voice brass, go for the single.

Remove Notes

This is usually the obvious answer to any polyphony problem, but it's always frustrating when you *have* to do it. Try to solve the problem using other methods first. If you have to delete notes, choose the least important ones first.

❑ **Unnecessary Drum-Hits:** Whenever you step-enter a crash cymbal, remove the hi-hat/ride-cymbal on the same beat and any within the following eighth-note beat. You can usually remove almost any percussion note on a crash hit except kick, snare and toms.

❑ **Pad Notes:** You could probably get by with a two-note pad chord instead of three at that point, especially if the pad's well buried in the mix. Try putting that third note back in a beat later (and a beat shorter !).

❑ **Inaudible Notes:** Take out anything that can't be heard with the volume up (similar to the effect of the crash- cymbal mentioned above).

Shorten Notes

❑ **Long Release Sounds:** Lots of pads, atmospheres and synth-effects have a long release phase – you might have a note-off occurring on beat two and the sound still gulping down valuable voices on beat three. Chop little bits off the note-lengths of these until the polyphony problem goes away.

❑ **Quantize Pads:** Avoid legato playing of pad sounds unless they're a dominant sound in the mix. You can afford to quantize pads fully (and shorten their lengths as necessary) to avoid *any* overlapping of notes or chords at all. With a good human feel from the other instruments, this technique should be unnoticeable.

❑ **Monophonic Instruments:** Remember that a great many instruments are *monophonic* – they can only play one note at a time. Obvious examples are sax, trumpet and flute, but basses are often played this way too. For this type of instrument, overlaps can (and usually should) be removed.

Move Notes

Certainly preferable to actually deleting them! The more quantized your arrangement is, the more likely you are to run into polyphony problems. The obvious solutions are to quantize to a lower percentage; not quantize at all; or to manually move notes off the beats *after* quantizing.

❑ **Split Up Drum-Hits:** Drum sounds are nearly always 'trigger' sounds: they play from start to finish in only a tick or so. Therefore splitting *stacks* of drum-notes, such as kick, hi-hat, tambourine and shaker onto different ticks (both backwards *and* forwards) could solve a few problems, and add to the feel at the same time!

❑ **Shift Notes Backwards:** MIDI traffic is nearly always greatest on the first beat of the bar, and for quantized parts this means the first *tick* of the bar. Moving a few notes backwards might prevent some drop-out – judge carefully which ones and how far so as not to start *dragging* the feel.

Sustain Pedal

The sustain-pedal (CC64) is a devilish little chap when it comes to polyphony-snatching. Even if you re-pedal once per beat, each of those beats could quite easily contain half-a-dozen or even a dozen different notes being sustained at different points. Only one suggestion here – don't use it if you don't have to!

And Finally . . .

Is the problem really solved? After making a few of the most obvious and least destructive changes, play the file from a few bars earlier: the problem might be a long note, or a note with a long-release, that was triggered several bars back.

▓ Mixing

When constructing a MIDI file section-by-section, it's usually best to mix and balance everything as you record it – if you copy and paste an unmixed section of music the result is that you have to mix it *twice* later. Following this principle, there should really be no such thing as a 'final mix'. You should be able to listen to the completed file a couple of times tweaking volumes, velocities and pan positions just to fine-tune the song.

The same thing could be said if you prefer to record each instrument a track at a time from start to finish, but this isn't always as easy to accomplish. In a perfect world, you'd have played the part with the dynamic variation (*light and shade*) needed, made a few edits to tighten this up and perhaps entered any controller fades and so on as overdubs afterwards, so that the file was still being at least roughly mixed as you built it up. In reality though, this method of working could require a little more editing and mixing work at the end.

As it's usually regarded as favourable to 'mix as you go', and the resulting mix will always be defined by either personal taste or the sound on the original record you're covering, this topic just takes a brief look at some ideas and general principles worth considering.

Essence

This should be a primary consideration: *What is the essence of the sound*? Is it a lush sound or a spartan sound? Is it largely piano-based with the other instruments sitting slightly behind, or maybe it rests on strong drums and bass? The aim during mixing is to try to bring out the essence of the sound, which usually relies on the best settings for all the major controllers – volume, expression, pan, reverb and chorus. Of course it's also going to involve considerations of note-velocities, strength of quantization, choice of patches. This is why it's best to get these things right *as you record*!

If you're working on cover-versions, the mixing job is easier in some respects. The essence of the sound should be obvious, and the mix is sitting in front of you begging to be copied. This is not to suggest that you should always blindly go with it – use poetic licence and artistic interpretation. And a fair degree of common sense: just because a record made in 1952 was mono and recorded in front of a reverb plate doesn't necessarily mean it sounds best that way.

Space

Consider the sounds in your file as posters on a wall: are they all tightly gathered together, overlapping or fighting for the same space? If you spread them around a bit, each one becomes clearer and more noticeable for having a stretch of blank wall next to it. Assigning each sound its own space in the mix adds to the clarity and interest of a file and helps to prevent the sounds merging.

Judicious use of panning (CC10) is a major leap in this direction, but 'space' can be created around sounds by using differing amounts of reverb (CC91) on them. Where pan sets the left-to-right balance, reverb controls the balance from front-to-back (or down-to-up depending upon how you hear it), so that a stack of *centre-panned* sounds can still be assigned their own space by creating large differences in their reverb settings.

Live Use

When considering the issue of 'space', there are a few practical points to remember: if you're going to use the file 'live', will you be using a stereo setup? All the careful pan-placement and stereo-sweeps might be wasted! Remember too that lead-vocals are usually panned centre – try to leave a space for them, especially if you intend to record the result. Bass and drum-parts are usually panned centre too (in General MIDI, the kit has to be), though drum-kit instruments usually contain their own individual pan settings anyway.

Drive

If the file is supposed to be a driving rock, pop or rave number, does it drive enough? The drive depends as much on note-velocities as it does on timing: accent the wrong notes and the song will start to drag, particularly if you do that to the bass and drums. Similarly, however successful you've been with the velocities, if you then proceed to quantize everything 100% the drive takes a huge step backwards.

Velocities

With some instruments in some tone-generators, the sounds gain a harder and more 'raspy' sound with higher velocities. This is usually most noticeable with guitar, brass and piano sounds. Try raising all the note-on velocities as much as you can (keeping an eye on available headroom!) and reducing the CC7 setting in the song-header. This could obviously work in reverse if you're trying to get a more gentle sound to an instrument.

Fig. 22 **Real-time mixing in *Cakewalk Pro***

Real-Time Mixing

Some sequencers have a *Mixer* option which lets you adjust all the elements of the mix in real-time as the file plays. The screen is often laid out like any 16-channel mixer found in an analogue studio, with faders, buttons and pots (Fig. 22). This can be a very useful option to have, but make sure that any changes you make *will* be recorded and check on how they'll be inserted into the file.

Some of these mixer-screens can also give access to parameters that are otherwise controllable only via System Exclusive, and may be used to select patches by name, often by letting you create custom *mixer-maps* to suit any device in your setup.

End Use

What will be the end use of the file? If you're planning to use it as the basis for a finished recording (adding live elements such as vocals and mixing to audio-tape or CD), consider using tape-synchronisation to record the live parts so that you're not committed to the final mix at this early stage.

If you expect the file to be used as a backing-track for live performance, remember that not everyone uses stereo gear so the carefully chosen pan positions and sweeps will be lost. This certainly isn't a reason to leave them out, but it's a good reason to have a listen to the file with CC10 controls filtered out to check the result.

Finally, remember that a home-studio mix isn't an accurate representation of a live-hall mix, even with the volume turned up. If you feel that certain elements in the file are important (the volume of a fill, or the difference in pan-position between two instruments), *exaggerate* them.

Detours

➡ For details on specific areas of the mix, check out **Drive** on page 125, the ***Close-Ups*** section of the **Channel Messages Menu** (indexed on page 172), and the **Instruments Menu** on page 145.

➡ Take a look at the topic on **System Common** (page 231) for more info on MIDI to audio-tape sync.

Cover-Version Problems

This topic is geared towards programming covers of existing records and, as you might have guessed, the problems that tend to present themselves in these cases. We'll assume that you're creating a cover-file which will ultimately be used as a backing-track in a 'live' situation. If you're not programming covers, you'll still find a few useful ideas here that are just as relevant to programming original material.

Poetic Licence

We've all heard wrong notes, bad timing, wild tempo fluctuations, poor mixing, uninspired playing and all the rest in records. Before multi-track recording became standard it was usual to record several 'takes' of a song and use the best. So when it comes to covering these records, some form of artistic interpretation is needed. Let's start with a quickfire list of things you'll come up against in cover-files before moving on to the more complex issues.

❑ *Wrong notes in the original* – it's usually best to replace them with the correct ones. If the end user hadn't noticed the wrong notes on the record it might reflect on your abilities!

❑ *Bad timing in the original* – this rather depends upon the effect it has. If it adds to the atmosphere or feel of the song you could leave it. If it sounds wrong, put it right – you can bet *they* would have too!

❑ *Wide tempo fluctuations* – either try to pick a good working average for the whole song, or enter extra tempo events where necessary.

❑ *Dull playing* – as an example, many old records consist of the same drum-pattern played repeatedly with no fills or variations. Bear in mind that as long as you're *improving* on the original there are unlikely to be any complaints. Adding a few drum-fills to help lift the song, or changing from hi-hats to ride-cymbal for the last chorus will probably be appreciated by the end user.

❑ *Unable to hear the notes* – sometimes a line vanishes into the rest of the backing, or you can hear the attack of the notes but they're too short to be able to pitch. If you can't hear them with the volume well up, can anybody else? Give it your best shot and try to mix the line in a similar way.

❑ *Can't match the sound* – a perennial problem in cover-versions. However, if you can match the notes, the timing and the feel, slight differences in the sound tend to be a lot less noticeable. Pick the closest sound you can for the actual recording, and reckon to rethink *when you've finished the file* – chances are it'll sound perfectly okay.

❏   *It's mono!* – ... and it might still be a great record but it sounds
     rather constricted when you program it this way. The advice here is
     the same as for 'Dull Playing' – the end user is unlikely to complain
     if you give the sound a little room to breathe. (Extravagant pan-
     sweeps are probably out though.)

Clicktrack and Cues

Some songs contain sections where the vocal line continues over a
sustained (non-rhythmic) backing, or the song pauses for a bar or two
before resuming. In these cases the vocalist (or lead-instrumentalist)
needs a **clicktrack** to indicate tempo or a **cue** to indicate when the
tempo resumes.

The obvious type of **clicktrack** is simple quarter-notes on a kit-
instrument such as a hi-hat, ideally with an accented first beat. The
danger is that because this has to be clearly heard by the vocalist it
will also be heard by the audience. A better form of clicktrack is a
rhythmic pattern (perhaps using congas, cabasa or rides) which is just
as easy to hear but not as obviously a clicktrack. Or try using an
instrumental rhythm such as a muted-guitar line or some form of
echo-effect (see page 140).

A **cue** may be needed if the lead-vocal is to start *after* a long sustained
chord with no rhythmic backing, or a pause in the song. A cue could
be anything: a 2-beat drum fill, an instrumental pickup line, and so
on. Once again, it has to be heard, so it should be imaginative.

Hint

➡ When saving as a type 1 Standard MIDI File, try to keep clicktrack and
   cues on a separate track so that they can be isolated and muted if
   necessary.

Dealing With A Vocal Pickup

As we've mentioned earlier in this section, files should have a one-bar
count-in to the song, and if the song begins with an instrumental
pickup this can be placed over the count-in bar. But if the song has
a *vocal* pickup it isn't just the tempo and cue that's needed, it's some
hint of the key.

There are two ways of getting around this: one is to place a cue-chord at the beginning of the count-in bar; the second is to construct a short introduction. A rule of thumb for an introduction is to keep it short (2 bars should do the trick) and make it sound like a natural part of the song. You could try using the first or last two bars of the chorus since they'll often lead into a similar vocal-line; or perhaps the song is built around a main theme or *hook* that you could incorporate? Is there a particular guitar or keyboard riff that you could use, maybe with some adjustments to the chord-sequence? If nothing obvious springs to mind, then you'll need to *compose* something suitable but it's best to keep it short and functional.

Hint

→ Try leaving a couple of blank bars after the count-in, and when you're further into the song use copy and paste to 'slot in' and re-edit sections that are already recorded, corrected and balanced.

Dealing With A Fadeout Ending

Another tricky problem — it's not usually desirable to program the fadeout ending into the file. Partly because any live musicians and vocalists have to try to fadeout in time with the file, and partly because a fadeout isn't much of an applause-grabber!

This means, of course, that you have to find a way to *finish* the file. As usual, there are whole hosts of possibilities and they're going to depend on the song you're working on. You might decide to hold the last vocal note while the accompaniment plays a short outro; or to finish with a sudden stop on the last vocal note. You might want to build the song up to a big finish or pull it down to a more understated ending.

The most popular ways of ending songs are either to finish on the last line of a chorus, or to find a way to use the title-line as a last line. In any event, it's usually most effective to finish with a vocal note, and a big finish is more likely to get applause than a small one. But before you decide *how* to finish, there's another pressing question . . .

Where Do I Finish?

The two most frequent scenarios are the vocal *repeat and fade*, and the *ad lib. guitar solo to fade*. The first case is easier to deal with: simply decide how many repeats you can use to indicate that the song is coming to an end without getting boring (remembering not to use the Beatles' *Hey Jude* as a model!). For a single line, three repeats usually does the job. Finding some way to use the title or hook-line at the end is a popular option.

The guitar-solo fadeout is more complicated: to be true to the record, of course you should use as much of the solo as possible. But, on the other hand, many people performing the file live won't want to finish with a guitar solo, especially if they don't have a guitarist in the act, and it never provides the big finish that a vocal-ending does. Let's take a couple of well-known songs as examples:

Lou Reed's *Walk On The Wild Side* finishes with a fadeout sax solo. It's well known and you'd feel cheated if it had been left out entirely. Try using the sax solo, as it is, gradually fading out, but before it fades entirely do a fast fade-up and a big finish – perhaps a final loud sax-line with full strong backing, or a vocal-repeat of the title-line.

Lionel Richie's *Running With The Night* ends with a long guitar solo. While it keeps the beat going and you can dance to it, it doesn't lead to a strong finish: two possible options are, first, cut it entirely and finish on the chorus preceding it (rather unfair to anyone looking forward to performing it live!), or keep it in but try to steer it back into a final chorus leading once again to a vocal finish and keeping everyone happy.

To some, it can seem almost sacrilegious to remove sections of a song, or to add extra choruses and additional vocal-lines on the end. But bear in mind that you're producing files for *live performance* – when the original artists perform their material live they have to consider exactly the same questions and arrive at similar results. If you have a live recording of the song you're working on, listen to how *they* solved the problem and try copying that.

Vocal Parts

In some MIDI file markets, especially the UK, it's usual to include the vocal melody-line on channel 4 of any cover-version file. Obviously, if the file is to be used live, the track will be erased but it's included to help vocalists learn the melody and structure of a song, and it's especially important if you've had to compose a slightly different ending! Remember that the vocal track is your lead-instrument which should grab attention and help you to sell the file, so choose a sound that complements the song and the mix, and try to emulate the phrasing of the original vocal-line.

Backing and harmony vocal parts are a different kettle of fish: acts that don't have backing-vocalists will probably leave these in so they're well worth taking some trouble over. Harmony vocals might also be used as a feed to a harmony-machine (see **Appendix Two** on page 283) so try to keep the playing legato and allow for slight differences in vocal phrasing by starting notes a little earlier and not clipping them too short. It's becoming an accepted custom to place harmony vocals on channel 5 to prevent the end-user having to reset the receive channel on the harmoniser for each file.

Hint

➡ You can take a lot of poetic licence with the choice of patch for backing vocals. Obvious choices are choir or synth-voice patches, but in rock numbers a harder sound such as brass, electric guitar or organ can add extra punch to a file where a choir sound might do exactly the opposite.

4

Tricks and Effects

In this section we take a look at some of the so-called 'advanced' programming skills. Of course, there's really no such thing – we're still using the same old MIDI messages and the same old sequencer functions, so if you're familiar with these (and you know an effective sound when you hear it), this is good simple stuff!

Apart from the **Drive** topic, all the effects and techniques listed here are interlinked and can usually be used in combination with great results (for example by double-tracking an echo effect, or applying a pan-sweep to a layered sound). Remember that most of these effects can be used on drums and untuned percussion sounds just as usefully as with tuned instruments.

▨ Drive

This is as much a musical question as a programming one: you've recorded a song with a driving rock feel, perfect in every respect but one – it drives like Miss Marple on a moped. Fortunately there are solutions to this, some of which are best used during the recording and editing stages, but one in particular that can add some push when you've completed the programming.

Remember – drive is in no way linked to *tempo*. In fact, when you've managed to make a file push effectively, you might even feel you need to reduce the tempo!

Getting Down To It!

The idea of **drive** is to create the effect of *pushing* the beat as if the song were trying to get faster. An easy way to do this when the programming is complete is to move the drums and bass tracks forward by a tick or two (depending on the song tempo). Even with fully quantized tracks you should still end up with a file you can groove to, if grooving is your thing.

Depending on your sequencer functions, you might be able to do this just by applying a negative delay to the tracks (but make sure you don't try to apply it to the header-bar), or you could physically *move* all the song-body events or patterns so they occur a couple of ticks earlier.

Hint

➡ The operation above illustrates a good reason for always entering a count-in bar before the song-body: without this area to move events forward into, you'd have to move all the other tracks backwards which can make them more complicated to work with in the editors.

Nothing good comes easy, as they say, and in this case they're right. 'Drive' equates to 'feel', and while the above tip can make a difference there's still no substitute for constant regard to the feel right from the start.

The Rhythm Method

A far more suitable way of getting drive into a file is to pay attention to all the primary rhythmic parts as you record and edit. For a rock number, these would usually be drums, bass, rhythm guitar and possibly keyboards. Drums and bass should always be kept quite tightly together as they provide the main push to the beat, and a fairly simple way of getting that push is as follows: keep the kick drum fixed dead on beats 1 and 3, but move the snares on 2 and 4 forward two ticks. Move any hi-hats occurring between beats forward one tick together with any hats coming a 16th-note before or after the snare hits. Then alter the bass-part to a similar pattern of timing (the easiest way to do this is with *Match Quantize* if your sequencer has that facility).

Okay, so it looks rather mechanical on paper! Elements of human feel are regained by techniques covered in **Cut**, **Copy**, **Paste** and **Feel** in the previous section, such as variation of note velocities and adding incidental notes. A second point is that with additional percussion parts (and indeed other *tuned* instruments) you can adopt a more relaxed approach.

The actual *rhythms* played by the drums can make a huge difference to the drive too – take a look at the next couple of pages and the **Drums** topic on page 146 for a few examples of driving drum-patterns and fills.

Secondary Rhythm Parts

With the vital push now coming from the drums and bass, consider the other main rhythmic elements of the file which could often be rhythm guitar or piano. These two couldn't be quantized even if you wanted to – you can't strum several guitar strings onto one tick, and keyboard 'chords' are in fact nearly always arpeggiated to some degree due to the design flaw that resulted in human beings having fingers of odd lengths.

Velocities, as usual, will have a great influence on the push-factor, but for rhythm parts played by naturally arpeggiating instruments the first few notes of the 'chord' should usually straddle the beat rather than begin dead on it. This is particularly true of the guitar parts (see **Rhythm Guitar** on page 150).

Have a listen to the file **DRIVE.MID**. The rhythm guitar part has been pushed forward, together with snares and hats. The bass line has been left slightly looser but is still playing *ahead* of the beat.

Avoiding Drag

Once you've got the more rhythmic parts sorted out it's time to think about the lines, fills, pads and so on. This is where the *more relaxed approach* mentioned above has to be qualified slightly: while not wanting to destroy the feel of the recorded parts, try to avoid them dragging behind. This isn't to say that notes must never occur late, but if a loud or chorded part is playing consistently behind the beat for several bars it's going to undo all your good work. Deal with this by simply moving *all* the events of that phrase forward until the *majority* are slightly early. This way you keep the internal feel of the phrase without sacrificing the drive.

A second point to consider is slow attack sounds such as pads, strings and some synth-patches: if the note-on is quantized you can find the sound isn't heard until well into the following beat. With some sounds, at certain tempi, you might have to move all these notes forward by up to 10 ticks to counter the effect.

When Push Comes To Shove . . .

Obviously if you try to drive a file too far you'll just end up with the effect technically known as *bad timing*. If you find that you're moving tracks, patterns and notes further and further to get that elusive push, check the velocities. If the velocity differences between the quarter notes and the eighth- or sixteenth-notes are too narrow, timing changes won't be enough to solve the problem. Try entering much bolder dynamic variety (or use your sequencer's *Compression* function).

More Drive Effects

❑   Use a tuned sound with a sharp attack to play a 16th-note rising line (as in the example below) to echo the lownote/highnote swing of kick and snare. This is usually best fully quantized as an undisguised synth-line, but you could try time-shifting it forwards a tick or so for added punch.

❑ For a driving feel coupled with a heavy 2nd and 4th beat, add a handclap to each snare hit, but move all the claps forward a tick or two. This adds a strong 'thickening' effect to the beat but, more importantly, causes it to start a little sooner. Obviously this is better suited to 1970s disco/soul styles than thrash-metal!

Have a listen to the drums in the file **ECHOPAN.MID** to hear the offset handclaps at work.

❑ Eighth-notes are great drivers: try adding a constant staccato 8th-note pulse on muted-guitar based about an octave below 'middle C'. Stick to the root note of each chord, reduce the velocities of the 'in-between' 8th-notes and shift the whole thing forward about 3 ticks. You can get a more raunchy sound using an overdrive-guitar patch and reducing the note-lengths to around 10 ticks. This idea is most effective if the bass-line is fairly sparse and non-syncopated.

❑ For a heavier rock drive, quarter-notes might be the answer. Try sticking to a strong 4-feel from kick, snare and open hi-hat (with 2nd & 4th beats pulled forward a little further than for an 8-beat feel) and use either a strong 4 on the bass coupled with staccato 8s (as above), or bass 8th-notes in alternating octaves as shown below.

❑ With slow numbers, ballads and so on, *drive* isn't really what's needed, but sometimes more movement and interest can help things along. Try dubbing a touch of latin percussion such as a light conga rhythm or a few cabasas. Two or three notes per bar is quite enough to do the job, but try to vary the patterns as much as possible: a constantly repeating conga pattern gets boring very quickly which defeats the purpose.

❑ Along similar lines, a simple but slightly syncopated muted-guitar line can help to push a slow or mid-tempo ballad along. It can also add a slightly 'funky' feel so it can work wonders added to the chorus of a soul-ballad.

❑ Adding incidental 8th- or 16th-notes to a ballad bass-line can make a huge difference to the song without touching drums or rhythm-instruments at all.

 Take a listen to **SMOOCH.MID** to hear the muted-guitar line in the background and the congas doing their thing.

Detours

➡ For more programming tips on drums, bass and rhythm guitar, among others, try the **Instruments Menu** starting on page 145.

Double Tracking and Delay

Double-tracking is very similar to layering (on page 138) in that the recorded track is copied to another channel and both are played together. The difference is that in this case the two tracks both use the same instrument. The danger of doing this with some sounds is that you'll get a 'flanging' effect giving an unnatural overall sound. To counter the flanging problem (assuming you don't want it!), double-tracking is usually combined with **Delay**.

Double Tracking

As an analogue studio effect (known as 'ADT'), double-tracking takes a sound that would normally be panned close to centre and doubles it, with one being routed to the right speaker and the other to the left. In MIDI programming terms, this is a piece of cake –

just copy the recorded track to another channel, pan one hard left and pan the other hard right, ensuring that all the other settings are the same, and you're done!

The result is roughly the same as if you'd panned the single sound dead-centre, but you'll hear an additional thickening, a spatially wider sound, and you'll leave room in the mix for other centre-panned sounds.

Triple Tracking

Along similar lines, there's *triple tracking*. In this case an additional copy of the track is panned centre. The result is obviously a very solid sound which might be useful to strengthen a weak lead-instrument, but bear in mind you're now using three voices per note so make sure your polyphony can stand it! A more interesting way to use triple tracking is to transpose the centre voice up or down an octave (and perhaps drop the volume) so that the main work is still being done by the left and right tracks, and the centre track adds some extra effect.

Flange

With some sounds (notably pianos) on some tone-generators, double-tracking may give a flanging effect – a sort of heavy chorus: if you're looking for this type of sound this is a great place to start! (Of course, just to get the flange effect there's no need to pan the two channels apart unless you want to *combine* it with double-tracking.)

Delay

At its most basic, delay is a good way to achieve double-tracking without the flange: just time-shift one of the tracks forward or back a tick or two and the flanging problem should go away. But delay has far more value as an effect in its own right. By moving the co-pied track 4 to 6 ticks later than the original and reducing its velocity you can produce superb results from any sound with a reasonably fast attack. Whether you choose to pan the sounds apart or keep them close depends upon the type of effect you want (panning makes a considerable difference); similarly how many ticks apart the tracks are placed will depend upon the type of sound, the tempo of the song, and how obvious an effect you want.

Have a listen to the file **DELAY01.MID**. The copied piano part on channel 3 has a delay of six ticks and reduced velocity. With the original panned slightly left and the copy panned hard right the total result is similar to a *concert hall* sound. For a larger hall, delay the copy by an extra tick or two and reduce the velocity slightly.

Velocity is an important factor in delays – the further apart the original note and the delayed note are moved, the more the velocity needs reducing to prevent it sounding like bad timing.

Separate Channels?

Delay effects usually require different channels for the tracks to avoid the age-old problem of retriggering. If you're using drumkit instruments or tuned percussive sounds such as xylophone however, you could keep the additional track(s) on the same channel as the original, provided that you can shorten the note-lengths enough. It's still advisable to keep them on separate *tracks* though to make for easier editing.

Hint

➡ Double tracking and delay effects are great candidates for using ghost tracks for the copies if your sequencer provides that facility (see page 86). This ensures that any changes you make to the original track will automatically update the ghosts. Changes in velocity, volume and pan can usually be set as track or playback parameters but make sure you set the delay here too rather than trying to physically move the ghost tracks (this will move the original as well!).

Multiple Delays

But why stop at one copy? Well okay, *polyphony* is a pretty good reason, but aside from that you could make several copies of the original and delay them all by different amounts. Once again, how many copies you make depends on the sound you're using: two or three is normally the limit, but for tuned percussive sounds with short note lengths it's quite possible to use more and it shouldn't upset your polyphony at all.

Play the file **DELAY02.MID**. The piece is the same as DELAY01 but this time we're using *two* copies and all three piano parts are panned to centre. Despite the extra copy, the effect is actually *less* pronounced in this file. Try panning channel 3 to left-50, and channel 4 to right-35 to hear how panning makes the effect come alive.

Hint

➡ When adding delays to single-note lines such as fills and melodies, try changing the notes of the copy to harmonise with the original rather than double it, for example, by playing the melody in 3rds or 6ths. Transposing the copy up an octave can also give great results.

Autopan

This is a trick along the lines of the boxed suggestion for DE-LAY02.MID above. Make three or four (or more) delayed copies, and pan each one differently so that the sound jumps around the stereo field as it fades away. This works best with non-sustaining percussive sounds: sounds that sustain tend to grab large portions of the stereo field for themselves *wherever* they're panned so the effect isn't as perceptible.

 AUTOPAN.MID gives an example of this effect using a marimba as the lead sound.

Hint

➡ A neat trick with autopan is to use four copies, and to give the first and third repeat a different patch from the original. This can give some weird and wonderful results, and usually needs just one channel for each patch.

Pre-Delay

This is a very simple idea which works with most types of sound, although it tends to need just a little more experimentation to get it right. Make the copy in the same way as usual but position the copied track to play a few ticks *before* the original. The volume of the copy will need to be lower than for a standard delay effect and, even so, it might still make the timing sound too anticipated. The solution is usually to then move *both* tracks back so that, for example, the copy starts 3 ticks before the beat and the original 3 ticks after it.

 Listen to the file **PREDELAY.MID**. This is our old buddy DELAY01 again, this time with the original piano track moved back to begin 4 ticks late and a pre-delay track starting 3 ticks early.

Pre-delay can also give the added impression of *driving* the tempo of a song, as you probably noticed in PREDELAY.MID. This feel can be useful in rhythm guitar and keyboard parts, but you could use it in drum parts by pre-delaying the snare hits, or all the tom-toms in a fill. The result is similar to a *flam*, but in this case the pre-delayed notes need to be a lot quieter (not much more than a hint of them!). Used on a conga sound, it gives a very cute sounding 'plop'!

 Have a listen to **SMOOCH.MID** to hear more examples of delay and predelay on the lead-guitar and sax lines.

> **Detours**
>
> ➠ Delay has a lot in common with echo, an effect with more regimented timing. Take a look at the topic **Echo Effects** on page 140 as a possible source of similar ideas.

Fades and Sweeps

Fades and sweeps are effects that use **Expression** and **Pan** to create smooth changes in volume or pan-position. Some of the effects use these two in their rôles as continuous controllers, so the results are much easier to produce if you can remap a volume-fader or modulation-wheel to CC10 or 11 (see **How To Access Controllers** on page 192).

Fade In, Fade Out

Expression fades are probably the most-used continuous 'effect' there is, employed to create dynamic colour in string or pad sounds, fade out the last chord of a song or introduce sounds gradually into the mix. The pros and cons of working with expression are covered in **CC11: Expression** on page 213, and of course there's no trick to it at all: to get a smooth fade simply takes a steady hand on the fader or wheel.

But there's no reason why a fade should be smooth. For a fade-in with a little more interest, try this: record the chord to be faded in, starting at the beginning of a bar. Step-insert a CC11 event just before the note-ons, and CC11s on every 8th-note beat of the bar. Set the values of these events to rise from 15 (as the chord is played), 30, 45, 60, 75, 90, 105, 127. The result is a *rhythmic* fade-in similar to a gated effect (see page 142).

You could even combine this with an 'economic' pan sweep (on page 136) by copying the CC11s and converting them to CC10s to make the sound stutter across the stereo field as its volume increases. Converting the copied CC11s to CC93s (Chorus) would make the sound gradually increase in thickness and presence, heightening the crescendo effect.

Crossfades

The crossfade is a method of *morphing* one sound into another: some synth-sounds gradually evolve into something that sounds quite different, and this effect can be emulated by actually *using* two different sounds and fading one out as you fade the other in. It works best using smooth fades, but you could try the 'stuttering' expression method mentioned above. As with all of these effects, it's easy to do.

Make a copy of the recorded track and assign it to a different channel with the same pan position. Choose two sounds to morph: for maximum effect go for a warm pad and a metallic or resonant pad. Now create an expression fade which starts at about 30 and rises to 127 over roughly a bar, on a track assigned to the same channel as one of the sounds. Copy this expression-bar to another track assigned to the second channel and reverse the events so it *descends* from 127 to 30. (Make sure the tracks *begin* with expressions set to 30 and 127 respectively too!)

To create a constantly alternating crossfade between the two sounds, copy these one-bar fades to every bar or every second bar, switching back and forth between fade-up and fade-down as shown in Fig. 23.

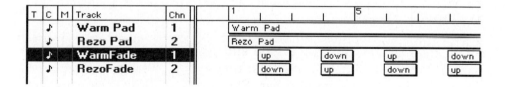

Fig. 23 **Alternating crossfades**

Load the file **CROSSPAN.MID** and mute the tracks labelled *Pan 1* and *Pan 2* (Tracks 6 and 7) to hear the *crossfade* effect. Notice that the volumes and chorus settings are different for the two channels to mix the sounds better. Try experimenting with different sounds and settings.

Dynamic Pan Sweeps

If your tone-generator doesn't support dynamic panning, this effect won't work. Take a look at the topic **CC10: Pan** on page 210 to find out more about it.

Dynamic pan sweeps are almost identical to expression fades: you simply play a sustained chord and use a remapped fader to move the sound around the stereo field. An effective way to use dynamic panning is in conjunction with expression. Say, for example, that you've recorded a pad track using expression to add continuous variation to the volumes of the chords: copy the expression data to a separate track and convert the events to CC10s. As the volume increases the sound will move to the right, and vice versa, creating an effect similar to waves rolling up the beach, but without the seaweed.

Rhythmic Panning

Of course, there's no reason why a pan sweep should be smooth. This is a neat effect to use with sustained sounds such as pads, using dynamic panning: try step-entering pan events as if they were notes with a particular 'rhythm' (16th notes, 8th-note triplets, funky syncopations, etc.) and give them all different values. You could start at 0 and move up to 127 in jumps of about 30 at a time and then back again, or use random values like 114, 52, 76, 10, etc. The rhythmic effect will be more noticeable if you keep the reverb setting to a bare minimum.

For a truly randomised panning effect in 4/4 time, try creating a *5-beat* pattern of pan-events and chaining them together: this gives the effect of a single 20-bar pattern and sounds very random indeed!

Economic Pan Sweeps

This is a quick and event-economic method of creating a pan sweep for a rhythmic track: make a copy of the track, edit it to reduce chords to a single note and convert the notes to CC10 controller events. Set a pan-position value for each one, either planned or random, and move each event (or the whole track) forward slightly so that each pan event will occur just before the note or chord on the same tick.

The benefits are twofold: you get complete control of exactly where each note or chord will be situated, and you cut out all the unnecessary pan data that would be sitting between each note-on doing nothing more than clogging up the arteries!

 Load the file **SPLITPAN.MID** to hear this in action on channel 3 (try muting channel 1 to hear the effect more clearly).

Crosspanning

This is a similar effect to *Crossfades* on page 135, but using Pan instead of Expression. Construct the tracks and 'fades' in exactly the same way but fade all the way from 0–127 and vice versa. With this effect, two sounds panned hard-left and hard-right gradually move towards each other and swap places. And, of course, you could combine this effect with a crossfade to get the best of both worlds.

 Load up **CROSSPAN.MID** again. The two fade tracks have been copied and converted to CC10s to create the *crosspanning* effect together with the same crossfades. To hear the crosspanning by itself, mute the tracks labelled *Fade 1* and *Fade 2* (Tracks 4 and 5) and raise the CC11 Expression setting of the track labelled *PAN 2* (Track 3) to 127.

Split Panning

This is very similar to *Economic Pan*, and it's also very simple and extremely effective: take any rhythmic part of the sort that would normally be panned close to centre, and step-enter pan events just before each chord to make them alternate between hard-left and hard-right: this gives the effect of two separate instruments 'in conversation'. It also gives a type of hypnotic result popular in techno and rave styles.

 Have another listen to **SPLITPAN.MID** to hear this idea strutting its stuff on channel 1.

Detours

→ For more on panning and expression, take a look at their own topics in the Close-Ups section of the **Channel Messages Menu** (pages 210 and 213 respectively).

Layering

A favourite studio trick, **layering** is playing the same line on two different sounds and mixing them together to create one new sound. In analogue recording, a favourite is to layer a solo instrument with a vocal: a good example of this is George Benson's lead-guitar/vocal layers.

Create The Layer

Layering a sound is a quick and easy process. Once you've recorded a track, simply copy it to another channel and set up this second channel with a different sound from the first. Hey presto, a layer! Of course, there are other considerations too. To start with, which sounds should you use? Secondly, does it actually sound like one instrument or is it still obviously just two instruments playing the same thing? This is where the mixing is needed.

Mix The Layer

If the result is going to sound like one instrument, an obvious point is that both channels must have the same pan positions. You would also expect them to have similar effect settings. But the chief element is the relative volumes of the lines. You won't usually change the velocities of individual notes because you want the lines to be dynamically the same. For a whole track, adjust the CC7 in the song-header; for a portion of a track, use a global command to change *all* the velocities, or insert a CC11 before the first note. The results will always depend on the two sounds in question, but you might find that one sound needs a hefty drop in volume for an effective sound.

Edit The Layer

Doing it by the book, that's a layer. But of course you don't have to stop there – try editing one or other of the sounds to improve on the effect:

❑ Try transposing one of the sounds up or down an octave (or even a few octaves).

❑ Try detuning one of the sounds for a 'chorusing' effect: either enter a small pitch-bend peak before the line or use RPN #1 (fine-tuning) – don't forget to reset these at the end of the line though!

❑ For a layer of two fairly percussive sounds, try shifting one of the tracks forward a couple of ticks to give a slightly 'thicker' sound.

❑ Experiment with sounds: try taking them out of their usual range (for example, take a marimba a couple of octaves below its usual range to layer quietly with a bass-line).

❑ Try creating a 'stacked' sound: instead of copying a part to one channel, copy it to two or three and give each one a different sound. This is a polyphony-hungry move, so it's best avoided with chorded parts unless you split the *chord* over three different channels.

Layer Suggestions

If you're short of an idea, try giving one of these a run up the flagpole:

❑ Layer a fast-attack sound (e.g., vibes) with a slow-attack pad or string sound for a rhythmic lead sound playing a slow line. Keep the pad sound mixed fairly quietly.

❑ A good old favourite is the piano/strings layer. This can cause problems with the sustain pedal (pianos have a natural decay and strings don't) so some heavy editing can be required.

❑ Use vibes or electric-piano to add a warmer sound to an acoustic piano patch.

❑ Add a filter-sweep synth sound to strings or choirs for a more interesting effect.

❑ Layer the bass line with a muted or staccato overdrive guitar (an octave higher).

❑ Layer an electric piano patch with a quiet glockenspiel transposed 2 or 3 octaves higher.

❑ Try layering an electric guitar solo with a guitar-feedback or harmonics patch, possibly transposed an octave or two higher and with a reduced volume.

▓ Echo Effects

Echo has a lot in common with Delay effects (page 130). The basic differences are that echoes are an audible effect in their own right while delay is a treatment applied to an existing track, and echoes usually involve a quantity of repeats with fixed timing (such as 16th notes, 8th-note triplets, etc.). Echo is generally used for short phrases as opposed to whole tracks.

Stab Echoes

Echo works best with a single loud chord such as a brass stab. Keep the note-lengths short, and make copies of the chord at regular intervals after the original, say every 16th note for 2 or 3 beats. Then work through the chords gradually reducing their velocities (or inserting a CC11 Expression event before each one): ideally the volume of the first repeat should be about 75% that of the original, and then dropping by about 10% for each chord. The velocities for each chord might then look something like this: 127, 95, 86, 77, 71, 65, 59, 53, 48, etc.

Line Echoes

You can also get a great effect by echoing 'one-finger' melody lines, particularly with percussive sounds such as guitars, pianos and tuned percussion. The setting-up is much the same as that for constructing multiple delays (page 131). Copy the line twice to two new channels, drop the velocities of the first repeat-track by about 30 and the second repeat by 50 (assuming your melody's velocities are maximised). Then time-shift the tracks to create the echoes. If your melody line is mostly playing quarter- and eighth-notes, try using eighth-note triplet timing for the echoes – this usually gives an excellent (and natural) echo effect!

Hint

→ If you're using different channels for the echoes, try using 'ghost' tracks (see page 86) and entering the velocity difference and delay as playback parameters.

Of course, if your original channel's notes are all short enough to have finished before the first echo plays, you can put all the echoes on the *same* channel without any retriggering problems.

Panning Echoes

Using either of the above types of echo (and, in fact, the following two), simply use *Economic Pan* (from page 136) to move the echoes around the stereo field. If you're using separate channels for the echoes, this just involves setting the correct pan position once before the first echo.

 Stoke up the trusty sequencer and play **ECHOPAN.MID** to hear *Stab Echoes* doing a bit of gratuitous panning.

Slapback Echoes

Slapback was an effect very popular in the rock'n'roll era, giving a weird, empty sound. The only difference between this and the *Stabs* mentioned above is that here you use just a single echo, usually a 16th- or 32nd-note after the main hit, and considerably quieter. Once again, it's most effective on drums and any other short, fast-attack sound.

Listen to the files **SLAPBAK1.MID** and **SLAPBAK2.MID**. The first is a drum-pattern with a slapback on the snares; the second contains brass stabs with a panned slapback.

Pre-Echoes

This is a tricky one to use successfully, but it's sometimes worth a try. Follow all the copying rules, but place the 'echoed' chords on the three 16th-notes *before* the stab and gradually getting *louder*. The pre-echoes generally need to be a lot quieter than they would if they were coming after the stab. Adding pan can heighten the effect: place the first pre-echo hard-left, the second L20, the third R20 and the stab hard-right.

Detours

→ Echo and Delay are so alike, even their mother couldn't tell them apart. Take a look at the topic on **Double Tracking and Delay** (page 129) for similar ideas.

Gate Effects

The **noise gate** is a much-loved studio tool for creating weird effects. Essentially, it's a cutoff switch: when the signal strength drops below a certain volume, the gate shuts and the sound is silenced. A good example is the gated-reverb used by Phil Collins on the drumkit.

How and Why?

Gate effects are created by step-writing CC11 Expression events (usually with values 0 and 127) to mimic the opening and closing of the gate. Their main use is in producing rhythms, but a by-product is that you can use them to capture just the sustain phase of a sound and give it a sharp attack.

Basic Gate

Here's a quick tutorial on putting together a simple gated rhythm. First choose a favourite pad sound and record a single chord held for 2 bars at about 100bpm. Then, on a separate track, insert CC11s at the positions and with the values shown in Fig. 24 below. Copy the expression data another three times to fill the 2 bars. Finally, play the file and congratulate yourself!

Track 2: Gate 1				
Meas:Beat:Tick	Chn	Kind	Values	
2:1:000	1	Contrl	11-Express	127
2:1:012	1	Contrl	11-Express	0
2:1:024	1	Contrl	11-Express	64
2:1:048	1	Contrl	11-Express	0
2:1:072	1	Contrl	11-Express	127
2:1:084	1	Contrl	11-Express	0
2:2:000	1	Contrl	11-Express	84
2:2:024	1	Contrl	11-Express	0
2:2:048	1	Contrl	11-Express	127
2:2:072	1	Contrl	11-Express	64

Fig. 24 **List-edit view of a gate effect**

The way to approach a gated rhythm is to decide what rhythm you want, and enter CC11:127s first as if they were the chords being 'played'. Then decide how long each chord should last and enter CC11:0s in the correct positions after the 127s. Finally have a listen and edit any 127s that should be quieter.

Panning Gate

To add a panning effect to the gate, copy all the CC11:127s to a separate track, convert them all to CC10s, and edit the values to create the desired pan movements. (Don't copy the CC11:0s – the track will be silent at this point!)

Have a listen to the files **GATE01.MID** and **GATE02.MID**. The first of these uses a sweep-pad with a panning gate effect. There are three different gate rhythms and two different pans: each set of data has been placed on a separate track to help you isolate individual effects and see what's going on a little more clearly. The second file illustrates gate effects with a drumkit: in the last few bars the controllers have been carefully placed to just miss the attack of the kick and snare giving a slightly electronic sound.

Cross Gate

A cross gate is similar to a crossfade (see page 135): when one sound cuts off, a different sound cuts in. Panning the two sounds to opposite sides gives a great effect. To create a cross gate, record two tracks of chords with different pad sounds, and construct a gate rhythm exactly as before for one of the channels. Then copy the gate data to the second channel, and switch all the 127s to 0s and vice versa.

 Listen to **CROSGATE.MID** to hear this one in action. The phrase is repeated with a split-panning effect (see page 137).

Drum Choke

Finally, here's an interesting way to 'choke' a particular drum or percussion sound without using expression, which would bring the whole drum-part to a halt. A few ticks after the drum-hit, insert the same drum-instrument again with a velocity of 1. On *most* tone-generators (though not all) this will steal the voice for that instrument in the same way that a closed hat chokes an open hat. This is especially effective on cymbals.

 As a *very* brief demonstration of the cymbal-choke, listen to the last chord of **ECHOPAN.MID**.

5

Instruments Menu

The wonderful thing about multi-timbral synths is the huge store of sounds you can get your hands on at the push of a button. And as technology progresses, the *quality* of the sounds gets better and better. You can now listen to a sound and think *Hey, it really does sound like an overdrive guitar!* And after you've hustled to the sequencer to record that screamin' solo, does it *still* sound like an overdrive guitar?

The plain truth is that the more lifelike the sounds become, the easier it is to kill them stone dead by programming for them as if they were just good ol'-fashioned synth sounds! In this section, we'll take a look at how to combine the sounds you've got with a few tricks and a little knowledge of the instrument and how it's played, to create more realistic instrument parts.

Because these sorts of technique are always easier to learn by listening, looking, and 'getting your hands dirty', this section relies more on the accompanying SMFs for illustration than plain text, so you'll find it useful to have your sequencer running as you read on. The example patterns and lines in each file have been split to different tracks to make it easier to analyse each one individually.

Drums

Since the arrival of the MIDI drumkit-patch included in most multi-timbral tone-generators, 'drums' can be anything from a snare to a clave to a scratch. To avoid confusion, this section deals with the standard rock kit comprising kick, snare, toms, cymbals and hi-hat – the domain of the drummer rather than the percussionist.

Practicalities

❑ Remember that the drummer is *human* – she has the usual total of two arms and two legs! So she isn't likely to hit snare, tom-tom and crash-cymbal at the same time unless she falls off the stool.

❑ It takes a finite time to move from crash-cymbal back to hi-hats so the drummer will usually return to the hat rhythm on beat two of the bar if the crash was on beat one.

❑ The drummer can't play a hi-hat or ride-cymbal rhythm while playing a drum-fill, other than with the left foot (pedal hat). Most drum-fills and flams require two hands.

Have a listen to **FLAMS.MID** for examples of one-bar fills using flams and short rolls.

❑ The drummer's innate human-ness means that she won't play every hit at the same volume, nor will they be *exactly* at the same time. Vary the note-velocities, and try to picture which hand is playing each hit.

Hints

➡ Consider investing in a set of drum-pads to enter your drum-parts. The techniques will take some practice and a little editing will usually still be needed, but the result should be more credible for being an accurate portrayal of how a drummer really plays.

Listen to **HIHATS.MID** and **DRUMPATT.MID**. Each of these files contains a collection of two-bar patterns demonstrating a variety of timing and velocity techniques.

❑ The drummer doesn't hit the same area of the drum or cymbal every time, partly due to human error and often due to a desire to vary the sound. Try using small spikes of pitch-bend to subtly alter the pitches of individual hits. Together with velocity variations, this technique can be particularly effective with ride-cymbal parts. (This doesn't apply to the kick, of course, where the beater is fixed in position.) The General MIDI kit incorporates a Ride Bell which does some of the work for you.

❑ Bear in mind that the tempo will change slightly even when the drummer is following a click-track; this occurs most often in fills, and helps to add to the 'push'. A fully quantized 'round-the-kit' 16s fill won't be as effective as a slightly 'speeded-up' fill.

Hint

➡ Try shifting each successive sixteenth-note forward by one tick, then two, and so on for a fill. This might mean that the next bar starts a few ticks early but it should be easy enough to 'lose' these ticks over the course of the bar to get back into position again.

Suggestions

- ❏ Try to alternate between crash-cymbals if your kit contains more than one, to give some variety. These should preferably have different pitches and pan-positions to emulate the live kit.

- ❏ When recording flams and rolls, use two different percussive sounds on the keyboard, and then edit one to match the other. Make sure you shorten all the note-lengths to avoid retriggering. (See *Drum Rolls* below.)

- ❏ For a very solid rock 4-feel, use the kick on all four beats (i.e., doubled with the snare on 2 and 4). Shift both kick and snare forward a tick or two on these beats to emphasise the driving feel.

- ❏ Avoid using exact triplet timing in swing and shuffle feels: it tends to sound too rigid and unnatural. The third tripletised eighth-note of each beat when quantized would occur on tick 64. For a more typical swing feel, keep these around the 60 mark.

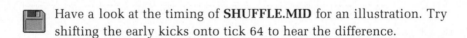

Have a look at the timing of **SHUFFLE.MID** for an illustration. Try shifting the early kicks onto tick 64 to hear the difference.

- ❏ If you record your drum-parts in real time always record both kick and snare at the same time, even if you later want to split them to separate tracks: you'll get a much better feel. Then record hi-hats and crash-cymbals in the same way. This helps to ensure that you don't have a hi-hat playing at the same time as a crash. If you later want to add a crash to a beat, always *convert* the hi-hat rather than *adding* the crash, and make sure you remove any hi-hats falling within roughly a quarter-note beat after the crash hit.

- ❏ Liven up an 8s or 16s feel by using fills in triplets; this works very well with slower 8-beat and 16-beat rock-ballad feels.

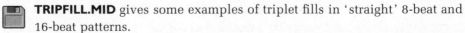

TRIPFILL.MID gives some examples of triplet fills in 'straight' 8-beat and 16-beat patterns.

❑   Accent all drum-notes that play on the 2nd and 4th beat of the bar,
and spread them onto separate ticks for a thicker hit (and therefore a
more noticeable beat). Handclaps are particularly effective when
moved a few ticks earlier than the snare; tambourine hits sound good
a few ticks later, as do rides.

Drum Rolls

Rolls are tricky things to program by step. Always try to get the best
result you can by real-time recording, either using drum-pads or using
two different (but similar) drum-sounds from your keyboard. The
success of a programmed roll will depend a lot on how your tone-
generator assigns voices to drum-sounds: some devices will cut off
one snare hit when they receive another; others will allocate a second
voice which makes for a far more realistic sound. Keep in mind (as
usual) that a drummer has two hands, so there will be little uniformity
in the velocities – even during a crescendo some notes will naturally
be quieter than the note preceding them.

 DRUMROLL.MID, as you probably guessed, gives some examples of
different types of drum-roll.

Cymbal Rolls

Programming a roll on a cymbal relies on re-allocation of voices (as
mentioned above) far more than a drum-roll due to the long decay of
a cymbal sound. If your tone-generator allocates one fixed voice per
kit-instrument, your cymbal roll will sound like a very fast gate-effect.
(Try converting all the snares on the track 'Roll01' in DRUMROLL.MID
to cymbals and see what result you get.) If your tone-generator doesn't
re-allocate voices, you can still get a reasonable result by alternating
between two different cymbals.

Very effective as 'decoration' in quieter sections of music, or to mark
the end of a fill or crescendo are *flourishes*. These are short rolls
consisting of maybe four or five notes increasing in velocity preceding
the strong beat.

Take a listen to **CYMBROLL.MID**. This contains three short patterns demonstrating a soft ride-flourish, a more expansive crash-flourish, and a similar flourish using an expression fade-in for effect.

Triggers

Keep in mind that drum-notes are *triggers* – they'll play the sound to the end regardless of the note-length, so keep all the notes as short as possible, especially when programming rolls and flams.

Detours

➠ For more hints and tips on drum programming, take a look at **Drive** on page 125 and **Cut, Copy and Paste** on page 98.

Rhythm Guitar

However hot your keyboard-playing skills, rhythm-guitar is one of the few instrumental parts that can't be recorded in real-time from a keyboard and regarded as finished. Editing is *always* required, often to the point where you might just as well step-record the lot! Creating an authentic-sounding guitar rhythm is simple, requiring just a little knowledge of the instrument and patient persistence; you could opt for a more detailed and precise rendition, but it isn't usually necessary. And if it were that important, a MIDI guitar (or *guitarist*) would be the answer!

Practicalities

❑ Remember that a guitar is *strummed*, so a chord will usually be spread across several ticks. At slower tempi a short muted chord might sound better on a single tick, but this is the exception rather than the rule.

❑ Consider which way the guitarist's hand moves – the majority of guitar rhythms involve alternating downward and upward strums: a downward strum plays the strings from lowest pitch to highest. In regular rhythmic playing, the guitarist will often continue the alternate down/up movement even if she doesn't actually *strum* on every stroke: this should be borne in mind when deciding whether to spread the chord from low to high, or vice versa.

❏ Guitarists don't always strum all six strings, particularly on a fast upward stroke. (In MIDI programming, the lower two strings can sometimes make the sound too thick in faster rhythms.)

❏ If a guitarist is strumming eighth notes on the same chord for a bar, each string will continue to sound until strummed again on the next stroke – this is where the patience comes in! You need to ensure that each note-off occurs as close as possible to the next note-on of that pitch *without actually overlapping*. Leave a 'gap' of one or two ticks to prevent retriggering.

❏ Guitarists usually start a downward stroke early so that the top string plays on the beat. So the first 'chord' of the bar might start around 5 ticks *before* the bar. An upward stroke usually *starts* roughly on the beat.

Load up **GUITARS.MID** for examples of a few rhythm guitar styles and programming techniques. Rhythms 5 and 6 use two guitars at once, panned apart. Notice the muted chords in Rhythm01, and the hammer-on ('sliding') notes in Rhythm02 and 05.

❏ There are a great many ways to 'voice' a single chord on guitar, so whichever voicing you choose will nearly always be possible, if not actually easy. It is sometimes necessary or desirable to use a believable voicing, so it's useful to know the tuning of the strings. From lowest to highest, the standard tuning is E, A, D, G, B, E (where the top 'E' sounds E3, a major third above 'middle-C', with the bottom 'E' two octaves lower).

❏ When working from a score, remember guitars are *transposing* instruments: they sound an octave lower than written, so 4th-space 'E' (the open top string mentioned above) will *sound* as 1st-line 'E'.

❏ For rock-guitar programming, using Overdrive/Distortion guitars, the power-chord is a useful tool. It consists of only root-notes and 5ths, and is very effective using a three-note chord (root/5/root), or just 2-note 4ths, 5ths and octaves. (In the 3-note chord, you'll get a less 'muddy' sound by lowering the volume of the 5th.)

Have a listen to the files **PORTA02.MID** and **POWERCHD.MID** to hear variations on the power-chord theme. In both files, the tracks to look at are named *Overdrve* (Track 6 and Track 2 respectively).

Suggestions

❏ For funk-guitar parts involving bending and sliding notes (or even chords), use two or more channels to let you apply pitch-bend to individual 'strings' without affecting the others. Alternatively try using a separate short note for each fret, as covered in the **Lead Guitar** topic following, for a more realistic sound.

❏ Because rhythm-guitar programming can be a time-consuming affair, try putting together two or three slightly different single-bar parts and using one of the techniques on page 101 to copy and paste them together. Combined with the obvious changes of chord and voicing, plus the occasional extra note or stroke thrown in for luck, this should give a good approximation of a 'live' guitar part.

❏ Instead of step-entering the notes, it's easier to play them in as a keyboard rhythm (this stops you forgetting what rhythm you were going to use halfway through!). Then position the notes, set the lengths and finally adjust the velocities. There should be at least one clear tick between the note-off and the next note-on of the same pitch, but try to avoid an audible gap.

❏ Bear in mind that changing from one chord to another can cause a short gap while the guitarist moves her hand; in this case only the open strings will continue to sound (perhaps the 'B' string in a G7 chord, for example).

Lead Guitar

In many cases, lead guitar work and guitar solos are as easy to program as synth solos: the proliferation of effects units has buried the idea of a 'typical' guitar sound and it's very often only the playing style that tells you it *is* a guitar. This topic (and its SMFs) therefore leans more towards programming for acoustic guitars, where the techniques are the same but the cleaner sound requires a little more programming precision for a successful result.

Practicalities

❑ Pitch is usually bent by up to a tone, so to be truly accurate set the pitch-bend range to 2. A smooth bend with a range of 4 is just about feasible, but that's the limit. If you're using a MIDI-guitar to input data, you'll probably find a range of ±12 is preferable to 2 in most circumstances.

❑ A useful guitar technique is the 'hammer-on' – a string is played and the guitarist then hits another fret (releasing the first) causing the pitch to change without plucking the string again giving almost a sliding effect. This can be done using pitch-bend by inserting a 0:0 (minimum) event before the note-on and a 0:64 (reset) where the 'second' note should sound. As the second note will naturally be quieter than the first, enter a CC11 Expression of roughly 95–105 at the same time as the reset. You could, of course, just enter two *note* events, the second having a lower velocity, but with some guitar-patches the attack of the second note might spoil the effect.

❑ Remember that finger-slide noises won't usually happen while the guitarist is playing a note. These occur as the left-hand slides along the neck, so try to judge the pitch and length of the slide-noise according to how far the finger is moving and how quickly. Slide noises are a useful way to earn credibility points, but choose your moment with care to prevent them overshadowing the guitar-line itself.

❑ Remember that each guitar-string is *monophonic* – for complete accuracy, a run of notes on the same string won't overlap (see the string-tunings on page 151).

Suggestions

❏   For pitch-bend slides covering more than two semitones, try step-entering the pitch-bend events so that each event raises or lowers the pitch by a semitone. For example, at a range of ±4, the semitone steps downward are 0:48, 0:32, 0:16, 0:0. This gives a good approximation of passing over each fret in turn. Adding CC11 events at the same time to reduce the volume of each successive 'note' will add to the realism.

Listen to **LEADGTR1.MID**. These guitar lines all use pitch-bend either in smooth slides (Patterns 1, 3, 5 and 6) or in a fretted style (2 and 4).

❏   When using a guitar-harmonics patch to create screaming high notes in an overdrive solo, try using a crossfade to get a smooth transition between the two (see page 135).

❏   Instead of using pitch-bend to produce the fretted effect (as in the first suggestion), try using individual notes for each fret. It takes a little longer as you have to consider note-length and velocity, but the results can be better for being a more accurate representation of the playing style.

Load up **LEADGTR2.MID**. The first three patterns give examples of string-slides using separate notes instead of pitch-bend events.

❏   For chorded solos and slide-guitar emulations, use one channel for each string if you prefer to use the pitch-bend method of sliding. Alternatively, if your tone-generator is recent enough to support it, you could experiment with CC84 Portamento Control but you'll lose the guitar-realism of semitone steps.

❏   When programming a muted-guitar line, remember that you don't necessarily have to use the Muted Gtr patch. Try using an overdrive or distortion sound with very short note-lengths for a grittier effect.

❑ Instead of using CC1 Modulation in guitar solos, try using upward
spikes of pitch-bend to mimic tremolos and trills (with the range set
to one semitone).

 Have another listen to **SMOOCH.MID** for some more acoustic lead-
guitar.

█ Keyboards

Keyboard instruments commonly found in tone-generators are piano,
organ, harpsichord, clavichord and accordion. Each of these is played
and programmed in a similar way, but each also has its own curiosities.
We'll start by covering the similarities.

Keyboard Playing

❑ The range of a keyboard chord is limited to the span of the player's
hand, so the maximum range for a one- handed chord will be a tenth
in slower parts or an octave in faster-moving styles.

❑ All keyboard notes have to be *triggered* in order to sound – pitch-
bend is definitely out! Keyboard-players instead rely on trills, grace-
notes and glissandi for their 'effects'.

❑ It rarely happens that every note from a chord falls on the same tick,
however hard the player is trying, and the notes won't necessarily
occur in order from lowest to highest – this human error is part of
the natural keyboard sound. Chords may be intentionally arpeggiated
in a similar way to a guitar chord, but the individual notes will
usually be further apart due to the different method of playing. Too
many arpeggiated chords in close proximity will sound like a badly
played guitar.

❑ Because each note in a chord is played by a different finger, human
error means that note velocities won't all be the same, and could
even vary widely within a single chord.

❏   When a keyboard-player plays a grace-note (*acciaccatura*), different fingers are normally used for the grace-note and the principal note, even when it's possible to 'slip off' a black key onto a white one. This means that, unlike guitar, there could easily be a slight overlap between the two notes, and the principal note will usually be louder than the grace-note. The exception to this might be when slipping from a *chord* on two black keys to two white ones to avoid awkward fingering – in this case some of the control is sacrificed and the principal chord will be softer as the grace-notes are taking the initial force of the fingers.

Piano

❏   Acoustic piano has a huge range of tone and dynamic expression as a result of velocity-sensitivity, so a piano part with similar or fixed velocities will always sound synthetic.

❏   A common question is *What does the left hand do?* There are as many answers to this as there are styles of music, and the answer will depend a lot on what the right hand is doing. If the right-hand is playing a high single-note line (as opposed to rhythmic chords), the left will often play sustained chords around the centre of the keyboard. In blues and rock'n'roll there are established piano-bass patterns. In rock and ballad styles, the left hand's main job is to avoid getting in the way of the bass-guitar so the playing may consist of rhythmic arpeggios (similar to a finger-picking acoustic guitar), or perhaps sustained or slightly rhythmic octaves.

Listen to **SPACEPNO.MID** and **DELAY01.MID** to hear a couple of examples of left-hand piano. The first of these shows both the chorded and the arpeggiated accompaniments.

❏   Piano-players have the benefit of a sustain-pedal to enable them to use the full range of the keyboard while keeping a smooth sound. Remember that sustain-pedal off (CC64:0) events don't occur *before* the next chord – if they did, there would be a brief silence which can sometimes act like a gate-effect and upset the apparent timing. Piano-players release the pedal as the next chord is played and depress it again before they let go of the notes they want sustained. The result is similar to quantizing the pedal events then moving them back a few ticks.

❑   The soft-pedal is a huge advantage on acoustic pianos, but a rather dubious one on synths. One of its functions is to lower the velocity range (think of it as giving you a whole new range from −30 to 97 instead of 0 to 127). In addition, it should produce a softer, warmer tone. Many manufacturers overdo the velocity scaling and completely ignore the tonal differences, so CC67 is usually best avoided.

 Have a listen to **PIANO.MID**. This file contains patterns including ballad, jazz, blues and bar-room.

Organ

❑   Organs have a *swell pedal* to control the volume – an obvious case for the Expression controller. The pedal should also affect the brightness or resonance of the sound. you might bo able to vary this in real time using CC74 or a NRPN.

❑   The organ sounds are the reason some tone-generators include a Rotary Speaker effect, usually with an adjustable fast and slow speed. For true accuracy, the speed should also accelerate and decelerate between the two which you should be able to access using either a dedicated continuous controller or data-entry (CC6). You might be able to get a good result by editing the vibrato setting, and truckloads of chorus can work wonders for a strong, thick sound.

❑   An organist may use both hands to create a rhythm in a chorded style, or play sustained chords with the left hand while playing rhythms or lines with the right.

❑   Use of *stops* can allow a line to be automatically doubled an octave or two higher or lower; these will of course be perfectly synchronized (i.e., just copy and transpose the organ track).

Harpsichord and Clavichord

❑ These two are very similar animals, both to each other and to the piano of which they were the forerunners. Neither has a sustain facility (other than physically holding the notes) so legato playing is needed to create a smooth sound. For programming purposes (when recording in real time), CC64 could still be used sparingly – justify this by deciding to emulate a harpsichordist with a great technique!

❑ The two have very different expression capabilities – the harpsichord is powerful and loud but has almost no touch-sensitivity resulting in very little difference in note-velocities. The clavichord is just the opposite.

❑ A common use of the clavichord in modern music is in playing chorded rhythms, to some degree emulating funk guitar styles. These are very often two-handed affairs, both hands positioned close together spanning a range of perhaps two octaves, and played in a choppy staccato fashion.

Accordion and Bandoneon

❑ The piano-accordion is similar to a traditional organ in that wind creates the sound. It has a shorter keyboard with a range of around three octaves from a 5th below 'middle-C'. The right hand plays the keyboard while the left operates the bellows and plays sustained accompanying chords by pressing buttons. The bandoneon is a similar instrument but lacks the keyboard – the buttons instead operate single notes which can be used to create chords.

❑ Being wind-controlled, the volume of notes varies according to the force of the air, so extensive use of CC11 Expression is needed to reproduce the 'fading in and out' effect – this is a vital part of a credible accordion sound.

 KEYBDS.MID contains a collection of patterns and effects from various keyboard instruments.

And Of Course . . .

Obviously a synthesiser is a keyboard instrument. The capabilities of a synth depend largely on whether it's monophonic or polyphonic: the only synth emulation you're likely to want is that of an old modular monophonic device. If you can set a channel to Mono mode you're done, otherwise you have to edit the note-lengths to remove overlaps. Set all note-velocities to the same value and perhaps add a touch of portamento. With a little editing of envelope parameters, vibrato and resonance (possibly via NRPNs), you can create some excellent analogue-synth emulations from such mundane patches as a piccolo or string sound.

Programming for modern synth sounds is left totally to you — there are no limitations, rules or playing techniques to follow and the result can sound as far removed from human playing as you want it to!

Detours

➡ For some of the possible pitfalls encountered with the sustain-pedal, turn to page 215.

Brass and Reed

Brass, reed, and indeed pipe, instruments have a lot in common when it comes to MIDI programming, which is why they're subjected to the indignity of being lumped together in the same topic. Each relies on breath-power to produce a note, which means that identical programming techniques can be used to good effect. Let's start with a few generalities.

A Few Generalities

❑ Notes can be 'bent' and, particularly in the case of brass instruments, the first note of a phrase often begins below pitch and slides up — this is more easily done by step entering pitch-bend events with low values than by using the bend wheel.

❑ Long notes are rarely held without vibrato — careful use of modulation (CC1) can be effective provided the values don't get too high, or step entering spikes of pitch-bend can give a more credible and slightly less regular result. Remember that notes won't have vibrato right from the start; it may be introduced for effect, or it may occur as a sort of pitch instability towards the end of a long note.

❑ All these instruments are monophonic (with the obvious exception of any 'ensemble brass' patches), so too many overlapping notes will detract heavily from the realism.

❑ As these instruments all rely on human breathing, allow your human to take a breath once in a while – she'll sound and feel a lot better for it. Eight bars of uninterrupted playing on a wind-instrument is the second most common scenario highlighting poor programming (beaten only by rhythm-guitars that sound like badly-played pianos).

Hint

➡ Try using CC2 Breath Control to record these parts if your tone-generator supports it. It's hard to look cool while you do it if you're using a mouthpiece attachment, but the authenticity of the results can be breathtaking.

❑ Brass, reed and pipe notes never just *end* as they do when you take your finger off a synth-key: use CC11 to create a slight diminuendo at the end of the last note of a phrase. When you've done this once you can probably copy the same CC11 events (with a little tweaking) to every instance in the file, so it's a pretty small job that pays big dividends.

❑ Brass and saxophone lines often end with a *trailing off* – a combination of lowering volume and falling pitch. While this could be effected using expression and sliding pitch-bend, the results are far better using short individual notes of gradually decreasing velocity. The alternative, as mentioned in the earlier guitar topics, is to use carefully chosen pitch-bend values for regular semitone falls, but expression is still needed so this is really taking the scenic route to the same destination.

Take a listen to **BRASS.MID**. This file contains several patterns covering the brass falls mentioned above, and stabs with a similar effect using pitch-bend instead.

❑ Bear in mind that the volume of the note is proportional to the air pressure; a wind player often hits a note quietly and then 'forces' its volume up, sometimes at the same time as forcing the pitch higher. The best way to mimic this effect is to use CC2, but if you don't have that option, some judicious use of expression helps to imitate the sudden changes of intensity often heard in long sax and horn notes. Use of a few upward pitch-bend spikes at the same time adds realism by mimicking the pitch-instability that naturally occurs.

Saxophones

❑ Together with guitars, sax patches are renowned for being rather poor efforts in most tone-generators. The result is that you have to work that much harder to get a believable result. Most often, good sax programming requires very wide velocity differences (particularly in runs, falls, grace-notes and 'bends') and subtle use of vibrato effects or modulation.

❑ Don't pay too much attention to *range* – between baritone, tenor, alto and soprano a range of roughly four octaves is covered and you'll be lucky if more than two of your sax patches sounds convincing. Pick the closest good one – an out-of-range alto will generally sound better than a bad soprano.

Play the file **SAXES.MID**. (If your alto patch is lousy, switch to the one you prefer.) This file contains sax rises and falls, grace-notes and bends. Notice the forced note at the end of the second pattern using a couple of expression events, the second timed to coincide with the start of the bend where the player is actually 'forcing' the note upwards.

❑ Try a little patch-editing to get a sexier sax for ballads and jazz. For example, set a slightly slower attack phase, reduce the brightness or resonance, decrease the vibrato rate and increase the depth a little. On many tone-generators, these parameters can be accessed via NRPNs and more recent devices may implement dedicated controllers such as CC74 Brightness. An increased use of pitch-bend and/or step-sliding notes can add to the 'lazy' atmosphere of the part.

Have another listen to **SMOOCH.MID** – the lead-instrument in the second section of the piece is an alto sax demonstrating a few of the techniques covered in this topic.

Pipes

❏   A common characteristic of flute and piccolo playing (among others) is *tonguing* – fast interruptions of the flow of air by a movement of the tongue similar to that of saying the letter 'T', which gives rapid short repetitions of the note. As with so many of these techniques, you could use sequencer 'tricks' to reproduce it (in this case a gate effect), but by far the best method is to actually enter a series of staccato notes of varying velocity – this way you should also hear the breath-noise attached to the attack of the note each time.

Have a listen to **FLUTE.MID** to hear an example of tonguing in the second pattern. The first pattern contains a flute trill of which the final note uses a few pitch-bend spikes rather than modulation to mimic a slight vibrato, as mentioned under *Generalities* on page 159.

❏   Instruments of the flute family have a peculiarity in that the higher register is reached by increasing the wind pressure. Therefore, a sudden high-velocity note can produce the note an octave higher giving the effect of 'harmonics'. This can be effectively imitated by *adding* the higher note to the lower one at a slightly reduced velocity.

❏ Human whistles are another type of patch that leaves a lot to be desired. Remember that people are pretty hopeless at whistling on key, so pitch-bend detunes or fine-tuning (RPN #1) can help. The *knowledge* that we're pretty hopeless makes us tend to *slide up* to notes, especially at higher pitches, rather than risk the humiliation of shooting for it and missing completely. A bend range of ±2 is usually best for this.

❏ A breath-noise patch (as contained in the General MIDI sound-set on #122) can be a useful addition to pipe and whistle lines on the appropriate notes, but be careful not to overdo it. Breath noises will be particularly noticeable in tonguing passages, staccato notes and phrases beginning with a loud note.

Brass

❏ Bear in mind that smooth pitch-bend slides (as opposed to semitone-steps) are quite legitimate in trombone parts due to the design of the instrument, almost to the point of being a *requirement*.

❏ Unlike many other instrument families, brass instruments use combinations of stops (or a slide in the case of the trombone) to specify a harmonic series, the actual note being made by similar techniques to those we use when whistling or singing. The pitch therefore isn't *fixed* as it is on, say, a piano. Use of a little pitch-bend or fine-tuning can add to the authenticity of this slight pitch variation, and can be useful to slightly *sharpen* a note temporarily as its volume is forced higher, but don't overdo it – there's no point in mimicking an incompetent trumpeter.

❏ If you have enough channels to do it, try creating your own brass section instead of using an ensemble brass patch. For best effect this takes a lot of patience, but it does give you scope to assign different pan positions to each instrument, in addition to the instrumental subtleties of different pitch variations, slides, etc. Tuning each instrument slightly differently using fine-tuning (RPN #1) can give a more genuine result still, and sharpening the lead-trumpet slightly is especially effective. A typical brass section could comprise two trumpets, trombone, alto and tenor. Of course you can add to or subtract from this setup to create the sound you want, or even use the ensemble brass patch monophonically on several channels instead of the different brass instruments. Record each 'instrument' separately instead of just copying and note-editing a track to allow the precise timing of the instruments to differ slightly.

❏ Brass instruments, especially trumpets, also use the *tonguing* technique to great effect.

❏ Brass stabs are particularly effective if you make the highest note louder and a few ticks longer than the others. They can also be an effective way of accenting the beat, especially in mid-tempo funk numbers, by adding a stab to every snare-drum hit on beats 2 and 4. Try spreading a four-note stab-chord across two successive ticks for a more rounded sound, or voicing the chord over a $1\frac{1}{2}$ octave range rather than in close position.

▓ Bass Guitar

The practicalities of playing bass are similar to those of lead-guitar, except that there are fewer strings attached. The same techniques logically apply regarding slides and pitch-bend, but the difference in pitch tends to make these subtleties unnoticeable most of the time.

Practicalities

❏ The bass-guitar's strings are tuned E, A, D, G, matching the first four strings of the guitar but tuned an octave lower. The lowest note is therefore E0 (almost three octaves below 'middle-C'). The bass is also a transposing instrument, so this note is written on the first leger-line below the bass-clef.

❏ The bass is usually played as a *monophonic* instrument: slight overlaps might occur where notes are played on different strings but these are usually kept to a minimum. Widely spread chords are occasionally used, particularly in 'new-age' music, and 10ths work well in slower ballad styles.

❏ As mentioned above, individual semitones are rarely heard in bass slides. The exceptions might be during solos, when the bass is up front in the mix, or for sections using the higher strings. Techniques to recreate the fret movement are covered in the topic on **Lead Guitar** (page 153).

❏ *Look ma, no frets*! The fretless bass got its name for a reason – slides will always be smooth, and in slower styles where the fretless is used most, slides are used to the max which can call for almost constant alteration of the bend range. Alternatively, you could set the range to 12 and work out the numbers yourself. Also worth a try is CC84 Portamento Control if your tone-generator is recent enough to support it. The same applies when using acoustic bass patches.

 Have a listen to **BASS01.MID** and **BASS02.MID** for a few bass-patterns containing bends and slides.

Suggestions

❏ Try to keep the bassline moving in time with the kick-drum: bass and drums are the cornerstone of the beat and need to work together to prevent the rhythm sounding untidy.

❏ Slap basses often lack the depth to carry the whole bass-line of a song: try using the slap-bass patch for just the slaps (either using program changes or a separate channel) and sticking to a fatter sound for the line itself. Remember that the slaps will be short, clipped notes.

❏ Try to avoid dull, metronomic bass-lines. A few slides and grace-notes can make a world of difference, but try adding a few incidental sixteenth-notes as well to liven up an eighth-note bassline and break the rigid feel.

BASSLINE.MID contains the same 4-bar phrase played twice: in the first section the bass plays a basic eighth-note feel. The second section is the same line with added sixteenth-notes. In this case the drums are also playing 16s, but the effect is at least as good when the drums are playing a solid 8s feel.

❏ Avoid making basslines too legato: rests are as rhythmically effective as notes. An example of this is the first section of BASSLINE.MID.

❑ Add chorus to a bassline to get a fuller sound that fills the stereo field. Remember that reverb is hardly ever added to bass instruments.

❑ Another way to get a 'wider' sound from the bass is to break with tradition and use double-tracking instead of panning it to the centre. This can be particularly effective if you have another low-pitched instrument panned centre such as a sustained string or pad note, or a full sounding rhythmic instrument such as a piano part or rhythm-guitar.

❑ Some bass patches have a usable working range of only an octave or so from the lowest note; above this point they start to sound thin. Doubling these notes quietly an octave lower will often solve the problem.

Detours

➡ The Drive topic on page 125 has a few more points to make about bass-guitar programming.

Strings

Strings are well-known to be a musician's best friend and can be used effectively in almost *any* style of music: if a file needs that certain indefinable 'something' and you haven't used strings yet, it's probably only a matter of time. But bear in mind that a fistful of notes and an ensemble-string patch do not a string-part make . . .

Practicalities

❑ String instruments are usually played with a bow, resulting in a smooth sustained sound, but the volume of the note varies according to the force of the bow on the string – for realistic string parts, use of expression is pretty much vital.

❑ As these instruments don't have frets, pitching of notes relies on the player's ear (or position of her finger to be more precise) so small tuning variations between notes are to be expected. Smooth pitch-bend slides are also possible, and notes may begin with a small slide up to pitch as with brass parts.

❑ String players often use tremolo – rapid vibrating of the finger on a note, or two alternate notes. The first of these is best emulated by using small pitch bend spikes back and forth between about 0:72 and 0:64 (at a range setting of ± 2). The second works most effectively by inserting short notes, though wide pitch-bend alternations can give a similar effect with this one.

❑ *Fiddle*, to be exact, is just a colloquial term for a stringed instrument, but has been adopted as a name for a violin played in a particular style. Its main distinguishing features are extensive use of pitch-bend, wide velocity differences in the more raucous playing style, and a sharp attack on accented notes which usually requires an expression-controlled volume drop after the note-on.

❑ Due to the arched layout of the strings, chords are limited to two notes which must be from strings positioned side by side, i.e., two outer strings or the two centre strings.

 STRINGS.MID contains several patterns including string runs and swells, fiddle and harp.

❑ The harp is a curious instrument in that it's tuned to the major scale of C flat, rather than a chromatic scale. A set of seven pedals allows individual notes to be raised in semitones thereby creating different scales. (For example, raising the C, E, F and G flats would give the harmonic minor scale of F.) The sweeping motion of the hands produces a glissando like that of a piano, but perfectly in keeping with the key of the music. The harp sweep in STRINGS.MID has the harp tuned to the major scale of F.

Suggestions

❑ Try creating your own string section (as with the brass section mentioned previously). If you can spare eight channels for the job, assign two each to cello, viola, second-violin and first-violin, each with slightly different detune levels and pan positions. If you prefer to use the ensemble strings patch for each of these, try adding a solo-violin patch tuned slightly sharp to double the lead-line for a more realistic sound.

Hint

➡ The more effort you put into creating a credible lead-instrument (lead-violin, lead-trumpet, etc.), the more successful your finished result is going to be, covering a multitude of sins in other parts.

❑ Resist the temptation to just play single 3- and 4-note chords unless your string-part is used as a pad *and* placed well back in the mix. Instead take a note from each chord to write three or four separate string-lines and record them this way (even if they're all on the same channel) – this will help your legato movement between chords no end, and add a little timing realism. You might even find that you can add extra notes to the individual lines to create additional movement within the 'chords'.

❑ If you follow the tip above and find your simple string-part suddenly has a bit more character, why not go the whole hog and move each line to its own channel, panning them apart a little (something like L25/Centre/R25). The extra movement you added to the lines will have far more interest if the notes occur at slightly different points in the stereo-field.

❑ When using strings as a pad-sound, try using a wider spread: a 'C' chord spread over a 10th (C, G, E) sounds warmer and more spacious than the more easily reachable C, E, G.

❑ For solo-string lines, playing octaves rather than single notes can thicken the sound well if your polyphony can stand it. Try lowering the velocities of one of the parts to give just a hint of its existence.

❑ String-patches can make excellent synth-lead sounds by adding a bundle of chorus (CC93) and using portamento (see page 221). If you've got easy access to envelope and filters (perhaps via NRPNs), try reducing the attack-time and experimenting with TVA/TVF settings too.

Shorts

This topic takes a briefer look at some of the other instruments you may run up against whilst programming one by one, with similar tips and snippets of information, plus a few general remarks and suggestions.

Tuned Percussion

❏   The tuned percussion category contains such instruments as xylophone, glockenspiel, marimba and vibes. Each of these is played with hammers, beaters or sticks (except for the celesta which is operated from a keyboard). Chords therefore consist of a maximum of two notes (unless you choose to imitate one of those smooth operators who use two sticks in each hand) and human error means that the notes won't necessarily be in perfect sync.

❏   Notes and chords are sustained by a *roll* played in similar fashion to a drum-roll. In fact most of the techniques of drumming can be applied to tuned percussion, together with glissandi as on keyboard instruments.

❏   Another form of tuned percussion is the kettledrum, often (though not always) used in pairs and referred to as timpani (timps to abbreviation-crazed musos). These are usually tuned a perfect 4th apart.

 Load up **TUNEPERC.MID** for some examples of tuned-percussion rolls and glissandi.

Percussion

❏   Tricky one; percussion instruments are many and varied, and most are associated with particular styles of music. For example, timbales are popular in reggae and calypso; cuica, guiro and whistle in samba and salsa; castanets in flamenco and so on. In rock music, the most common percussion instruments are cowbell and tambourine, but a little well-placed cabasa or a few congas can add interest to a slightly flat rhythm arrangement.

 Take a listen to **PERCUSSN.MID** – there are no particular thrills here, but there *are* a few patterns you might find useful.

❑ Some of the sound-effects found in tone-generators can make useful percussion sounds: such things as gunshots, footsteps and door-slams can replace or add to a snare hit. A heartbeat sound can be very atmospheric used rhythmically if you can match the song tempo to the speed of the sound's 'double-hit'.

❑ Pay attention to the timing of some of the longer percussion sounds: vibraslap and guiro are 'long-play' sounds that might be more effective shifted a few ticks earlier. Percussion instruments with a less marked attack, such as cabasa, can often benefit from the same treatment to prevent them dragging the tempo.

Vocals and Choirs

❑ Obviously these can be used as straight synth sounds with no constraints, but vocal sounds can be particularly effective with the famous slide-up to pitch (especially good on the *Doo* and *Ooh* type patches). For more realism, try emulating vocal vibrato with pitch-bend spikes, or creating a multi-channel choir with separate detunes.

❑ If you can spare four channels, try the 'two-thirds trick': write two harmonised vocal lines, record each of them twice (don't just copy each track) and tune one of the doubled tracks slightly sharper than its original and the other slightly flatter. Then pan each pair roughly two-thirds of the stereo-field apart, i.e., one pair to hard-left and R20, the other to hard-right and L20. This trick (with the addition of chorus sometimes) has all the right ingredients to create a rich ensemble sound with almost any instrument playing harmonised lines as accompaniment.

Harmonica

❑ Technically a reed instrument, and programmed in a similar way to saxes. Semitone-step glissandi and wide velocity differences to emulate different forces of breath are common. Vibrato tends to be very controlled so you'll get more realism using pitch-bend spikes and alternating-note trills than with modulation. Like all breath-powered instruments, the brightness will vary according to the intensity of breath so try experimenting with CC74 Brightness as well as note-velocities and expression to imitate the muted sound and changes in tone of blues-harmonica.

Have a listen to **SHORTS.MID** to hear a few of the suggestions in this topic in action.

General

- ☐ One of the problems you can find in tone-generators is poor keyboard-scaling of some of the sampled sounds: on one note the sound is smooth and warm, a semitone higher it's suddenly harsh. For chorded parts, it's easiest to reduce the velocity of the offending note; for solo lines insert a pitch-bend event (127:127) and play the warmer sound a semitone lower. If the line stays in that higher register covering various notes, try this: record the line as usual, then convert all the 'harsh' notes to the highest 'warm' sounding note, switch on RPN #2 (coarse tuning) and use CC6 Data Entry events before each note to re-pitch it correctly.

- ☐ No decent windchime/mark-tree sound? Try a descending glockenspiel arpeggio covering a couple of octaves, transposed to start somewhere between C7 and C8. (And this one you can pan sweep too!)

- ☐ No tabla or 'talking-drum' in your kit? Try pitch-bending a conga with a range-setting of around 12 semitones.

- ☐ For an effective, though untuned, filter sweep, try pitch-bending a seashore patch (GM patch #123) with a high range setting (and a CC10 sweep if you have dynamic panning).

- ☐ Try doubling a bass-line with a piano or honky-tonk patch, shifted forward a tick or two. On fast-moving or 'feature' bass-lines this can give a great sound.

Detours

- → For more ideas along similar lines to those above, take a look at **The Big Idea** on page 265.

- → There are a few more mentions of percussion instruments in **Drums** (page 146) and **Drive** (page 125).

6

Channel Messages Menu

Overview

Close-Ups

All the messages passing between MIDI devices fall into one of two categories: **Channel** or **System** messages. **Channel messages** are events containing a *channel setting*, to direct an event to one channel only. There are five types of channel message: Note On/Note Off; Control-Change; Program-Change; Pitch-bend; Aftertouch. These are the basic event-types from which MIDI files are constructed. **System messages** don't contain a channel setting, and are directed to your MIDI system as a whole. These are covered in detail in their own section on page 224.

This section is split into two parts, **Overview** and **Close-Ups**. The first of these covers general information about each type of channel message, while the second is an exposé of the private lives of better-known controllers.

▥　Intro

What Is The Channel Messages Menu?

The Channel Messages Menu is intended to be part-tutorial and part-reference guide on our best buddies, the Channel Messages. If you're a newcomer to MIDI, read through this *Overview* section absorbing as much as you can and keeping an eye on your MIDI Implementation Chart to see which controllers apply to your device, and experimenting with different controllers to hear what effect they have.

Included in the *Overview* are explanations of notes, controllers, program changes, pitch-bend and aftertouch, so all the building-blocks of MIDI programming are covered. If you're using this section as a tutorial, you'll find more details on channel messages in the topics about **General MIDI** (page 50) and the **Song Header** (page 57). The second part of the section, *Close-Ups*, is an in-depth look at some of the control changes you'll use most often, with a healthy mix of tips, explanations and warnings.

Control-Change Classifications

We have loosely grouped the Control Change messages under three categories: Continuous, Variable and Switch/Fixed controllers (see *Technical Notes*, below).

❑ **Continuous Controllers** are the controllers you might have a hand (or foot) on most of the time while you play, constantly adjusting the value (an example being CC1 – the modulation control).

❑ **Variable Controllers** are controllers that are set to an initial value (0–127) and usually left at that value for a while (if not for the whole song).

❑ **Switch and Fixed Controllers** are controllers that are either *switched* on or off (CC64 sustain pedal for example) or send out a *fixed* message.

Technical Notes

There is some crossover between Variable and Continuous controllers: CC10 (Pan) for example would usually be set in the song-header and left at the same setting throughout the song. Or you might choose to pan a sound harder right for the chorus and pull it back in for the verse – it still fits our Variable definition. But what if you want to program a pan sweep across the stereo field and back again? Is CC10 now suddenly a continuous controller? Does it matter? No, not really. These definitions are included simply to split the controllers into vaguely recognisable 'families' to aid explanation and understanding. As with all MIDI events, they're simply tools to help you create music – *how* you use them is up to you.

It should be stressed that these categorisations are entirely of our own devising. For the sake of accuracy, the current MIDI specification for allocation of Control Change numbers (as defined by the MIDI Manufacturers Association and the Japan MIDI Standards Committee) is as follows:

0–31	**Continuous Controllers 0–31 MSB**
32–63	**Continuous Controllers 0–31 LSB**
64–95	**Switches (On/Off)**
96–121	**Undefined Controllers**
122–127	**Reserved for Channel Mode messages.**

Clean Up!

Most of the topics covered in the **Overview** have a *Clean Up!* section at the end to point you towards a few possible glitches in the finished file associated with the different data-types, and how to avoid them.

The importance of cleaning up a file is straightforward: however well it's running on your setup, another user's setup may not be so forgiving (and some tone-generators are very fussy indeed!). Secondly, the more unnecessary data you've got in a file the longer it's going to take to load into your sequencer or file-player. You could opt to do a clean-up operation after finishing the file, but it would be very laborious work and, in truth, you probably wouldn't bother! It's far easier to clean up each section as you record it, knowing that you can then copy and paste the section safely.

▓ Controller List

What Is A Controller?

A Control Change (or *controller*) is a message that alters the way a note or channel sounds or behaves by sliding it, sustaining it, adding reverb to it and so on. A controller event contains four parameters: position within the song (bar/beat/tick number), controller number, value for that controller and the channel on which it's to be sent.

The following is a list of various functions accessed by Control Change commands and the CC number to which they are usually mapped. Not all devices will respond to all controller numbers, nor will you necessarily have access to all these functions. But if you do, this is probably where you'll find them:

Function	Number	Range/Value
Bank Select MSB	0	0–127
Modulation MSB	1	0–127
Breath Control MSB	2	0–127
Foot Pedal MSB	4	0–127
Portamento Time MSB	5	0–127
Data Entry MSB	6	0–127
Main Volume MSB	7	0–127
Balance MSB	8	0–127
Pan MSB	10	0–127
Expression MSB	11	0–127
Effect-type selector #1	12	0–127
Effect-type selector #2	13	0–127
General Purpose 1 MSB	16	0–127
General Purpose 2 MSB	17	0–127
General Purpose 3 MSB	18	0–127
General Purpose 4 MSB	19	0–127
Bank Select LSB	32	0–127
Modulation LSB	33	0–127
Breath Control LSB	34	0–127

Foot Control LSB	36	0–127
Portamento Time LSB	37	0–127
Data Entry LSB	38	0–127
Main Volume LSB	39	0–127
Balance LSB	40	0–127
Pan LSB	42	0–127
Expression LSB	43	0–127
General Purpose 1 LSB	48	0–127
General Purpose 2 LSB	49	0–127
General Purpose 3 LSB	50	0–127
General Purpose 4 LSB	51	0–127
Sustain Pedal	64	0 or 127
Portamento Pedal	65	0 or 127
Sostenuto Pedal	66	0 or 127
Soft Pedal	67	0 or 127
Legato Pedal	68	0 or 127
Hold 2	69	0 or 127
Sound Controller #1	70	0–127 (Sound Variation)
Sound Controller #2	71	0–127 (Harmonic Content)
Sound Controller #3	72	0–127 (Release Time)
Sound Controller #4	73	0–127 (Attack Time)
Sound Controller #5	74	0–127 (Brightness)
Sound Controller #6–10	75–79	0–127 (undefined)
General Purpose 5	80	0–127
General Purpose 6	81	0–127
General Purpose 7	82	0–127
General Purpose 8	83	0–127
Portamento Control	84	0–127
Reverb Depth	91	0–127
Tremolo Depth	92	0–127
Chorus Depth	93	0–127
Celeste (Detune) Depth	94	0–127
Phaser Depth	95	0–127
Data Increment	96	0 or 127
Data Decrement	97	0 or 127
NRPN LSB	98	0–127
NRPN MSB	99	0–127
RPN LSB	100	0–127
RPN MSB	101	0–127
All Sounds Off	120	0
Reset All Controllers	121	0
Local Control On/Off	122	0 or 127
All Notes Off	123	0
Omni Mode Off	124	0
Omni Mode On	125	0
Mono Mode On	126	0
Poly Mode On	127	0

Undefined Controllers

You'll notice that many numbers don't feature in the list. These 'missing' numbers are classed as *undefined* controllers, which manufacturers can map to particular features of their device not covered by the existing controllers. NRPNs (page 190) are a similar, but more recent, way of doing the same thing, but with a lot more scope to become standardised.

Some of those listed are technically 'undefined' (according to *Technical Notes* on page 175), but are in fact usually mapped to these CC numbers if they're implemented at all. This is part of an on-going standardisation which is a pretty good indication of how the MIDI standard continues to evolve. As time passes, manufacturers follow each other with the inclusion of new features, most requiring control-change access. So the 128 controller numbers are gradually being assigned uses, and these are not necessarily in keeping with the original MMA/JMSC specification.

Range/Value Variations

The possible values for the controllers vary as well, depending upon what job they have to do. As you can see from the list, there are three possibilities:

0–127:   These are low-resolution 128-position controllers. (Two low resolution controllers used together give a high-resolution controller, as you're about to discover . . .)

0 or 127:   These are 'switch' controllers: they control a 2-position parameter, toggling it Off or On respectively.

0:   These controllers are 'fixed': they contain no variable value parameter because they have only one function. For example, when your tone-generator receives CC125, it turns Omni Mode On – it can't just turn it on slightly!

Channel Message Groups

Control changes 120 to 127 are called the **Channel Mode Messages** – rather than giving options of a *directly* musical nature, they handle the slightly more technical side of MIDI channel control. The remaining controllers (0–119) are referred to as the **Channel Voice Messages**.

Clean Up!

To reiterate an important point made elsewhere in the book, always check each channel's last controller values at the end of a MIDI file. Make sure in particular that all CC11s are 127, all pitch-bends are zero (centre-point) and that all CC64s are zero. This is of extra importance in commercial programming: you can't be sure that the file your user plays next will have a GM Reset or CC121 at the beginning of it – if it doesn't, she may be left with channels detuned by a semitone or totally inaudible!

Controller Resolution

From looking at the *Range/Value* column in the preceding **Controller List**, you can see that the possible values for various controllers vary, and that some are described as MSB or LSB. This is because different controllers have to do different jobs, requiring different levels of precision.

MSB/LSB – High Resolution

Controllers with MSB or LSB after their Function name are intended to work in pairs as a single **high-resolution** controller. For example, CC7 and 39 are the MSB and LSB controllers for main volume, and there are also hi-res pairs for modulation, expression and so on.

Each of the two controllers in the pair has the usual 128-point range, so when they're used together to address the same parameter this gives a potential *combined* range of 16,384 values (i.e., 128 squared). In other words, for each point along the 128-point scale of the MSB there are another 128 tiny divisions, courtesy of the LSB, allowing minute tuning of the value. It's pretty easy to see that most of the time this fine-tuning is unnecessary: using CC7 to raise a channel's main volume by 1 gives an almost unnoticeable result, so why would you want to raise it by any less than that?

In practice, the controllers mentioned above, along with most of the others in the list, are never actually used in their hi-res form for exactly this reason. Three hi-res pairs that *are* used that way are the RPN and NRPN controllers (101,100 and 99,98 respectively), and Bank Select.

And *Still* No Saxophone . . .

Being able to control over sixteen-thousand parameters from a single pair of controllers is pretty impressive, but consider the Bank Select pair (CC0 and 32). Together they have the usual 16,384 possible values, but they still don't do much by themselves. Add a program change command into the equation to select one of the 128 patches from each of these bank positions and you can start to see the expandability that high-resolution controllers bring to the MIDI specification: you can potentially access a mind-boggling 2,097,152 sounds!

MSB – Low Resolution

As you've seen from the Technical Note in the **Intro** topic, the hi-res capability of certain controllers is built into the MIDI specification. In reality though, most MIDI equipment doesn't transmit or recognise the LSB controller, so the most frequently used control-parameters are handled by the MSB only, thus saving a lot of mucking around and reducing the controller data clogging up the system by 50%. The MSB by itself, as we know, gives a potential range of 128 values, losing the *fine-tuning* capabilities of the controller-pair. For this reason it's called a **low resolution** controller.

Abbreviation Alert!

Yes, it all comes down to abbreviations again. **MSB** stands for *Most Significant Byte* and **LSB** is *Least Significant Byte*. What these are and how they work is covered elsewhere (see below), but if you've had enough of it all and don't want to get bogged down in any more that's fine. The only thing you really need to know is which controllers *must* work as a high-res pair (only Bank Select, RPNs and NRPNs in most devices) and in which order they should be transmitted (always MSB first). Each of these works as a *pointer* to a parameter to be changed: Bank Select needs a program change after it to actually select a sound, while RPNs and NRPNs need CC6 (Data Entry) to select a value for the chosen parameter. So the use of any of these high-resolution controllers will always require at least three events. To make sure these are all transmitted in the right order, it's vital that they're placed on separate ticks.

> **Detours**
>
> ➝ For a detailed look at MSB/LSB, bits, bytes, and the amusingly-named 'nibble', jump to **Binary Code** (page 237).
>
> ➝ **Pitch-Bend** and polyphonic **Aftertouch** are both high-resolution controllers, but in both of these cases the MSB and LSB are built into a single message. Their topics are on pages 200 and 204 respectively.

Continuous Controllers

A thumb-nail definition of a continuous controller would be a controller that creates its effect by sending out a stream of gradually changing values for a particular parameter of the sound. For example, when you pitch-bend a note, its pitch changes smoothly over time due to the tiny differences between each pb event; if you simply inserted one pb event the result would be a sudden jump from one pitch to another.

From the Controller List on page 176, these are the continuous controllers you're most likely to have access to and use regularly:

CC1	**Modulation**
CC2	**Breath Control**
CC4	**Foot Pedal**
CC8	**Balance**
CC11	**Expression**
–	**Pitch-Bend**
–	**Aftertouch**

Pitch-bend and aftertouch are, of course, types of controller, but they have dedicated methods of data-entry rather than being assigned CC numbers, and are always classed as separate event-types in their own right. Pitch-bend and aftertouch are covered in detail, together with CC1 and CC11, in their own topics further ahead in this section. CC2, CC4, CC8 and Aftertouch are not recognised elements of General MIDI specification.

CC2 – Breath Control

This controller lets you play a brass or reed instrument on the keyboard and recreate the nuances of sound in the same way that the 'live' player does – by blowing into a mouthpiece. In truth, though this facility has been around for about 10 years on a few devices, the effect often produced was a bit of a squeak and a lot of dribble. However, breath control is finally starting to enjoy a second wind (tut!) with the new wave of 'virtual synthesis' and the arrival of the dedicated MIDI wind-controller (see page 31).

CC4 – Foot Control

Often used to adjust the 'scale mode' (i.e., alter the pitches of individual keys on the keyboard) to emulate scales other than the chromatic. Useful for achieving an authentic rendition of a sitar, etc., but rarely implemented.

CC8 – Balance

Used to adjust the relative volumes of the two parts of a dual-voice sound and, once again, rarely implemented.

Clean Up!

The clean-up operation for continuous controllers is exactly the same as that for pitch-bend (see Fig. 29). Inevitably, when programming expression, modulation or pan sweeps there'll often be unnecessary controller events before the note-on and after the note-off which should be erased. All you need is the last setting for the controller before the note was played, the sweep itself while the note continues and the reset event (e.g., CC1:0) after the note off.

Remember that the higher the resolution of your sequencer, the more continuous events it can record (including pitch-bend and aftertouch). Most higher-level sequencers have a *Reduce Continuous Controllers* facility to combat this by thinning out the data. Don't be afraid to use it – the reduction usually looks pretty drastic, but you'll be surprised how little data is needed to produce the same effect.

▪ Variable Controllers

Variable controllers are control commands for which a value is usually set just once per channel (e.g., in the song-header) for the whole song.

Any of these may of course be used more than once but, in contrast with Continuous Controllers, they tend to be one-off occurrences rather than a stream of events.

It should be pointed out once again that these functions won't necessarily be implemented on your device; similarly, your device may have functions which aren't listed here.

CC0	**Bank Select MSB**
CC5	**Portamento Time**
CC6	**Data Entry MSB**
CC7	**Main Volume**
CC10	**Pan**
CC32	**Bank Select LSB**
CC38	**Data Entry LSB**
CC84	**Portamento Control**
CC91	**External Effect Depth (Reverb)**
CC92	**Tremolo Depth**
CC93	**Chorus Depth**
CC94	**Celeste Depth**
CC95	**Phaser Depth**

From this list, the controllers that meet with General MIDI approval are CC6, CC7, CC10 and CC38. (CC91 and CC93 may also be regarded as GM-compatible, despite not being included in the official specifications.)

The controllers for portamento, main volume, pan, reverb and chorus are dealt with in the *Close-Ups* section of the **Channel Messages Menu**, indexed on page 173.

CC0 and 32 – Bank Select

Bank Select became a part of MIDI specification in 1990 to allow easy access to more than the 128 sounds offered by the Program Change message. As another high-resolution pair, they have the capability of addressing 16,384 banks of sounds. Bank selects are always placed before the program change to which they refer, and always on separate ticks to ensure that they all get acted upon: if the two controls are on the *same* tick they don't arrive at the same time because MIDI's binary code is sent in *series* – something's got to get there first – and if it's the wrong one, then one or both may be ignored.

Though the Bank Select controllers are now an established fact of life, their exact implementation still tends to vary between manufacturers. Roland devices, for example, require the inclusion of CC32 but always with a value of 0, thus giving 'only' a potential 128 banks (effectively a low-resolution controller).

Remember to use Bank Select messages only when actually *changing* banks – to change to a different sound within the *same* bank should require only a program-change.

CC6 and 38 – Data Entry

These form another high-resolution (MSB/LSB) pair, though they're rarely used together (RPN Fine Tuning being one of the few occasions). As the name implies, Data Entry doesn't have an inherent function: it changes the setting of a function you've previously specified, usually in conjunction with the 'pointer' controllers, RPNs and NRPNs (see page 188). The data-entry controller is also often used as a Continuous Controller, depending upon which parameter it's being used to control.

CC92, 94 and 95 – Tremolo, Celeste and Phaser Depth

Though implementation of these is far from being universal, technology is now allowing manufacturers to build a better range of effects into their tone-generators. Presumably, if these are considered useful enough, they'll soon find their way into the standard MIDI spec (and if these don't, others certainly soon will – the lack of flexible onboard multi-channel effects processing is still one of MIDI's main failings).

Clean Up!

CC7 Volume shouldn't be used within the song body, so make sure you've remapped the volume slider on your keyboard to CC11 Expression, either at the keyboard or the sequencer end. Make sure changes to settings such as pan position, data entry setting for RPNs and so on aren't repeated unnecessarily when copying and pasting.

Switch and Fixed Controllers

Switch Controllers

Like a light switch, this type of controller has two positions: On or Off. Standard MIDI specification defines the following switch controllers:

CC64	**Sustain Pedal/Hold 1**
CC65	**Portamento Pedal**
CC66	**Sostenuto Pedal**
CC67	**Soft Pedal**
CC68	**Legato Pedal**
CC69	**Hold 2**
CC122	**Local Control**

Of these, only CC64 may be used within a commercial General MIDI file. Portamento and the Sustain Pedal have topics of their own on pages 221 and 215 respectively.

Switch controllers should only have either 0 or 127 (Off or On) as their value. Technically, however, these function just like any other controller in that any value will be acted upon, so a value of 0–63 will give the 'Off' message, while 64–127 will be interpreted as 'On'.

CC66 – Sostenuto Pedal

A type of 'selective' sustain pedal found on acoustic grand-pianos. Pressing down the pedal (i.e., sending CC66 : 127) while holding notes on the keyboard will cause these notes to be sustained after you release them – any notes you play after depressing the pedal won't sustain.

CC67 – Soft Pedal

This piano pedal should work in two simultaneous ways: when the pedal is depressed (CC67 : 127) the sound should be slightly 'softened' in terms of volume, and there should be a noticeable difference in the tone-colour of the sound, mimicking the reduced piano-string 'twang' that occurs on the real instrument. (Some lesser tone-modules and even dedicated electric-pianos simply reduce the volume and leave it at that.)

The two piano-pedal controllers above are best avoided in programming, unless you're expressly recreating piano works, and even then the MIDI musician has easier methods at her disposal. The sostenuto effect can be easily emulated either by lengthening the desired notes manually in *Edit*, or by overdubbing them afterwards.

As far as the soft pedal goes, the note-velocity range of 0–127 is usually expressive enough. If it isn't, try copying the piano part to a second channel (panned to the same point in the stereo field) and expanding the range of velocities on that track so that when the original part's velocities are low, these are *very* low, and when the original part's velocities are high these are *very* high. This procedure should be used with some caution, as it may cause a *flanging* effect.

CC68 – Legato Pedal

This chappie hit the MIDI spec in 1992 and hasn't yet been widely used. When legato mode is switched on (CC68:127), playing a different note changes the pitch of the current note without retriggering the attack phase of the sound's envelope.

CC69 – Hold 2

This is another type of sustaining pedal, very rarely implemented, and used only for sounds with two 'sustain' phases in their envelopes.

CC122 – Local Control

The setting of this switch dictates whether a multi-timbral synthesizer's built-in tone-generator will respond to note-data from its own keyboard or from an external source such as a sequencer or MIDI file-player, as described in more detail in the topic on **Local Control** (page 38). The benefits of local control are immense for programming purposes, and if you choose to you can access the setting with CC122 from your sequencer rather than trawling through indecipherable parameters on your synth!

However, the real value of CC122 is for 'live' use: imagine you have a MIDI file-player sending data into your synth, and your synth is connected to a tone-module. Sometimes you need to use your synth-keyboard to control the module during a song (so Local Off, CC122:0); other times you want to use the keyboard to add an extra sound from your synth to the incoming file data (Local On, CC122 : 127). In fact, when you've got your gig-set sorted out, you could even put Local on/off controllers at the start or end of particular MIDI files so that it's all done for you (and they say musicians are lazy!)

Clearly CC122 has no use in commercial programming (it's unfair to do things like that to other people's gear, and it's not good for business!).

Fixed Controllers

Fixed controllers are controllers that carry out one simple command that has no variables (unlike a Program Change which must have a patch-number, or a Note-On which must have a velocity). There are six fixed controllers in wide use although none is included in the General MIDI spec. These are:

CC120	**All Sounds Off**
CC121	**Reset All Controllers**
CC123	**All Notes Off**
CC124	**Omni Mode Off**
CC125	**Omni Mode On**
CC126	**Mono Mode On**
CC127	**Poly Mode On**

These controllers (together with CC122 Local Control) are collectively termed the **Channel Mode Messages**. Each of these controllers, if inserted into your sequence, should have a value of zero (e.g., to reset all controllers, send CC121 : 0).

Omni, Poly and Mono modes have been previously covered in the topic imaginatively titled **MIDI Modes** (page 40) and should be self-explanatory.

CC123 – All Notes Off

Often used as a 'safety net' at the end of a file to send Note-Offs to any notes left hanging for some reason (though this will have no effect on notes sustained due to an unresolved CC64 or CC66 message). Hanging notes are most often caused by splitting a Note-On from its Note-Off when cutting and pasting (i.e., cutting a sounding note 'in half') or as a result of retriggering. The MIDI-mode setting controllers (CC124–127) also send an All Notes Off message as they change the mode.

CC120 – All Sounds Off

Almost identical in result to CC123, with the difference that notes being sustained by an open CC64 or CC66 pedal will also be silenced.

CC121 – Reset All Controllers

Generally used at the start of a MIDI file, and rather similar in effect to the GM Reset, CC121 returns a few possible mischief-makers to their defaults (i.e., curing any hanging pitch-bend wheels and sustain pedals, returning CC1 to zero, returning CC11 to 127 and so on).

If you're producing MIDI files that don't conform to one of the established protocols, use CC121:0 as the first event of each channel to replace the SysEx reset.

Clean Up!

Two main contenders here for the Sloppy Editing Of The Year Award:

- ❏ **Pedal Repetition:** Make sure that events for pedal-switches have alternate values 127, 0, 127, etc., with no repetition (especially when copying and pasting), and that the controller isn't constantly being turned on and off while you're just holding a chord (for example, you might tend to tap out the beat on the sustain-pedal as you play).

- ❏ **Pedal Closure:** Check that the last pedal event of the file on any channel has the zero (Off) value.

▦ RPNs and NRPNs

Registered and **Non-Registered Parameter Numbers** are fairly recent additions to the MIDI specification, brought about by the obvious drawbacks in a system that allows only 128 of anything. As with any recent developments in the MIDI spec, only equipment manufactured later will be able to implement them. Consult your manual's MIDI Implementation Chart to see if your tone-generator is up to the task.

Like socks, RPNs and NRPNs work in pairs. As high-resolution controllers, each pair can therefore address up to 16,384 separate parameters (i.e., 128^2). Both pairings act as switches: two controllers switch on access to a parameter, a data entry or data increment controller sets a value for it, and two controllers are then used to close the 'switch' again.

What's All This *Registered* Business Then?

The difference between the two types is a simple and extremely practical one: Registered Parameters are *universal* – in other words, for any device that can implement RPNs, value 0 will always address pitch-bend range, value 1 will address fine-tuning and so on, according to the list below. As MIDI spec evolves, the list continues to grow and should eventually be able to provide universal access to basic sound-editing and effect-processing parameters which are currently the non-standard domain of the NRPN.

Non-registered parameters are *not* universal. They always use the same two controllers (99 and 98) but there the similarity ends – the *values* for the controllers and which features they will address are the choice of the individual manufacturer. They were introduced as a means of giving access to a wider range of parameters specific to particular devices – the kind of stuff that otherwise calls for manic button-pushing or delving into the user-unfriendly world of System Exclusive. Handy though they are, very few devices actually implement NRPNs yet.

Registered Parameter Numbers

RPN controllers are 101 and 100, and the values of these controllers 'point' to a parameter to be accessed. The possible parameters are:

Pitch-Bend Range:	101:0 100:0 6:???
Fine Tuning:	101:0 100:1 6:??? 38:???
Coarse Tuning:	101:0 100:2 6:???
MIDI Tuning Standard Bank Select:	101:0 100:3 6:???
MIDI Tuning Standard Program Select:	101:0 100:4 6:???

Fine and Coarse Tuning are used to ensure that all MIDI devices are in tune with each other, or to intentionally detune a channel for effect. *Coarse* tuning moves in increments of a semitone while *Fine* tuning moves in cents (100ths of a semitone). In both cases, the centre-point (no change of tuning) is a value of 64 for CC6, so detuning a channel by a semitone would require a pointer to coarse-tuning and a CC6 value of 63.

MIDI Tuning Standard is a new addition used to set different types of tuning. Most of the music we hear is based upon scales using equal temperament tuning but this is just one of a large number of tunings used among the different cultures of the world. This is the way to get the best out of that bank of Ethnic instruments lurking in a dusty corner of your tone-generator!

RPNs are most frequently used to set or alter the pitch-bend range (also sometimes referred to as pitch-bend *sensitivity*). Controller 6 is for Data Entry and is used to set the *range* for the parameter, so to set a pitch-bend range of ± 7 semitones you would enter the following:

101:0
100:0
6:7
101:127
100:127

the events being placed over 5 consecutive ticks. Whichever parameter you're addressing, the high-res pair that close the 'switch' will always be 101:127, 100:127.

Bear in mind that the GM, GS and XG Resets automatically set the pitch-bend range to ± 2 semitones. If you're using one of these resets and this is the range you require for a particular channel then these five events need not be entered for that channel.

Fine Tuning also uses the Data Entry LSB controller (CC38 following CC6), giving a range of -100 cents to $+99.99$ cents, thus requiring six events to create the message. The complication of Fine Tuning is that you're using a 128-point scale to address a 100-point value. So to raise or lower the tuning of a channel by 50 cents requires a CC6 setting of 96 or 32 respectively. Raising the tuning by 30 cents needs a CC6 setting of 83. And doing almost any of this needs a calculator. The good news is that the LSB controller can be given a value of zero since additional refinement in *100ths of a cent* should be unnecessary.

Non-Registered Parameter Numbers

NRPN controllers work in a similar way to RPNs, by using various combinations of values for CC99 and 98 to specify the parameter and a value for CC6 to specify the setting for it. Also in exactly the same way as RPNs, after setting all the NRPN parameters that you need to, the NRPN 'switch' should be closed by inserting 101:127, 100:127.

It's only necessary to close the switch once *all* the required RPN and NRPN parameters have been addressed and set. In this way, you can enter a stream of 3-controller messages and add the two final 'closing' events at the end, as shown in Fig. 25 below.

Trk	Hr:Mn:Sc:Fr	Meas:Beat:Tick	Chn	Kind		Values
4	00:00:01:02	1:3:015	4	Contrl	101	0
4	00:00:01:03	1:3:016	4	Contrl	100	0
4	00:00:01:03	1:3:017	4	Contrl	6	9
4	00:00:01:03	1:3:018	4	Contrl	101	0
4	00:00:01:03	1:3:019	4	Contrl	100	2
4	00:00:01:03	1:3:020	4	Contrl	6	66
4	00:00:01:03	1:3:021	4	Contrl	99	1
4	00:00:01:03	1:3:022	4	Contrl	98	99
4	00:00:01:04	1:3:023	4	Contrl	6	52
4	00:00:01:04	1:3:024	4	Contrl	99	1
4	00:00:01:04	1:3:025	4	Contrl	98	33
4	00:00:01:04	1:3:026	4	Contrl	6	74
4	00:00:01:04	1:3:027	4	Contrl	101	127
4	00:00:01:04	1:3:028	4	Contrl	100	127

Event List - Track 4: a hot lead!

Fig. 25 **RPN and NPRN events in Cakewalk Pro**

What Do They Do?

NRPNs commonly address basic sound editing parameters such as envelope settings (attack, decay, release), vibrato settings, effects and filters. You may also be able to access settings for individual drums in a kit (such as effect-send levels, pan-position and volume) and global channel settings such as key-shift (transpose) and modulation depth. Your tone-generator's manual should give you some clues to the parameters you can reach and the corresponding NRPN values.

Compatibility

Of the two, only RPNs are included in the General MIDI specification, and only RPN #0, #1 and #2. The actual implementation of pitch-bend range leaves a lot to be desired on some devices. If you feel an urge to point your hard-earned cash in the direction of a new synth, check that you can set *individual pitch-bend ranges* for each MIDI channel. If you can't, some basic pitch-bend effects may be difficult or even *impossible* to produce, and playback of files supposedly using these effects could sound pretty appalling.

Clean Up!

When copying sections of the song, make sure that the copy doesn't repeat the RPN/NRPN settings (such as pitch-bend range) made in the original section and not altered since.

Make sure also that any channel using RPNs or NRPNs has the switch 'closed' with 101:127 and 100:127 after all the necessary changes are made. This is to prevent any rogue Data Entry messages changing the range during live overdub-performance of the file.

Make sure the RPN/NRPN groups of controllers are always in the correct order and on separate ticks.

How To Access Controllers

You will no doubt have noticed that there's a whole bunch of controllers, many of which you'll need to use at least occasionally, and your synth/master-keyboard or whatever seems to be distinctly lacking in the knobs-and-sliders department! So how do you get to them all?

Controller Remapping On Input

An indispensable facility found on most software-sequencers is Controller Remapping. If your keyboard has a volume-slider which by default sends out CC7 data, you can use this facility to tell your sequencer to convert all CC7s it receives into CC11s (for example) before recording them and echoing them to its soft-thru socket. This is known as *remapping* the controllers. You can therefore use the same facility to create a pan-sweep using the slider (remap to CC10), or enter CC1 modulation if you've got some grievance against the mod wheel. Similarly (if you're a big fan of the mod wheel as a method of entering data) you could opt to use the wheel to control a different parameter.

Controller Remapping should be as easy as selecting the original and the target controllers by name or number from a list. In some sequencers (such as Big Noise's *Cadenza* in Fig. 26) it's also possible to remap aftertouch and pitch-bend to other controllers which can give some interesting performance effects.

Fig. 26 **Easy controller remapping in *Cadenza***

Controller Remapping On Output

A second option, if your keyboard supports it, is to change the controller-number transmitted by your keyboard's slider or wheel itself. Most *master*-keyboards in particular will allow this; some allow only a limited range of controller-numbers to be sent, but they're generally the most useful ones.

Controller Remapping In 'Edit'

If neither of the two previous suggestions work, it may be possible to remap controller events automatically once they've been recorded, similar to 'search and replace' in word-processors.

Finger Power!

If there's nothing else for it, you have to bite the bullet, record your CC7s and then go through manually changing them all. (Or upgrade your sequencer of course!)

Switch, Fixed and Variable Controllers

The suggestions here are intended purely for Continuous Controllers; to use a switch or fixed control event, or a one-off 'variable' controller, it's far easier to go into *Edit* and insert it manually.

Detours

→ If you're reduced to finger-power to remap CC7s to CC11s, there's another method you might be able to use instead. Take a look at the heading *No Remap Facility?* on page 210.

Note On/Note Off

As the whole basis of music, *notes* are obviously going to be pretty vital in MIDI. Musically speaking, you know how to play them; in sequencer terms you know how to record them. To be able to edit them afterwards, it's handy to understand a bit about them as MIDI messages.

What Is A Note?

When you play a note on the keyboard, your brain controls your hand. It says things like 'Play a C# now' and 'Time to let go of that F'. In MIDI terms, the sequencer is the 'brain' and the tone-generator is the 'hand', but the conversation from one to the other is identical. So a MIDI note is actually *two* events: 'Play it now' and 'Stop playing it now', otherwise known as **Note-On** and **Note-Off** respectively. It follows that if the tone-generator receives a note-on instruction and doesn't receive a corresponding note-off it just won't let go!

The Note Event

Very often, in List (numerical) Edit mode, your sequencer will still represent a note as a single event for ease of working. This event will *usually* contain five parameters: position within the song, note name (e.g., C#3), length (in ticks), velocity and MIDI channel.

The actual display varies between sequencers, so you may have an entry for the *note-off* position as well as the length (or perhaps instead). Similarly you might have an entry for the *note-off* velocity, although it's so rarely implemented that it's unlikely to have any effect on the sound. You might also have a mention of the note's MIDI note-number.

Note-On Velocity

Note-on velocity dictates the **volume** of the note, ranging from 1–127. 'Velocity' is speed: sensors beneath your keyboard detect how fast the key is travelling which is directly related to how loud it will sound. The exact timbre of the sound will usually change in response to different velocities as well, to mimic the 'live' instrument – the 'rasp' of a brass or reed instrument, or the increased brightness of a piano or guitar. In some tone-generators, the velocity is linked to tone and frequency modulation circuits which can give dramatic differences in the sound.

Note-Off Velocity

Note-off velocity is the speed with which you let go of the note. It might be listed in your sequencer's editor, but it's very rarely implemented. Where it *is* used, the effect it might produce is to trigger a final phase of the sound (or even bring in a whole *new* sound) as you release the note, allowing you to adjust the volume of this as well.

Note Name

The note-name will often be in a recognisable form of letters and # signs followed by a number to indicate which octave the note is from. Once again sequencers vary in their numbering system of the octaves, but the most usual is the C–1 to G8 system where the piano 'middle C' is C3.

When looking at drum-notes, which are usually on channel 10, some sequencers have a facility whereby you can specify certain tracks as drum-tracks and the list-editor will display the name of the kit- or percussion-instrument for each event, corresponding to a previously defined drum-map. The reasoning is that it's far more intuitive to work with the *names* of kit-instruments when editing than to try and remember the drumkit layout and corresponding note-numbers.

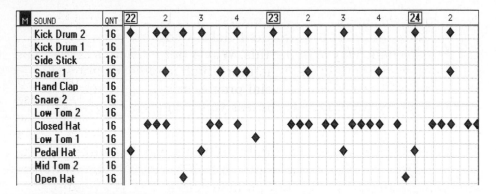

Fig. 27 **Drum-Edit screen in** *Cubase*

For exactly the same reason, many sequencers also have a dedicated *Drum Editor* (as shown in Fig. 27 above). This makes it easy to see at a glance which kit-instruments are playing at any point, and the editor usually has some extra editing options such as the ability to 'transpose' all the mid-tom notes to low-tom in one quick operation.

Clean Up!

Retriggering – trying to play the same note twice at the same time on the same channel – is one of the primary causes of glitching in MIDI files. Normal real-time recording from the keyboard obviously shouldn't create any retriggering problems, but go into *Edit* and it's easy to stretch a C#2 until it overlaps the note-on of the next C#2. The effect this usually has is that the first note will end suddenly as the second note strikes, but the second note will be shortened to only one or two ticks in length, giving either a sudden silence or a staccato blip *followed* by sudden silence.

Some sequencers cheerfully ignore retriggering until you save the song as a Standard MIDI File, when the conversion process starts chewing up the offending notes. If you're using a well-respected, forgiving type of tone-generator, you might not know anything about retriggering problems until you reload the SMF.

Particular care needs to be taken when programming rhythm-guitar parts by a combination of real-time and step recording (see **Rhythm Guitar** on page 150): you'll naturally want to stretch notes as far as possible but it's by no means a casual or random exercise.

Remember that drum-kit notes can retrigger too – once again, step-programming of flams and rolls, and editing generally, is the culprit.

Here, however, there's no good excuse! The length of drum-notes is irrelevant, so shorten them all to 4 ticks – your sequencer probably has an automatic way of doing this. Why **4** ticks? There's at least one GM synth from a certain manufacturer which *ignores* any notes shorter than 4 ticks! For non-commercial programming, shorten them all to one tick for maximum safety (unless you *bought* the aforementioned synth!).

Split Notes – Sequencers are rarely built in a way that allows this to happen since it serves no useful purpose: if you cut a section of music (or *split* a pattern in two) at a point where a note is sounding you may be able to remove its *Note-Off* event, resulting in a hanging-note. The only solution is to track down and delete the note-on, reset your tone-generator and replace the note correctly.

Program Change

The **Program Change** is the command that sets up a particular sound or patch on a particular channel. The Program Change message has only one variable parameter – the patch number – with 128 possible values. As usual, it also has a position within the song and a MIDI channel assignment.

Program-Change Numbers

In computer terms 'zero' is regarded as a number, which can cause confusion when using different devices and software – some sequencers use program changes that match the patches (usually 1–128) while others use the 'minus-one' system (0–127). So you could find that the patch-number and the program change number don't match: your tone-generator's manual may say that patch number 10 is a Glockenspiel but you have to enter program change #9 in your sequencer to call it up. A few of the more caring, sensitive sequencers will let you choose the system you prefer.

Bank Select

Many tone-generators contain several hundred sounds organised into *banks*, meaning that the program change needs a bit of help! This help usually comes in the form of one or more control changes placed before the program change to direct it to a particular bank. Since 1990, control-changes 0 and 32 have been included in MIDI specification as a high-resolution Bank Select command, though the implementation of them can vary – even to the degree that some of the guys who write the user-manuals get it wrong! Make sure that any combination of bank selects and program change you use are in the correct order and on different ticks.

General MIDI has only one bank, so bank selects should never be used in a commercial GM file, although the GM header-bar does leave space for their future inclusion in the specification. The exact layout of the song-header is shown in HEADER.MID and described in detail in the topic appropriately titled **Song Header** on page 57.

Some older (pre-August 1990) tone-generators may have the usual stack of sounds arranged into banks so that you can only access a maximum of 128 patches by program change, and bank-changing is done by a combination of pushing buttons and swearing. If this is the case, you may find that you can copy all of your most-used sounds to a user-bank (but keep a patch-list, or you'll *still* be pushing buttons and swearing!).

Accessing Program Changes

There are two simple ways to input a program change: creating the event manually in *Edit* mode in your sequencer or thumping the appropriate button on your keyboard while recording. As you probably won't be using program changes while recording the song-body anyway (see below) the 'step' method is usual.

A less obvious (and not General MIDI compatible) way to do the same thing is via System Exclusive, either sending a single SysEx string containing a program change command for one channel, or by a bulk dump from your tone-generator after you have manually set it up the way you want it: the bulk dump can then contain *all* the initial settings for each channel, plus the device's global settings, replacing the song-header bar (see **System Exclusive**, page 225).

Patch Lists

A more intuitive method of inputting program changes from within your sequencer is to use the patch-list function found on a lot of more recent softwares (see the example in Fig. 28). The concept here is similar to the one behind the Drum-Edit screen mentioned in the previous topic: it's far easier to work with instrument-*names* than with patch-*numbers*.

Using Program Changes

Commercial Programming

The obvious place that you'll use program changes is in the song-header to set up each channel as required. General MIDI specification recommends that they are not used within the song-body for several reasons.

1   Some tone-generators 'glitch' slightly or create noise when changing patches, particularly during heavy MIDI traffic – it's preferable that any glitching that's going to happen occurs only in the header.

2   If the file is stopped and then restarted from elsewhere in the song some of the sounds may be wrong. Some sequencers and MIDI file-players have *Chase* or *Update Events* facilities which try to keep up with control and program changes as you wind and rewind, but many don't.

3   It can make life slightly harder for an end-user trying to edit the file. It could be argued that a commercial MIDI file should be of such a quality that editing is unnecessary and shouldn't be a consideration when programming, but you may like to take this into account.

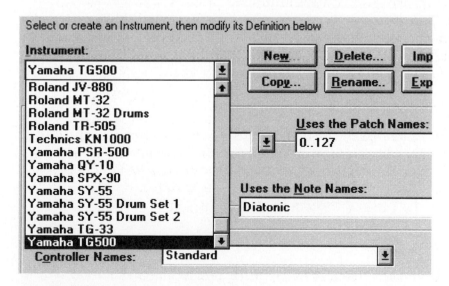

Fig. 28 **Defining a patch-list in** *Cakewalk Pro*

The bottom line is, if at all possible, try to stick to the single song-header program change for each channel, and make maximum use of the 16 channels available. If you do have to use a program change within the song-body, try to ensure that there's plenty of 'space' before and after it.

Non-Commercial Programming

As usual, you can do whatever you want! If it sounds okay to you, and your tone-generator(s) accept it then go with it, but be aware of point 2 above – if your sequencer doesn't have a *Chase* facility then the recording and any subsequent editing could be a bit of a nightmare. It's usually best to make the most of the full 16 channels, even if you choose to merge some of the more sparsely-used channels later.

Some tone-generators allow you to play one note, for example, a violin note lasting 3 bars, change to a trumpet patch immediately after the note-on and play a trumpet-line while the violin note is still playing – this can be a handy option if you somehow manage to run out of channels and refuse to sacrifice any existing notes! On some devices however, the long note is immediately cut. In addition, some devices can take quite a while to process a patch-change so a gap of *at least* a beat may be required before the next note-on.

Clean Up!

The most important thing to avoid with program changes is repetition when cutting and pasting sections. This shouldn't usually cause any timing glitches on the channel, since it's not actually *changing* the patch, but it's unnecessary and looks sloppy to anyone digging around in your files!

Remember that once you've used a Bank Select and Program Change combination to enter a bank, you should subsequently need to use only Program Changes to change patches *within that bank*. The bank select is needed only for actually *changing* banks.

Pitch-Bend

Pitch-bend is a high-resolution continuous controller shown as a separate entity in list-editors. Pitch-bend allows you to 'slide' a note up or down in pitch in a controlled way and by a pre-specified amount. This is similar in effect to **portamento** – the essential difference is the complete hands-on control you have over pitch-bend in both the timing and the pitch-range.

Accessing Pitch-Bend

On keyboard instruments, pitch-bend is controlled with either a dedicated wheel, or a lever (which usually controls CC1 Modulation as well) – moving the lever to the left lowers the pitch, moving it to the right raises the pitch. Of course, you can enter pitch-bend events manually in step-record mode too but it's a time-consuming and hit-and-miss approach. It's definitely preferable to record even a badly-executed bend in real-time and then edit it (better still, keep trying for a *well*-executed bend!).

On a MIDI guitar, just *looking* at the instrument makes it chuck out bunches of pitch-bend messages, so it's advisable to disable the reception or transmission of pb data at your sequencer or guitar respectively when you're not playing lead parts. Guitarists access pitch-bend by simply bending a string and due to the high-resolution of pb messages the string doesn't need to move far before pb messages are transmitted.

Accessing Pitch-Bend Range

The pitch-bend range (or *sensitivity*) is the maximum change of pitch gained by moving the lever fully left or right and is measured in semitones. The General MIDI default setting is ± 2 semitones. The standard method of setting the pitch-bend range is by using RPN controllers (see page 189).

A brief point to consider on the subject of pb range: 99% of tone-generators have independent range settings for each channel (using RPN #0) as required by General MIDI. However, here are a couple of multi-timbral 'GM' synths on which the setting is either user-definable but *global* for the whole device or, worse still, is *fixed* at ± 2! This will obviously limit your use of pitch-bend, and will make playback of commercial GM files often sound abysmal.

Pitch-Bend In The List-Editor

As we've already mentioned, pitch-bend messages are almost always transmitted and recorded in high-resolution, giving 16,384 possible settings over the *entire* pb range (in other words, if the range is set to ±2, then the *entire* range covered by the lever will be 4 semitones). These may be shown in your list-editor in one of two ways.

I Two separate 0–127 controllers representing the MSB and LSB. The MSB can be regarded as the 'coarse' tuning of pitch-bend, each successive step representing one *one-hundred-and-twenty-eighth* of the whole range. If you record a smooth downward pb movement and look at it in the editor, you'll see the MSB entries gradually dropping from 64 towards zero while the LSB entries look rather more randomised. When it comes to editing any less-than-perfect bends it's the MSB you'll nearly always need to change, often ignoring the LSB. In this method of listing pb events, the centre-point (no bend) is 0 64. This method of listing pitch-bend data is shown in Fig. 29 on the following page: as you can see from the graphic representation to the extreme right of the picture, the degree of bend is largely being governed by the MSB value (VAL2 column) – there's certainly no obvious correlation with the extreme movements of the fine-tuning LSB controller in the VAL1 column.

2 A few sequencers actually display the whole 16,384-point pb resolution as a single parameter, ranging from $-8192 > 0 > 8191$, where zero is of course the centre-point (no bend). For the technically minded, this is a translation to decimal (base 10) of the two binary data-bytes that form the pb message.

The Mathematics Of Pitch-Bend

Amid the screams and wails that always accompany any mention of maths in music, it's worth mentioning the logical points of pitch-bend. Firstly, if your pb range is set to ±1 semitone each MSB step will be a tiny step along the route from one note to the note a semitone away (and the LSB steps are totally unnoticeable!). However, if the range is set to ±24 semitones, then each MSB step will obviously be twenty-four times as wide so fine tuning of the LSB is more likely to be needed when editing.

Secondly, the setting of each MSB/LSB pair enables you to work out the current pitch of the note. For instance, if your range is set to ± 2 semitones, then a setting of 0 32 (or -4096) would mean a downward bend of a semitone; a setting of 0 80 (or 2048) indicates an upward bend of a quarter-tone.

Clean Up!

Normal use of the pitch-bend lever in real-time recording means that inevitably you'll sometimes move the lever when no note is sounding: perhaps you want the note to start a semitone lower and 'bend up to itself', or maybe you bend a note a semitone up *from* itself, let go of the note and then release the pb lever.

The example in Fig. 29 (recorded to a timebase of 384 tpq) shows both situations for the same note. (The length of time between the events has been exaggerated for clarity, but the quantity of useless data has, if anything, been minimised!)

START-POS	LENGTH	VAL1	VAL2	VAL3	STATUS	CHN
0029.04.108	=====	14	62	===	Pitch-Bend	4
0029.04.164	=====	78	49	===	Pitch-Bend	4
0029.04.199	=====	51	37	===	Pitch-Bend	4
0029.04.223	=====	102	24	===	Pitch-Bend	4
0029.04.256	=====	77	12	===	Pitch-Bend	4
0029.04.280	=====	0	1	===	Pitch-Bend	4
0029.04.318	=====	0	0	===	Pitch-Bend	4
0030.01.000	164	F#4	83	83	Note	4
0030.01.002	=====	111	13	===	Pitch-Bend	4
0030.01.038	=====	81	30	===	Pitch-Bend	4
0030.01.071	=====	55	46	===	Pitch-Bend	4
0030.01.090	=====	79	61	===	Pitch-Bend	4
0030.01.109	=====	17	77	===	Pitch-Bend	4
0030.01.142	=====	122	94	===	Pitch-Bend	4
0030.01.173	=====	23	80	===	Pitch-Bend	4
0030.01.214	=====	82	69	===	Pitch-Bend	4
0030.01.275	=====	125	65	===	Pitch-Bend	4
0030.01.316	=====	0	64	===	Pitch-Bend	4

Fig. 29 **Unnecessary pitch-bend events (*highlighted*)**

The highlighted events are occurring either *before* the note-on or *after* the note-off and so should be removed: as you can see, that's quite a lot of useless data! The event on 29.4.318 could be moved closer to the note-on, allowing a previous note to be lengthened if required, and the resetting event on 30.1.316 could be moved closer to the note-off (i.e., to around 30.1.168) provided the sound used doesn't have a lengthy release-phase.

Bear in mind that this pitch-bend data could just as easily be modulation (CC1) or expression (CC11) to name but a few – in all cases, the same events are redundant.

The higher the resolution of your sequencer, the more continuous events it will record. After cleaning up as above, use of the *Reduce Continuous Controllers* facility found on most higher-level sequencers will thin out the amount of data without impairing the overall effect. Remarkably little continuous data is *needed* to produce the effect you want.

Detours

→ For more background on high-resolution controllers, take a look at **Controller Resolution** on page 179.

→ The heady world of the MSB and LSB is covered in more technical detail in **Binary Code** on page 237.

Aftertouch

Aftertouch is a type of pressure sensitivity that kicks into action after the key has been pressed down and is resting on the keybed, usually producing a frequency modulation effect. Unlike pitch-bend, after-touch is not a universal controller, and neither form is included in General MIDI specification. There are two different types of aftertouch, and there are three implementation possibilities for each unit in your MIDI setup (keyboard, sequencer and tone-generator).

Three Implementation Scenarios . . .

The three possibilities are: implement one type of aftertouch, implement both types, or implement none. Clearly the lowest common denominator is going to be the winner here: if your tone-generator doesn't recognise either form of aftertouch, you won't spend an afternoon trying to get your keyboard to transmit it. Similarly if your keyboard sends only one type and your tone-generator responds only to the other, it's a no-score draw.

Two Types Of Aftertouch . . .

As already mentioned, aftertouch is pressure-sensitivity measured by how hard you press down on the keys while holding them – this is picked up by sensors in the keybed. Some keyboards use a single sensor running the span of the keybed and picking up the total pressure on the keyboard: this gives the first type of effect, **Channel Aftertouch** (also known as monophonic aftertouch). Other keyboards have individual sensors for each key, and transmit individual pressure readings – this is called **Polyphonic Aftertouch**. Of the two types, polyphonic aftertouch is clearly going to be the more expressive, but by definition must be the more data-hungry as well.

Channel aftertouch as a MIDI message consists of a single data byte in the form of 'This is the total amount of pressure at this point in time', making this a low resolution message. Polyphonic aftertouch messages contain two data-bytes: 'This is the amount of pressure *on this note* at this point in time', a high-resolution message. And if you're playing a three-note chord, there'll be a similar message for each note, and more messages whenever the pressure changes on one of the notes.

Being a low-resolution message, channel aftertouch results in a similar amount of data to modulation (CC1), with a similar effect. However, with the mod wheel, data is sent only when you move the wheel, which you're not going to do constantly. And modulation *is* a universally implemented controller.

. . . And A Partridge In A Peartree

To most people, being presented with a MIDI file chock full of aftertouch is about as welcome a gift as a fat bird in a bush. The time a file takes to load is directly proportional to the amount of data it contains – if the user of the file can't implement aftertouch, she's not going to be amused at having all this unnecessary data slowing down her access and filling the buffers. In addition, at least one workstation won't even load a file containing aftertouch.

So for commercial programming under any protocol, the bottom line must be: avoid using polyphonic pressure like the plague; avoid using channel pressure like a touch of the sniffles, and rely instead on the mod-wheel if you can!

Clean Up!

As with all continuous data, particularly on sequencers with a higher timebase (192 tpq and above), and *especially* with polyphonic after-touch, use the *Reduce Continuous Controllers* facility to thin out the data.

Detours

→ For the MIDI-newcomer who obediently jumped forward to read the **Overview**, it's now time to carry on from where you left off – fire up your sequencer and skip back to the **Recording Session** on page 63.

→ **Binary Code** on page 237 strips off the gloss and delves into the seedy backstage world of the high- and low-res controller.

→ More background on high and low resolution messages can be found in **Controller Resolution** on page 179.

CC1: Modulation

Modulation is an abbreviated term for *Pitch Modulation*. In musical circles this is better known as *vibrato*, used widely in stringed, wind and reed instruments. On a keyboard the effect is usually controlled either by a dedicated wheel or by a lever moonlighting as a pitch-bend control. Modulation in a wind-synth is controlled by the mouthpiece in a similar way to the acoustic instruments it imitates.

Modulation For Acoustic Instruments

As usual when trying to mimic the behaviour or playing of an acoustic instrument, it takes a little care to get the modulation right. The most believable effect is always produced by a continuous sweep, starting from CC1:0 after the note-on, pausing briefly at the upper level and then falling fairly quickly before the note-off. Bear in mind that acoustic players don't apply vibrato to a note and keep the vibrato effect going as they move to the next so some accuracy of playing (or tidying up afterwards) is called for to make sure that the modulation 'drops off' in time.

Care is also needed with the level of modulation in acoustic instruments – too much can make a warm sexy saxophone line sound like a dentist's drill. This requires some self-control while using the wheel – the limit tends to be only about CC1:60 before it starts to really *sound* like a synth-effect which means that you're trying to make very fine changes over a restricted range of the wheel. The solution to this (if your tone-generator will let you do it) is to reduce the *Modulation Depth* – this lets you make more extravagant movements of the wheel with less danger of the drill-effect. (You should be able to include this in your file with a SysEx or NRPN message.)

Don't forget Channel Aftertouch (if all the necessary devices support it): for keyboard players it's sometimes easier to get smooth realistic gradations of effect by varying pressure than by using a lever or wheel. Or, to get the best of both worlds, try remapping aftertouch to Modulation. This helps to ensure that the effect tails off and finishes before the note does.

Brass Realism

The trouble with the modulation effect for acoustic instruments is that however carefully you apply it, it tends to be a very regular sound lacking in realism. There's a second way to get a modulation effect, without using the mod-wheel. It takes a bit more patience and possibly more editing, but the results can be excellent – use the pitch-bend control! Set a pitch-bend range of ± 1 semitone (the minimum possible) and step-enter in a graphic-editor small peaks of pitch-bend. Use varying values between about 0:75 and 0:90 alternating with 0:64s. This technique can very effectively mimic the natural vibrato or *shake* in pitch that occurs in long reed or brass notes.

Hint

➡ Try combining these small pitch-bend peaks with a mild gate using CC11 Expression (see **Gate Effects** on page 142). This can give excellent results with saxophone and trumpet patches.

Modulation As A Synth Effect

Using modulation as a synth-effect means never having to say you're sorry – you can do whatever you like with no considerations of realism. You could decide to give a sound a slight *edge* by inserting a CC1:20 or so at the start of the track (remembering to enter CC1:0 at the end to reset). Or try layering two sounds (see page 138) and giving one a modulation setting of 0 and the other a high modulation setting with a lower volume.

Modulatin' Rhythm

For a very synthetic effect on synth-lead lines, try following the **Gate Effects** principle (see page 142) using CC1 instead of CC11, varying the values between 0 and 127. The result is unusual, and not something you'd use too often, but it's a different way to create 'rhythms' in pad-type sounds. This one is most effective if you use simpler rhythms, such as an 8th-note pattern.

Clean Up!

The usual suggestions with continuous controllers apply: if you're working at a high resolution (192 tpq and above) use *Thin* or *Reduce Continuous Controllers* to cut down the quantity of data to what's actually *needed*, and make sure you don't have modulation events occurring where no notes are sounding.

▪ CC7: Main Volume

Volume – turn it up, turn it down, easy! Sadly not. MIDI provides three different ways of controlling the volume of the sound, and event-for-event CC7 is beaten hands-down by the other two: *note-on velocity* and CC11 *Expression*. Let's take a look at what to use and where to use it.

Volume Or Expression?

For each channel of note-data you use in a file there should be just **one** Control Change 7 event, which is placed in the song-header. Any changes in volume (such as fades) during the song-body are controlled with CC11. The reason for this is simple and extremely practical: you can balance all the note-data on a channel *with itself* so that the feel is right and the fades start and end with the right volumes, and then use the CC7 event to balance that *channel* with the others. If you'd used CC7 all the way through, you'd have to increase or decrease *every occurrence* in the song which gives problems of headroom: if one CC7 event is already at 120, you can only increase them all by 7 so some notes might *still* be too quiet. By the same token, if you raised all CC7s by 30, your fadeouts would no longer fade *out* – they'd just fade down!

Volume Or Velocity?

The other obvious method of controlling volume is by *note-on velocity*. It's worth trying to get as much volume out of the notes this way as you can. The higher the signal strength, the lower you need the master-volume on the tone-generator which will improve the signal-to-noise ratio of its output.

Most sounds (in most tone-generators) are constructed to give harder or raspier tonal characteristics as their note-on velocity is increased: with some rhythm guitar parts, for example, you may get a better result by maximising the velocities so that the highest is 127, and reducing the CC7 event's value to balance the channel.

One of the sounds with the most noticeable velocity-to-brightness correlations is the acoustic steel-string guitar. Listen to the file **BRIGHTNS.MID** to hear how this works in practice. The file consists of an 8-bar phrase repeated. In the first playing the notes have low velocities and a high main volume setting. In the second, the velocities are maximised and the main volume lowered. Notice the increased brightness in the second phrase even though the overall 'volume' seems the same.

Of course, there's no need to lose this brightness during quieter sections of the song where you'd expect to reduce the velocities – just keep the velocities maximised and 'bracket' the section with step-entered CC11 Expression events to make it quieter.

Volume In The Song Header

Try to start with the CC7 values set at a maximum of 100 for each channel in the song-header, and keep them there as long as you can. By doing this, if you record a sax-solo somewhere in the song which doesn't seem to pump out as it should, even with maximised velocities and full expression (CC11), you can turn up the CC7 value. If you'd started with them all at 127 you'd have to *turn down* all the others – same result, but unnecessarily time-consuming.

Volume Fader

Most keyboards have a volume fader sending out CC7s: use your sequencer's controller remap facility to remap incoming CC7s to CC11s. You might be able to remap the fader on your keyboard itself but this should be regarded as the last resort, especially if you use the same keyboard for live performance (see page 192).

No Remap Facility?

You may be using a setup that has no *remap* facility either on the sequencer or the keyboard so your fader can only send out CC7s. If this is the case you have two options: your sequencer might have a 'search-and-replace' function or some kind of 'mathematical' editor that will locate and alter all the CC7s to CC11s automatically. Failing that (and as long as you're not producing commercial SMFs) try switching the two: use CC7 throughout the song-body as an expression control and use a single instance of CC11 in the song-header as the master control. It's a less than perfect way of working since few tone-generators show the current CC11 setting on their front-panel displays, but it does give the same ease of volume-editing.

Detours

➡ For more on the different methods of controlling volume, take a look at **CC11: Expression** on page 213.

▓ CC10: Pan

For newcomers to MIDI and/or multi-track recording, the **pan** control (short for panoramic) is often seen as something of a toy – it's great to be able to move sounds around and create a stereo recording. But apart from its obvious use as an effect it's also a very handy mixing tool for creating a sense of *space* around the various instruments. In this topic we'll take a look at some of the practical applications of panning.

Spaced Out

Arguably the main use of the pan control is to assign each instrument its own space within the mix. It's usually a good idea to try and keep the mix balanced though – panning the pad and organ hard left and the flute-line hard right gives the uncomfortable impression that you're working on a slope and the sounds have *slid* into the wrong speaker!

Think of the stereo speakers as scales, with the sounds as weights – instruments that play chords are heavyweights, instruments that play single notes are lightweights. Try to keep the heavyweights balanced: either pan them in opposite directions or leave them (or it) close to centre. Lightweights can then be panned to more extreme settings without affecting the balance too much, unless you get two light-weights on the left at the same time with nothing on the right.

Of course, there are more imaginative options in the programmer's toolkit than assigning fixed positions for each sound which still keep the scales balanced: double- and triple-tracking, split-panning and delay (all covered in the previous chapter) are just a few of the effects that can spice up your mix.

Out In The Field

Remember to make use of the full stereo field for best clarity: it's tempting to think that a pan of 30 or 40 is the limit, and that anything wider will leave 'holes' between the sounds. Try this when you've finished a file: to all the channels panned between 5 and 15 (left or right) add 5. To all the sounds panned between 16 and 30 add 10, and so on, then listen to the file again. You'll notice that a lot of the sounds seem clearer and the mix is spacious and less muddled. This isn't to say that you'll always want that space or clarity of course, but the revelation can be startling if you've always stuck to a limited range.

Hint

➡ When a 'lightweight' instrument needs a little more volume, try giving it a more extreme pan setting instead: sometimes the extra space and clarity can give a better result than more volume.

Piano Realism

(This one requires a few channels, so you have to pick the right song for it!) Set up about 6 channels with a piano sound and exactly the same volume and effect settings, record a piano part and copy it to each of these 6 channels. Next, assign specific note-ranges to specific channels (such as C1 to G1 on channel 1, G#1 to D2 on channel 2 and so on) and pan each channel to a different point in the stereo field, with the lowest notes to the left and the highest to the right. The effect is that of sticking your head inside a concert-grand and adds amazing life to a piano-part. Even reduced to a more manageable three channels, the result is still good. It does of course require a fair bit of editing to make it work, since the events falling outside a channel's note-range should really be deleted, together with any redundant sustain-pedal events.

 Load the file **SPACEPNO.MID** for an example of this idea in action.

Dynamic Panning

Of course, panning can also be an excellent source of effects, one of the most popular being the pan-sweep: you hold a note or chord and *sweep* the sound across the stereo field. Or, without **Dynamic Panning**, you don't.

According to MIDI specification, panning is **fixed**: once a sound has been triggered, its position in the stereo field can't be altered, unlike the expression and modulation controllers. Pan wasn't really designed to be a continuous controller. However, some friendly instrument manufacturers have gone ahead and done it anyway.

Load the file **DYNAPAN.MID** into your sequencer and hit *Play*. You should hear a single chord play, and pan back and forth across the stereo field a few times. If you do, your tone-generator does have Dynamic Panning.

If you don't have Dynamic Panning, don't be too disheartened: it's still possible to program very effective pan sweeps using very fast single notes with a CC10 event placed between each, but for a continuous effect you'll find that sounds with a slow attack-phase are to be avoided.

Detours

➡ For more on panning effects take a look at section **4: Tricks & Effects** on page 124.

▓ CC11: Expression

The most important aspect of the **Expression** controller is in comparison with the Volume controller, and this has been covered a couple of pages back in **CC7: Main Volume**. This short topic takes a peep at a few matters that concern Expression alone.

High Expression

The expression value set in the header bar is fixed by default at 127: after all, you might not make any changes to it during the song so this ensures that you're gaining maximum output. Obviously if the channel starts with a fade-in you'd set your CC11 header event to the required starting value, but you'd normally fade all the way up to 127 and use the note-on velocity of the note(s) to adjust the final volume attained, so that CC11 is once again running at full power.

Invisibility

Expression is a tricky thing to keep track of. Few devices display the current CC11 settings for channels on their screens which can mean it's the last thing you think of when notes suddenly vanish. So when you record a section of music that ends with a fadeout, it's useful to enter the resetting CC11:127 as soon after the note-off as you can (but watch out for sounds with a long release-phase – if you enter it too soon you might get a sudden sharp attack from the note similar to a gate-effect).

Some pattern-based sequencers automatically send out resets to unresolved controllers (low expression, sustain pedals left on, hanging pitch-bend, etc.) at the end of a pattern, meaning that everything can sound just fine until you mixdown or save and then reload as a Standard MIDI File.

Expressive Expression

Remember that *Expression* got its name for a reason – it's a dynamic continuous controller with as much value in real-time recording as note-on velocities have, but with more flexibility. For example, when recording a pad sound you can (and naturally will) vary the note-on velocities, but once the chord is playing it'll remain at that volume for perhaps a bar or more. Real-time use of expression (using a remapped fader or a swell pedal) lets you introduce some dynamic colour to sustained string, pad and organ sounds whether chorded or one-note lines.

Copy and Paste, Pros and Cons

When you cut or copy and then paste a section of music containing CC11 data, check what it is and where it is first. Be careful not to remove resets (11:127) or to copy 11:0s to places they weren't supposed to be. Copy and paste can be a useful tool for fadeouts though – record one smooth fadeout and then copy it to all the channels to be faded. You might need to paste the data in slightly different positions depending upon the individual characteristics of each instrument, but it makes life a lot easier than recording separate fades for each channel and trying to make them match.

Clean Up!

Many files finish with the last chord fading away, so for most channels the final event will be CC11:0. If you (or your end-user) next plays a file with a GM, GS or XG Reset at the start all will be well, but remember that not everyone uses GM/GS/XG files and of those that do, not all sequencers will load the SysEx reset. To minimise the chance of problems occurring, enter a CC11:127 at the end of each of these channels' data.

You might raise the CC11 control after performing a fade just by sliding the fader back up again. It's a good habit to get into, but remember that all those intermediate events between the 0 and the 127 are unnecessary, as are events recorded after the note off has occurred and the release-phase has finished.

Detours

➡ Take a look at the topics on **Fades and Sweeps** (page 134) and **Gate Effects** (page 142) to see the Expression controller getting down and boogying.

▨ CC64: Sustain Pedal

The **sustain** pedal (also oddly known as the *Damper Pedal*) controller is one of the *Switch Controllers* and, in this sense, is easy to use with no hidden assets, tricks or effects. It is a wee bit of a troublemaker though, which is the reason it gets a topic to itself.

Pedal Power

Like all the other *On/Off* switch controllers, values should be either 0 or 127 unless your device is compatible with the 'half-damper' technique which uses values from 1 to 126. Tone-generators without the 'half-damper' implemented (i.e., most of them!) will interpret a value between 1 and 63 as *Off* (0) and a value between 64 and 126 as *On* (127).

Make sure that all uses of CC64 on a channel are in pairs (*On*, *Off*, *On*, *Off*, etc.) and that the final CC64 event on any channel has the zero (*Off*) value. Some tone-generators get extremely confused when they come across consecutive switch controllers with the same setting and give unexpected results.

Copy and Paste

All the usual potential pitfalls of cut/copy/paste apply to the sustain pedal – be careful not to remove *Off* events or to copy *On* events to an unwanted position. In either of these cases, the sustaining caused might sound so bad that you'd investigate and sort it out, but in some cases the effect might not be noticeable: it's not just the clash of non-harmonizing notes that's undesirable but the extra voices being snatched from your valuable polyphony.

Polyphony

As we've mentioned elsewhere in the book, the sustain pedal snatches voices like there's no tomorrow. For this reason alone, it's preferable to avoid using it if possible. Many keyboard players find themselves automatically using the pedal when entering note-data for any instrument at all and this tends to create areas of high polyphony spanning the end of one bar and the beginning of the next where changes of chord usually occur.

Hint

➡ For pianists and keyboard players who can't touch the keys without the 'sustain foot' getting busy, try filtering out the CC64 messages, or just unplugging the pedal.

All the issues of polyphony are fully covered in **Polyphony Problems** on page 112, but as a final and vital point on the subject: before using a sustain-pedal check out the voice requirements of the sound you're using. In a low-polyphony device (i.e., below 32 voices), using CC64 and playing in a normal piano style with a dual- or multi-voice sound is musical suicide if you're hoping to include a few more instruments in the file too!

Clean Up!

The sustain-pedal issues of avoiding repetition of identical events and leaving pedal-on events 'hanging' at the end of a file apply to any other pedal-controllers you might use, such as portamento, soft, sostenuto, etc.

CC91: Reverb Depth

Reverb is the effect the music industry thrives on – a touch of reverb added to a dry mix can transform a rather dull sound into a commercial, sparkling work of great artistry. Or transform it into the work of a one-man-band in a tunnel. As with any effect, it's not what you've got, it's how you use it that counts.

Lift and Separate

These are the two primary functions of the reverb effect. If you listen to a file *dry* and then hear it again with reverb added, you'll notice a definite *lift* in the sound to the point that instruments with more reverb seem to be literally *higher up* in the speakers. Where the pan effect adds a horizontal dimension to sound, reverb takes care of the vertical dimension. In recent years, 3-D effect devices have broadened the dimensional range to the point where the sound can appear to move from floor to ceiling, and even wind up behind you!

The element of *lift* relies on comparative differences between the sounds: if you apply a CC91 setting of 64 to every instrument you'll notice very little difference. The sound will certainly seem a little more roomy, but there'll be no effective change from the dry mix.

The second aspect of reverb, the *separation* of sounds, is indelibly linked to the first. Giving each sound it's own space also relies on different reverb settings (think of these as being different *heights*).

For maximum effect, reverb should work hand-in-hand with pan (CC10) in making separate spaces for sounds. Imagine a large grid on the wall between your speakers: to put a sound in the upper-left 'box', pan it hard-left with a high reverb setting. The lower-right 'box' would be a hard-right pan and a low reverb setting, and so on.

Make the most of the full 128-point reverb scale: as with the pan-controller, it's tempting to think that a reverb-depth of 30 is like having *no* reverb, and 100 is always going to be way too much.

 Load the file **REVERB.MID** and hit *Play*. The file consists of the same 4-bar phrase played twice: first dry, and then with reverb added.

The Bottom Line

The golden rule with reverb is: *don't apply it to bass instruments*! In most music recording, the bass end is kept as tight as possible. Other effects (such as Chorus) can work positively with bass sounds, but reverb tends to give a boomy, messy result. You've probably noticed that when you apply full reverb to your drum-kit, the reverb send-level of the kick is still much lower than that of the snares or toms for exactly this reason.

Nevertheless, rules are made to be broken. Using a fretless bass (or similar warm sound) in a slow piece of music, a small amount of reverb can help the bass to sit among the other instruments more comfortably. In fact, for this style of music, you'll probably raise *all* reverb levels compared to the same instruments' settings for a rock number.

Effective Effects

As is the case with any effect, its success lies in the way one setting is juxtaposed with another. In a file with fairly high reverb settings for most instruments giving something of a *floating* air to the music, try assigning a very low CC91 value to a lead or fill instrument to make it cut through and add an element of surprise.

When using Layering, Double-Tracking or Delay effects (see the **4: Tricks and Effects** section starting on page 124), try assigning one sound a very high reverb level with reduced volume, and setting the other a very low reverb level. The contrast can highlight the dimensional aspect of reverb very well, particularly when layering two different sounds playing a monophonic line.

Time and Type

Depth controls the volume of the reverb effect, but it's just one of the parameters that it's desirable to have some control over. (It's also the only one included in the MIDI specification, so any others you can access will usually be via NRPNs or System Exclusive messages.) The most useful parameter to experiment with is Reverb Time – how long the effect takes to decay. Setting a higher value for this can be very effective in slower (or less frenetic) music, and can add considerably to the total *lift*. Try setting all the relative depths for each instrument and then adjusting the reverb time.

The second parameter worth looking at is the reverb *type* – most tone-generators offer several different types such as Small Room, Large Room, Plate, Concert Hall, etc. These may be coupled with more exotic options like Early Reflections or Delays.

Where reverb depth should be variable for each channel, the other parameters are usually *global* so a bit of advance planning is needed to choose settings that will suit the *whole* mix.

CC93: Chorus Depth

The chorus effect works by a combination of delaying and detuning elements of the sound to create a richer, thicker texture. The result is similar to that of having several voices or acoustic instruments playing in unison, with the full force of human error helping to 'fatten' the sound.

Thickening Agent

The main use of chorus is to *thicken* a sound – in other words, to give the impression that more than one instrument is playing the line. Used sparingly, it can do wonders for thin monophonic sounds such as piccolos and oboes, or solo string-lines. Heavily applied to almost any instrument, it begins to sound distinctly unnatural and synthesized which can be useful at times.

Hint

➡ Try adding maximum chorus to a drumkit. The result can be unusual, and a very useful way to get a slightly different drum sound if you're stuck with General MIDI's single kit!

Some of the most effective uses of chorus tend to be in conjunction with sounds that are already fairly thick: you can get a wonderfully atmospheric 'wash' behind a file by adding quantities of chorus to a pad or a Rhodes electric-piano emulation, or some organ sounds. It's also an excellent way to fatten up a weak bass-sound, and to add extra punch to brass and orchestra stabs.

Load the file **CHORUS.MID** and hit *Play*. The file contains the same
4-bar phrase played twice: listen to the effect created by adding chorus
to bass, drums and pad for the repeat.

Bridging The Gap

The thickening effect of chorus can really start to make its mark when
you're programming a file with sparse instrumentation. In this
situation, you can often find that as soon as you widen the pan-range
from about left/right 15 there seem to be empty 'holes' between the
instruments. Adding a small amount of chorus tends to blur the edges
of the sounds making them expand to fill up some of this 'dead' space.

Chorus Vs. Volume

Another little idiosyncrasy of chorus is that it can give the impression
of adding volume. This is worth keeping in mind for those moments
when a solo or lead-line isn't pumping as it ought to even with the
velocities maximised. For example, if you've recorded a rhythm-guitar
track which breaks off to take a solo halfway through, instead of
adjusting expression (CC11) settings for the whole track to push out
the solo, just insert a chorus value of 40 to 60 before the solo and a
zero at the end. The result will usually be far more effective than a
simple rise in volume.

Spice Of Life

In exactly the same way as pan, reverb and any other effect at your
disposal, remember that variety is the spice of life. The most colourful
and vibrant effect in the world isn't worth much if you apply it
liberally to every instrument in the mix. Don't feel you have to use
chorus just because it's there – try to restrict its use to sounds that
need more presence or richness to highlight their individual character.

Chorus Type and Rate

The *depth* of chorus effect is often just one of a range of editable
parameters (though you might need to use SysEx or NRPNs to get at
any others). Adjusting the *rate* of chorus can give good results, and

create some weird and wonderful effects at extreme settings. You might also be able to select different chorus *types* such as Symphonic, Flanger, Phaser or Rotary Speaker. The last of these is primarily intended for organ sounds, and might be used together with real-time control over the *rate* setting to simulate acceleration and the speed of rotation.

These are more than likely to be *global* settings across the whole device, so if you choose a flange-effect for one sound you'll probably be stuck with flange or nothing for all the others.

CC5 and 65: Portamento

Portamento (or 'glide') is without doubt a *synth effect* and it's one of the oldest in the book. It's mainly used for synth-leads and sound-effects, having little in common with acoustic instruments. The effect is a regular 'sliding' from one note to another in a similar way to **pitch-bend**, but in this case it's the time taken rather than the distance that has to be specified. Portamento isn't included in the General MIDI specification, but it is supported by most tone-generators.

How's It Used?

Portamento uses two separate controllers: CC5 is used to set the **Portamento Time**, how long it takes to change the pitch by a semitone, which has a range of 0–127. CC65 is the **Portamento Pedal** which turns the effect On and Off (values of 127 and 0 respectively).

The portamento control started life in the older monophonic synths, and its main use is still in playing monophonic lines. When chords are introduced, the sliding becomes haphazard as any note from the first chord could slide to any note of the second. Remember too that the effect doesn't require the playing to be *legato* – the pitch will always slide from the last note you played however long you pause between the two.

Load and play the file **PORTA01.MID**, then start playing on ch1 – all the setting up has been done for you. The effect is extremely noticeable when you move in intervals of over a 4th, so if you don't hear any difference your tone-generator probably doesn't support it.

Changing Times

When programming a portamento line, you'll usually just turn the pedal *On* at the beginning and *Off* at the end. Very often though, the *time* will take a bit more thought and variation. For example, if the line moves in small intervals you can find the effect is hardly noticeable, so you might need to turn up the time-control. But as soon as you jump an octave, for example, you might find yourself waiting a beat or so for the correct pitch to be reached, so you'd need to set a lower time-value.

The time controller can be used as a continuous controller by using Controller Remap to map your volume or data-entry slider to CC5, but this will cause a vast number of unnecessary events to be recorded. The easiest way is to record the line with a low time-value (or with the portamento pedal turned off), and then step-enter the time-controller events where and when you need them.

Ghost Notes

A common trick used with portamento is to insert *ghost note*s into the line. These are notes used just for their pitch, as a *source note* to determine where the slide will start: their velocities and lengths are set to minimum so that they can't be heard. For example, if you've recorded a phrase that ends on C3 and the next phrase starts on C4 but you want a *downward* slide to the C4, simply add a higher ghost-note before the C4. The actual position of the ghost note doesn't matter, as long as it occurs *after the note-on* of the C3.

Ghost notes are also a useful way to avoid having to make changes in the time-controller: if you want a note to slide to the next more quickly, you can cheat by inserting a ghost note that's closer in pitch to the next. The slide won't actually start from the original note now, but no-one should be able to tell you've cheated just by listening!

This highlights another point worth remembering – the volume of the slide will be the note-on volume of the note it's sliding to. It sounds obvious, but it's the reason the ghost-notes must have a minimum note-on velocity: if they didn't, you'd hear a slide *to* them as well as *from* them!

Load the file **PORTA02.MID** and have a listen. The lead-line on channel 4 uses portamento, and includes sweeps, ghost notes and changes in portamento time. The panning effect on the sweeps will only have an effect if your tone-generator has Dynamic Panning (see page 212).

Portamento Control

A more recent addition to the portamento stable is CC84 **Portamento Control**. This controller allows you to specify the *source note* from which the slide will occur (in a similar way to using ghost notes) by entering the required MIDI note number as the value for CC84 and the slide will then take place when the next note-on message is received. The major advantage of this controller is its ability to work *polyphonically*, to glide from one chord to another in the manner of a pedal steel guitar. At the time of writing, Portamento Control has not yet been widely implemented by manufacturers.

Clean Up!

As with any on/off switch controller, make sure the last pedal event for any channel using portamento is 65:0.

7

System Messages Menu

MIDI consists of two types of message, **Channel Messages** and **System Messages**. Channel Messages are covered in detail in the **Channel Messages Menu** beginning on page 172.

System Messages are split into three groups: **System Exclusive, System Real Time** and **System Common**. The link between these groups is that their messages are not directed at a particular channel but at your **MIDI system** as a whole, to be interpreted either by the single device to which they were addressed ('**Exclusive**') or to any device that can respond to system messages ('**Common**'). A sister-message to *Common* is the **Real Time** group which controls the timing synchronization of non-MIDI devices. System Messages are transmitted on an additional (un-numbered) channel, though your sequencer might fill the 'channel' section of your list-editor with a '1' when you use one of these events.

However your Channel or System messages are presented to you on your sequencer screen or in manuals, they're actually transmitted between devices in the computer's native language, **Binary Code**, which is the rather tenuous justification for including the topic here. You don't really *need* to know about it, but it does give you an insight to what's going on behind that friendly *Edit* screen.

System Exclusive

As you can see from the various types and functions of Channel Messages, MIDI as a language has been buckled down pretty tightly to ensure that for all the things musicians commonly need to control in their music, at least one of these should do the job.

Your Flexible Friend

But however comprehensive MIDI is, it's a fairly static specification, as it has to be: it can't go changing every couple of months. But still every couple of months manufacturers bring out new MIDI equipment with enhanced features and greater levels of user-control. To be able to actually use these features, some degree of flexibility within the MIDI spec is clearly called for.

This flexibility is provided in two ways: firstly by using the undefined and NRPN Control Change Commands to which manufacturers can assign their own uses for individual devices, and secondly by using **System Exclusive** messages.

Pros. . .

System Exclusive (**SysEx**) messages are messages usually directed to one specific device in your MIDI setup. The inclusion of SysEx in the MIDI specification means that manufacturers can provide a way of accessing different features of their equipment that aren't accessible using Channel Messages. So when a new device is released with a great new feature, the manufacturer can simply create new SysEx messages which address this feature. However, as System Messages are sent to all MIDI devices in your setup, there must be some method to make sure these SysEx messages won't affect any equipment they weren't intended for.

To make all this work, manufacturers are assigned their own ID number by the MIDI Manufacturers' Association which they must include in all SysEx messages for their devices; only equipment with the same ID will be able to respond to the message. Many manufacturers also include a **Device ID** to prevent other devices in your setup *made by the same manufacturer* trying to respond to the message.

On many sequencers, particularly at the higher level, SysEx can be recorded in real-time ('*dumped*') from your device and saved/re-loaded with the MIDI file or in a file of its own. A collection of settings that might take you half an hour to write clearly on a piece of paper can be recorded or sent as SysEx messages in just a few seconds. You can also often write SysEx messages yourself within your sequencer.

. . . And Cons

So it's dead useful isn't it? And if you're content just to dump and send packets of SysEx data between devices (and there's no reason why you shouldn't be) you can happily just say 'SysEx? It's that dead useful stuff' if anyone asks. However if you need to actually *write* the messages yourself, you have to understand their 'language' and construction.

SysEx messages are commonly displayed in hexadecimal (base 16, often abbreviated to **hex**), using the numbers 0–9 together with letters A–F giving a total of 16 'numbers'. A number written in hex always has an 'H' suffix (such as 41H) to avoid confusion. For the sake of comparison, we normally use the 'decimal' system (base 10) using the numbers 0-9. The number we write as 98 in decimal means that we have 9 sets of ten + 8 units. The same number translated to hex gives us 62H (6 sets of sixteen + 2 units – go on, add 'em up !). The hex number 7FH translates to decimal as 127: 7 lots of sixteen + F (15) lots of units. Not too bad so far . . . but the flexibility inherent in SysEx also unfortunately has its downside. The message always begins with F0H which tells the device to expect a SysEx message, followed by the manufacturer's ID, the device ID (if one exists) and the message-data itself, and ends with F7H. Also straightforward enough, but this is where the edges blur: the construction of the message-data portion of the SysEx is undefined and different manufacturers tend to adopt different forms for their messages. Some devices also require inclusion of a *checksum* before the End Of Exclusive (F7H) flag. The checksum is a form of error-checking system for the data (see **System Exclusive: Analysis** on page 233).

It can be seen from the above that writing SysEx for a particular device requires you to spend some quality-time getting to know the back of your user-manual intimately, but if you persevere you should find that you can 'unlock' software access to parameters that previously were reachable only with a lot of button-pushing on your tone-generator.

Universal SysEx

Paradoxically, not all System Exclusive messages *are* actually exclusive: of the 128 possible manufacturers' IDs, the highest numbers have been reserved for **Universal** SysEx messages. One example of a universal message is **MIDI Time Code** which enables a sequencer to run in synchronization with other devices. Other types of Universal SysEx message are:

- ❏ **Master Volume:** the message governing the global volume setting of a device

- ❏ **Master Pan:** governing the pan position of an entire device's output

- ❏ **Time Signature:** containing the time-signature and current metronome rate.

- ❏ **MIDI Machine Control:** to control other hardware such as tape-recorders, video, DAT and so on

- ❏ **MIDI Show Control:** to control theatre equipment such as lighting, pyrotechnic effects, etc.

General MIDI System Exclusive

Another example of a universal message is the GM Reset, which is recognised by all GM-compatible devices regardless of manufacturer. There are in fact two universal SysEx messages concerning General MIDI, 'Turn GM On' and 'Turn GM Off', the second of which is intended for tone-generators which can implement General MIDI but have other operating modes (additional sound-sets, etc.) as well. The *Off* message isn't included in the GM specification.

The 'Turn GM On' message is F0,7E,7F,09,01,F7 and it's the message we refer to as the GM Reset – whenever this message is received by a GM-compatible tone-generator it automatically resets the device to GM defaults (see **General MIDI**, page 50) in preparation for receiving a GM file.

The 'Turn GM Off' message is F0,7E,7F,09,02,F7 which returns the tone-generator to its own standard operating mode. You'll notice that only one section of the message (the *data* portion) has changed in this command. Here's a brief explanation of the separate elements of the messages:

F0	**Start of SysEx**
7E	**Universal (reserved) ID number**
7F	**Device ID (another reserved number for General transmission)**
09	**Means 'This is a message about General MIDI'**
01	**Means 'Turn General MIDI On'. 02 here means 'Off'**
F7	**End of SysEx (EOX).**

Replacement Song Header

A useful way of employing SysEx is to use a spare track on your sequencer to record a dump from your tone-generator containing all your specially edited sounds and settings and so on, and have this data play back before the actual song-data begins, automatically loading all the correct sounds and parameters back into your tone-generator every time you play back the file (see page 112 for more details). This collection of SysEx messages can entirely replace the Reset, Controller and Program Change event-setup outlined in the **Song Header** topic.

Bear in mind though that no other data should be transmitted at the same time as System Exclusive – make sure you position your count-in or song-body data to begin *after* the SysEx has been played through. Remember, too, that even though a SysEx message may appear as a single event in your sequencer, it can actually be a fairly lengthy message that's being transmitted and will take longer to be transmitted and implemented than a program-change or note event.

Chain Trick

Another use for SysEx is in controlling two tone-generators connected in a chain (as in Fig. 7 on page 35). Sending a channel message such as a program change on a particular channel would select the same patch number in both units. To select *different* patch numbers (or controller settings, etc.) for each device, separate SysEx messages provide the solution.

Points To Ponder – The Good, The Sad and The Cuddly

The Good
Check to see if your tone-generator implements NRPNs (Non-Registered Parameter Numbers): these may save you having to get bogged down in SysEx at all!

The Sad
Not all sequencers (even some quite recent ones) fully implement SysEx: some won't load or save SysEx in a SMF, and quite a few lower and mid-range sequencers give you no facility to write your own SysEx strings so that even if you know what the string is, you still have to coax your tone-generator into dumping it to the sequencer in real-time.

The Cuddly
Use our nice friendly Decimal to Hex converter on page 241 when trying to work out the values for your own SysEx messages.

Detours

➡ For a more in-depth look at a lengthier piece of System Exclusive, jump to page 233.

System Real Time

That Syncing Feeling

The main use of **System Real Time** messages lies in the synchronisation of timing between several MIDI devices, or between a MIDI device and audio tape using additional hardware to 'translate' the messages into a form that can be recorded to tape. MIDI-to-Audio synchronisation is covered in the next topic, **System Common**. System Real Time is the collective name for the following group of messages:

❑ **MIDI Clock:** a 24 tpq 'beat' which can be thought of as a kind of metronome, forcing the receiving (or slave) device to keep time with the sending device (master).

❑ **Start/Stop/Continue:** these three messages tell the receiving device to start playing the song (or re-start from the beginning), stop playing the song, and carry on playing from the point it was stopped.

❑ **Active Sensing:** a type of error-checking signal sent roughly 3 times per second to ensure that data is being received. If the receiving device stops getting *active sensing* messages, it assumes that something's gone wrong and automatically turns off all notes to prevent them hanging.

❑ **System Reset:** a resetting command, just as you'd expect it to be. Few devices respond to this message as it can cause devices such as sequencers to wipe all data in memory as they do it, whether you'd previously saved or not.

Syncing Midi Devices

This is the simplest form of synchronisation. For example, to sync your sequencer with a drum-machine your sequencer will be set to generate its own timing messages (**Internal Sync** or **Transmit MIDI Clock**) and the drum-machine should be set to receive them (**External Sync** or **Receive MIDI Clock**). Sending a pulse of only 24 tpq makes MIDI Clock a low resolution message, so sequencers with a higher resolution (as most have) use this pulse to determine the positions of the *intermediate* pulses.

As well as actually running a sequencer and a drum-machine in sync, a little extra control is needed. For this reason, there are three additional messages to tell the slave device when to start, stop and continue playback.

MIDI Clock is the simplest form of sync, very easy to use when connecting two or more MIDI devices that can send or receive MIDI Clock pulses. On occasions though, it's useful to be able to synchronise a MIDI device (such as a sequencer) with a non-MIDI device like a video or audio tape recorder. That usually requires use of a **System Common** message, MIDI Time Code.

System Common

System Common is the name given to the following group of messages:

❏ **MIDI Time Code (MTC):** an adaptation of SMPTE time-code, MTC is a higher resolution message at 100 pulses per second and used mainly for syncing MIDI with audio or video tape. It also contains a second type of message, MTC Cueing, for *remote control* of external devices, but this has been largely overtaken by MIDI Machine Control.

❏ **Song Position Pointer:** a MIDI Clock message to keep track of the current position in a song when you rewind or fast-forward by counting the number of clock-pulses passed since the start of the song.

❏ **Song Select:** a little-used message enabling you to select a particular song- or pattern-number (from 0–127) on the sequencer which would then select the same number in the slave so that both devices would play the same song or, in the case of a drum-machine, the correct chain of patterns.

❏ **Tune Request:** a message to ask analogue synthesizers to retune their oscillators, which had a nasty habit of gradually drifting out of tune.

Syncing MIDI With Audio Tape

The option of syncing MIDI with audio/video tape is invaluable to both the recording and the film and television industries. Put simply, it means that as much of the music as possible is kept in the digital domain. As has been already mentioned, sequencers record binary code (1s and 0s) and these streams of numbers can't degenerate over time or get chewed up in the car stereo the way analogue recordings can. The action of the heads touching the analogue tape as it records or plays also causes the surface of the tape to gradually deteriorate.

It's only very recently that **hard-disk recording** has become possible and the price tends to make the option prohibitive to many. So to record a song that requires non-MIDI ingredients (such as vocals) the solution is to program your MIDI data, synchronise your sequencer to a multi-track tape recorder to record the vocals in time with the music and then mixdown the two synchronised elements to a third tape-recorder to create your master recording. This means that a method of keeping the tape-recorder in time with the sequencer is needed.

FSK

FSK (Frequency Shift Keying) is a type of MIDI Clock message altered to a format that can be recorded onto audio tape. A *MIDI Clock-to-FSK* converter is usually needed to do this, though some higher-level sequencers have this facility built in. The FSK signal is recorded to an empty *outer* track on the multi-track tape recorder (to minimise crosstalk between the FSK and adjacent tracks), and the FSK converter then patiently keeps track of your position within the song as you record and play, rewind or fast-forward the tape and translates these signals back to ordinary MIDI Clock messages to keep the sequencer in time.

FSK is relatively cheap and easy to use in a home-studio setup, but it's vital to check that your FSK converter can handle **Song Position Pointers**.

Time Code

A second method of synchronising MIDI and tape is **time-code**. Time-code is usually referred to as SMPTE (pronounced 'sempty', an acronym for Society of Motion Picture and Television Engineers) but SMPTE is actually just one of various possible time-code formats (in the same way that a particular brand-name has become the generic name for any vacuum-cleaner!). Time-code is a high-resolution/high-precision format, its primary use being in the synchronisation of MIDI and video for applications such as film-scoring.

The essential difference between time-code and MIDI Clock is that the latter is tempo-based (being 24 pulses per quarter-note, if the tempo is raised the speed of the pulses increases) whereas time-code is based on time as the names suggests, measuring position in hours, minutes, seconds and frames. The actual number of frames per second varies according to different tape-formats (black and white/colour, film/video, etc.) and different countries have adopted different frame-rate standards ranging between 24 and 30 fps (frames per second).

Time-code is used in the same way as FSK, by recording ('striping') the code onto an audio-tape track, or to the audio track of a video tape. It obviously carries far greater precision than FSK and has the benefit of not committing you to the tempo you've selected, but its negative points are that the hardware required is a good deal more expensive and demands a higher audio quality.

System Exclusive: Analysis

F0, 41, 10, 42, 12, 40, 00, 7F, 00, 41, F7

If you're new to the whole idea of System Exclusive, jump back to the main **System Messages** menu on page 224 for a very quick intro and then read the topic entitled **System Exclusive** before coming back here.

This topic sets out to show how an Exclusive message is constructed, taking the **GS Reset** message as an example. This can't be regarded in any way as an exhaustive reference on SysEx due to the flexibility allowed to manufacturers in constructing messages for their equipment, but it'll hopefully give you some clues.

Listed above is the System Exclusive message that sets Roland equipment to GS mode, in other words resets it to factory defaults and prepares it to receive further **Channel** or **System** messages.

What *Does* It All Mean?

This is what the message is telling the device, section-by-section, in both technical terms and in plain English:

F0	**Start Of Exclusive ('This is a SysEx message')**
41	**Manufacturer's ID number ('I'm only talking to Roland devices')**
10	**Device ID ('This device has multiple channels')**
42	**Model ID ('An unspecified GS system')**
12	**Type of Command ('I'm going to transfer some data')**
40,00,7F	**Address ('GS System Parameters')**

00	Data ('Reset the GS system')
41	Checksum ('I've checked to make sure I'm talking your language!')
F7	EOX ('This is the end of the message')

So What's All This *Checksum* Stuff Then?

The unpleasant side of System Exclusive is the checksum, a method of error-checking each message before it's transmitted to prevent it fouling up the target device. Fortunately, not all manufacturers include the requirement for a checksum in their SysEx. Unfortunately, among those that do, despite the vast lists of addresses, commands and data-ranges lurking in the back of your manual, often the only reference you'll find to the checksum is the word 'sum' inserted in the given SysEx strings. So unless your sequencer can calculate the checksum for you, you're up a gumtree. Or you were ...

The formula for calculating Roland's checksum is: 80H minus [Address bytes + Data bytes]. If the sum of address and data bytes is greater than 80H, then subtract 80H as often as necessary to give a result equal to or smaller than 80H before subtracting it from 80H.

Do What?

Yup, it's a bit daunting on first sight. Here's the easier step-by-step six-point formula, using the decimal system. (Remember – though the address and data bytes will vary from message to message, the 80H remains a constant. 80H = 128 in decimal.)

1 Convert address bytes and data bytes to decimal (using the Conversion Table on page 241)

2 Add together the address and data bytes.

3 If the result is between 0 and 128 inclusive, subtract it from 128 and go to step 6.

4 If the result is greater than 128, subtract 128 from it. If it's still larger than 128, take away another 128, and so on until it's between 0 and 128 (inclusive).

5 Subtract this result from 128.

6 Convert this final answer back to hex – this is your checksum!

A Quick Example

Pretending we don't already know it, let's work out the checksum for the GS Reset in the topic-header.

1 The address bytes are 40H, 00H, 7F.
   40H = 64
   00H = 0
   7FH = 127.
   The data byte is 00H which of course equals 0.

2 64 + 0 + 127 + 0 = 191.

3 191 is greater than 128 so we go to step 4.

4 As 191 is greater than 128, we have to subtract 128 from it. This gives 63 which is within the required range.

5 Subtract 63 from 128: this gives us 65. This is the checksum in decimal.

6 Convert 65 to hex: this gives us 41H. So the figure we enter for the GS Reset checksum is 41.

For Comparison . . .

As previously mentioned, not all devices require the inclusion of a checksum in their SysEx messages. An example is Yamaha's XG data. The XG reset is F0,43,10,4C,00,00,7E,00,F7.

F0	Start Of Exclusive
43	Yamaha ID
10	Device ID
4C	Model ID
00,00,7E	Address (XG system)
00	Data (initialise XG settings)
F7	EOX

Since all the XG SysEx messages are constructed in this way, they're almost as easy to use as a control-change: rather than entering the controller value, you enter the correct Address and Data values (in hex) and you're done.

Using SysEx Resets

As previously mentioned, both GS and XG devices are General MIDI compatible, so it should be possible to program a file for commercial purposes using GS/XG data and have it playback reasonably well on a General MIDI device. To make this happen, the file must include both the GM reset (see page 227) and the GS or XG reset.

In this way, the GM-only device will read the GM reset and ignore the other resets and the non-GM data contained in the file, while GS and XG devices will respond to their own resets. To make this work, the GM reset must always be first in the list, followed by either the GS or the XG reset (or both in that order). For example, when creating an XG file, enter GM, GS and XG resets in that order and the file should play credibly on any devices following one of the three protocols.

Specifics

Remember, *all* SysEx messages begin and end F0 ... F7. Other information specific to your device such as manufacturer, device and model IDs can be found towards the back of your user-manual along with command IDs and the various system parameter addresses. The manual should also contain details on how the messages are constructed.

If the checksum formula covered in this topic doesn't work for your manufacturer's device and there's no formula in the manual, see if you can dump a SysEx message from it to your sequencer to analyse: you might be able to spot some kind of numeric relationship in there. Failing that, call their Tech Support line – they're usually very helpful.

Detours

➟ Take a look at pages 52 and 54 for more on Roland's GS and Yamaha's XG respectively.

■ Binary Code

This is an explanation of the binary numbering system, how it relates to MIDI and the implementation of Channel Messages in binary code. If you're newcomer to MIDI, you may prefer not to read this just yet! On first sight it looks very 'technical' and important, but in fact you can still use MIDI to its fullest extent without even knowing that binary code exists! On the other hand, if you're a real techno-head you'll love it . . .

What Is Binary?

Binary code is MIDI's 'behind-the-scenes' way of working with both System and Channel messages. In all our normal dealings with numbers we use the **decimal** numbering system (otherwise known as 'base 10') which uses the figures 0 to 9 in various combinations. The figure we write as 14 denotes one lot of 10 plus four lots of 1. 253 represents two lots of 100, five lots of 10 and three lots of 1. We're all brought up with this counting system so we find it fits our uses perfectly.

Binary is otherwise known as 'base 2' and uses the figures 0 and 1. So, instead of indicating **x** lots of 10 or **x** lots of 100, a binary number consists of **x** lots of 2, **x** lots of 4, **x** lots of 8 and so on. So expressing the decimal number 14 in binary gives you:

128s	64s	32s	16s	8s	4s	2s	1s
0	0	0	0	1	1	1	0

so 14 in decimal equals 1110 in binary. The binary system fits a computer's uses perfectly because it has only to interpret a choice of two possible options for any parameter, 0 or **Off** and 1 or **On**. One binary figure (0 or 1) is called a '**bit**', short for BInary digiT.

Okay, So What's Binary Code Then?

Binary code is the form in which all these 0s and 1s are actually transmitted. A single bit contains too little information to be of much use by itself, so numbers are sent in groups of 8 bits called '**bytes**', which could look something like:

01010001

The bit which relates to the **1s** is referred to as the Least Significant Bit and the bit relating to the **128s** is the Most Significant Bit. In the example byte above, the Least Significant Bit is 1 and the Most Significant Bit is 0. The data is transmitted in order from the Most to the Least Significant Bit just as we write our hundreds before our tens.

A byte is made up of two 4-bit '**nibbles**' (what else?); in the above example these are 0 1 0 1 and 0 0 0 1.

Construction Of Channel Messages

As discussed in much simpler terms in the *Basic MIDI Events* sub-heading of **Viewing MIDI Events** (page 23), different types of channel message (note on/off, controllers, pitch-bend, etc.) each have different parameters to be set (i.e., *pitch* for a note, *controller number* and *value* for a control change and so on). Therefore, in the same way that your sequencer's edit facility shows a list of parameter settings for each event, a list of these same settings must be included in the event's binary counterpart.

The first byte of the message is called the '**status byte**' and consists of two distinct nibbles: it tells the tone-generator which of the five types of channel message it is (first nibble) and what channel it's on (second nibble). The system numbers the channels 0 to 15 so to enter a channel nibble to access channel 6, work out the binary version of 5 and enter that. Each type of channel message has its own code nibble (listed below). The status byte always has the Most Significant Bit set to 1 so the receiving device can tell it *is* a status byte. The following example shows the status byte for a Control Change Command on channel 6:

1 0 1 1 0 1 0 1

The first nibble (1 0 1 1) is the code for control changes; the second nibble (0 1 0 1) is 5 in binary (in case you didn't work it out earlier in the paragraph!) which corresponds to channel 6.

Following the status byte come the '**data bytes**'. Depending on the type of channel message it is, only one data byte may be required. Data bytes always have the Most Significant Bit set to 0. The two data bytes might, for example, be to tell the sound-generator to set control change 93 to 41. If so, the data bytes would look like this:

0 1 0 1 1 1 0 1   0 0 1 0 1 0 0 1

The first byte above is the Control Change Number (93) and the second is the value for it (41). As the Most Significant Bit is always 0 in a data byte, the highest number that can be transmitted is 127 $(64 + 32 + 16 + 8 + 4 + 2 + 1)$ which should sound familiar!

Channel Message Bytes

(MIDI channel nibble equals 1 in the following list.)

Message	Status Byte	1st Data Byte	2nd Data Byte
Note On	10010000	Pitch	Velocity
Note Off	10000000	Pitch	Velocity
Controller	10110000	Control Number	Value
Program Change	11000000	Patch Number	–
Poly Aftertouch	10100000	Pitch	Pressure
Channel Aftertouch	11010000	Pressure	–
Pitch-bend	11100000	MSB	LSB

Hey Big Bender!

As you can see, the data bytes for pitch-bend messages differ from the other types of message: they go back to all that acronym stuff! The reason for this is that pitch-bend requires a much higher resolution than other messages to make it bend smoothly.

So the pitch-bend message *combines* two data bytes which gives it a much larger possible field of values (16,384 in fact, compared to a paltry 128). It accomplishes this in a fairly simple way: as usual in data bytes, both bytes have a Most Significant Bit of 0, leaving two sets of 7 bits effectively adding up to a 14-bit message. The first byte contains the higher numbers (8192, 4096, 2048, 1024, 512, 256, 128) and is called the Most Significant Byte (**MSB**), while the second byte contains the lower numbers (64, 32, 16, 8, 4, 2, 1) and is referred to as the Least Significant Byte (**LSB**). The centre-point (no bend) is 8192, as shown in the example below:

    0 1 0 0 0 0 0 0   0 0 0 0 0 0 0 0

A Touch Too Much . . .

You'll notice there are two types of aftertouch, **Polyphonic** and **Channel**, one of which requires two data bytes, the other needing only one. Channel aftertouch uses one data-byte to express the *total pressure* on the keyboard at any time; Polyphonic aftertouch needs a byte containing the MIDI Note Number of the note in question, plus a second byte to express the pressure on that note.

Different tone-generators and keyboards have wildly differing implementations of aftertouch: some will transmit one or both or neither, some will not transmit either but can receive one or both, and some just look in the other direction and pretend it's not happening to them. As always, check your MIDI Implementation Chart for the specifics of your device.

Running Status

A related issue that does affect MIDI-users is that of 'Running Status'. As we've explained, every event you see in your sequencer's list-editor will be transmitted as a status-byte plus one or more data-bytes. For a long stream of continuous-controller events on a particular channel, therefore, an identical status-byte is being transmitted for each.

Running Status is a method of reducing the amount of data passing through the system by removing the status-byte from streams of identical message-types: in the above case, the tone-generator will go on interpreting incoming data-bytes as controller-messages until it receives a different status-byte.

Most of the time, you shouldn't be aware that this is happening. However, some older devices won't support Running Status so your sequencer will usually give you the option to turn it off.

Detours

➡ To see how the LSB and MSB relate to the MIDI channel messages, take a look at the **Controller Resolution, Pitch-Bend** and **Aftertouch** topics in the **Channel Messages Menu** (page 172).

Decimal/Hex Conversion Table

Decimal	Hex	Decimal	Hex	Decimal	Hex	Decimal	Hex
0	00H	32	20H	64	40H	96	60H
1	01H	33	21H	65	41H	97	61H
2	02H	34	22H	66	42H	98	62H
3	03H	35	23H	67	43H	99	63H
4	04H	36	24H	68	44H	100	64H
5	05H	37	25H	69	45H	101	65H
6	06H	38	26H	70	46H	102	66H
7	07H	39	27H	71	47H	103	67H
8	08H	40	28H	72	48H	104	68H
9	09H	41	29H	73	49H	105	69H
10	0AH	42	2AH	74	4AH	106	6AH
11	0BH	43	2BH	75	4BH	107	6BH
12	0CH	44	2CH	76	4CH	108	6CH
13	0DH	45	2DH	77	4DH	109	6DH
14	0EH	46	2EH	78	4EH	110	6EH
15	0FH	47	2FH	79	4FH	111	6FH
16	10H	48	30H	80	50H	112	70H
17	11H	49	31H	81	51H	113	71H
18	12H	50	32H	82	52H	114	72H
19	13H	51	33H	83	53H	115	73H
20	14H	52	34H	84	54H	116	74H
21	15H	53	35H	85	55H	117	75H
22	16H	54	36H	86	56H	118	76H
23	17H	55	37H	87	57H	119	77H
24	18H	56	38H	88	58H	120	78H
25	19H	57	39H	89	59H	121	79H
26	1AH	58	3AH	90	5AH	122	7AH
27	1BH	59	3BH	91	5BH	123	7BH
28	1CH	60	3CH	92	5CH	124	7CH
29	1DH	61	3DH	93	5DH	125	7DH
30	1EH	62	3EH	94	5EH	126	7EH
31	1FH	63	3FH	95	5FH	127	7FH

8

Troubleshooting Menu

This section attempts to help you unravel why it goes 'ping' when it should go 'bleep', why it goes in but it won't come out, or why it just won't go at all.

Bear in mind that extreme frustration and panic play havoc with your logic: some of this stuff will seem laughably obvious right now, but when it's still going 'ping' after two hours' fiddling you'll be glad of any help you can get!

■ Checklist

Got a problem? Take a look here first – this is a quickfire list of some of the most common causes, solutions and suggestions to point you in the right direction.

❑ For computer users, are you actually *running* your sequencing software?

❑ Is each device's power-switch turned on? If devices are connected in a chain, data won't pass *Thru* a device that isn't switched on.

❑ Are the master-volume knobs turned up?

❑ Are the MIDI cables correctly connected? (See **MIDI Setup Diagrams** on page 33).

❑ Is the amplifier turned on/headphones plugged in?

❑ Have you connected an audio lead to each device giving an audio output?

❑ Have you tried using different MIDI cables?

❑ Have you checked that nothing is muted that shouldn't be?

❑ Have you checked for *visual* indications that data is being transmitted (sequencer and tone-module displays)?

❑ Has a device been accidentally set to respond only to sync (MIDI Clock) messages?

❑ Is the sequencer's MIDI Thru (or MIDI Echo) activated?

❑ Have you tried connecting the MIDI-controller directly to the tone-generator (by-passing the sequencer)?

❑ Have you checked that your MIDI-controller is capable of transmitting this kind of data, and that your tone-generator is capable of responding to it?

❑ Have you tried transmitting the data on a different MIDI channel?

❑ Have you tried rechannelizing the sequencer track to a different MIDI channel?

❑ Have you checked the channel settings on the tone-generator?

❑ Have you got data for this channel on *another* track too? Maybe *that* track is causing the problem. Try mixing the two tracks down to one (temporarily) for a clearer view of *all* the channel's events.

❑ Have you checked the record and playback filters, and any track settings or playback parameters on the sequencer?

❑ Have you made sure the sequencer's output port you selected is the right one (i.e., it exists, there's something connected to it, etc.)?

❑ Have you checked your **Local Control** and **MIDI Mode** settings? (See pages 38 and 40 respectively.)

❑ Have you tried performing a *system reset* on the tone-generator, or hitting the *Panic* button on the sequencer or synth if they have one? (First make sure you note any settings you'll want later though!)

❑ Try removing add-ons (such as mergers, splitters, effects units) from the chain and trying again.

❑ Try turning off Running Status on your sequencer, especially if you're using an older tone-generator.

❑ Did you unplug (or plug in) a MIDI cable during sequencer recording or playback? If you're transmitting under Running Status, the receiving device may not now be receiving any status bytes.

Loading, Saving and Using Files

'I can't find the file'

❑ Is the correct disk in the drive?

❑ For computer users: have you selected the correct drive and path to the file?

❑ Have you selected the correct file extension (e.g., *.MID)? Try *.* to display *all* files.

'I can't load the file'

❑ Is the disk in the drive?

❑ For SMFs, is your sequencer *capable* of loading/importing Standard MIDI Files? If not, it won't do it however nicely you ask.

❑ Have you selected the correct file extension (eg *.MID)? Try *.* to display *all* files.

❑ *Can* your sequencer load files with that extension?

❏ Are you trying to load a sequencer-specific file into a different sequencer? It almost certainly won't work. Several sequencers may use the same extension (.SNG is an obvious example) but these are still incompatible.

❏ Has the file been assigned a *Read Only* status? Change the status of the file (or make a copy of the file and change the status of that).

❏ Has the file somehow just been saved as a name but no data? Check the file size. If it has, you're stuck!

❏ Are you trying to load it into a MIDI-file player or keyboard? Many of these devices will only read type 0 SMFs.

❏ Is it a type 1 SMF with more than 16 tracks? Some devices won't load the file at all; others will load only the first 16 tracks.

'The file is all on one track'

❏ It's probably a type 0 Standard MIDI file. It should play perfectly, but your sequencer might have a facility (such as *Remix* or *Split By Channel*) to split it up, creating new tracks with one channel's data on each. (Don't forget to mute or delete the original mixed track before playback.)

'This SMF has tempo-changes and/or track-names missing'

❏ Type 0 files don't contain track-names (they only have one track after all!). Some sequencers can't load track-names from a type 1 file either. In a General MIDI file you can look at the Program Changes to see which instrument is on each track, name the tracks yourself, and resave the file; or load the file into a different sequencer if you have that option.

❏ Some of the older sequencers (the kind that have trouble with track-names) have trouble with tempos too – they load only the first tempo of the song. Even some recent sequencers are a little unreliable with tempos when loading or saving type 0 files. If it matters, you'll have to insert your own and then save in a different file-format.

❏ Check you've got the tempo-track (or *Conductor/Mastertrack*) activated. Some software sequencers automatically turn it off when they load a Standard MIDI File.

'The *SMF* I just loaded sounds terrible!'

❏   For a type 0 file, check that the track isn't set to transmit on a particular MIDI channel – the rechannelize facility should be over-ridden because each event on the track contains *its own* channel setting.

❏   Check that no device in your setup has a *Transpose* function switched on.

❏   Check the pitch-bend range settings for any channel containing pitch-bend data (see below).

❏   Are you sure the file follows the same protocol you do?

'My MIDI-file player won't play my Standard MIDI File'

❏   You've probably fed it a type 1 file: a lot of MIDI-file players will only swallow a type 0.

'I've just played a file my friend gave me and it sounds all wrong!'

❏   The problem of *protocols* rears its ugly head. Possibly your friend gave you a General MIDI file and you don't have a GM tone-generator – use the **General MIDI Maps** (on page 61) and **Protocol Conversion** (page 289) to convert the program changes in the file to call up similar instruments in your own tone-generator. You might need to tweak the volumes and so on too.

❏   Presumably you've considered the possibility that your friend just isn't an awfully good programmer?

'All the pitch-bend in this file sounds wrong'

❏   Check the setting of the pitch-bend range (RPN #0) in the file and make sure the controllers are in the right order and on separate ticks.

❏   Does your tone-generator allow individual pitch-bend range settings for each channel? If a channel on the file uses a range you can't set, you might have to delete all the pitch-bend data for that channel.

■ Monitoring and Recording

The easiest way to solve problems concerning the MIDI input and output of data between devices is to remove links from the chain; for example, connect the master-keyboard directly to the module, by-passing the sequencer, and see if that does the trick. And don't forget to check the audio end of things (amplifier switched on, headphones plugged in, etc.) – because they're the least technical, it's easy to forget they're there!

'There's no sound from my slave instrument when I play to it via the sequencer'

❑ Have you made all the MIDI connections necessary? See **MIDI Setup Diagrams** on page 33.

❑ Have you made the necessary audio connections? And turned the amplifier on? Fed the meter?

❑ Check the sequencer to see if there's any data being received. If there isn't, check to see if a filter is set to ignore note-data. Check the sequencer's MIDI Thru is on. Try a different MIDI cable.

❑ Did you accidentally send a CC7:0 or CC11:0 which turned the channel volume down? Send :127s to fix this.

❑ Is the slave set to receive on a different MIDI channel? Try rechannelize on the sequencer. Try setting the slave to Omni On mode (see **MIDI Modes**, page 40).

❑ Have you selected the correct output port on the sequencer?

❑ Try playing a file from the sequencer to see if it responds to that.

'There's no sound from my multi-timbral synth when I play it through the sequencer'

❑ Check the obvious: is everything switched on? Are the MIDI connections correct? Is the volume turned up?

❑ Check the **Local Control** and MIDI Thru settings of your synth (see page 38).

❑ Check there are no sequencer input/output filters preventing the data *returning* to the synth.

❑ Did you accidentally send a CC7:0 or CC11:0 which turned the channel volume down? Send :127s to fix this.

❑ Check synth channels haven't been muted.

'There's no sound from the slave on some of the notes I play on the master-keyboard'

❑ Check that the keyboard isn't in *Split* mode with different areas assigned to different MIDI channels. Try connecting the keyboard directly to the slave to find out, or set rechannelize to Off/Any.

❑ Check your sequencer's *Remote Control* settings if it has this facility – you may be playing notes that have been set as function-keys instead.

❑ Make sure your slave device's channel settings aren't set to respond to a limited note-range – you might be playing notes outside this range.

'I'm getting no response from pitch-bend lever/modulation wheel/aftertouch, etc.'

❑ Check the input/output filters on your sequencer.

❑ Has your master-keyboard been set to not transmit this type of message?

❑ Has your tone-generator (or perhaps one channel on it) been set to *ignore* this type of message?

❑ Check Controller Remap – perhaps the controller has been mapped to something else. Try *recording* while using this controller and look at the result in *Edit* mode.

❑ Does your keyboard really send aftertouch? Does the slave device respond to it? (Check the MIDI Implementation Tables in your user-manuals).

'I'm getting no response at all from one particular MIDI channel'

❑ Has that channel's sequencer track been muted? Or the channel on your tone-generator?

❑ Have you accidentally sent a CC7:0 or CC11:0 on that channel? Try sending :127 values to raise them.

❑ Are you sure you're actually *sending* data to that channel?

❑ Has that channel been set up with no patch? Tone-generators using the bank-select/program-change combination won't have a patch in each of the two-million positions, and won't necessarily default to the *nearest* patch in these cases.

'The notes are playing on the wrong channel'

❏ Check the sequencer-track's rechannelize setting, or your MIDI-controller's transmit channel.

'It's not playing the sound I wanted'

❏ Are you transmitting on the correct channel and/or output port? Check the rechannelize setting of the track you're recording, or the transmit channel of your MIDI-controller.

❏ Have you accidentally sent a program change to it?

❏ Is there another track with data for the same channel on it? Perhaps that contains a rogue program change?

❏ Perhaps a different patch has been set as a playback-parameter rather than a program change event?

'The sound I'm playing seems very quiet'

❏ Have you sent a CC7 or a CC11 command turning it down by mistake?

❏ Is there another track with data for the same channel on it? Perhaps that's sending a CC7 or 11?

❏ Have you accidentally removed a CC11:127 (or not entered one) after performing a fade-out?

❏ Did you just playback a section of the file containing CC7 or 11 data and stop playback while it was being transmitted? Rewind and play the portion of the file containing the reset event. Turn on Chase Events.

❏ Have you set a track-parameter to reduce the velocities of all notes recorded and played back?

'When I play my synth through the sequencer I get a flanged sound'

❏ You probably have **Local Control** On when it should be Off (see page 38).

❏ Perhaps you're playing notes that have already been recorded for the same channel, causing retriggering.

'When I play my synth through the sequencer I hear two different sounds at once'

❑   As above, you probably need to turn Local Control off.

❑   Do you have a tone-generator in your setup that's receiving the data too?

❑   Have you accidentally switched your synth to a layer/stack/multi mode?

'All the notes I play are out of tune'

❑   Did you record a pitch-bend sweep earlier for this channel and stop the sequencer recording before releasing the pitch-bend lever? Or perhaps you accidentally removed the reset event. Enter the *zero* pitch-bend event in the right place. Or move the pitch-bend lever to reset the channel.

❑   Did you just play back a section of the file containing a pitch-bend sweep and stop the sequencer halfway through? Move the pitch-bend lever to reset the channel. Make sure Chase Events is activated if you have it.

❑   Check you haven't activated a transpose function on any device in your setup.

❑   Less likely, but perhaps you've accidentally entered the RPN controller for fine or coarse tuning instead of pitch-bend range? (see page 189).

❑   Perhaps you *are* playing all the wrong notes. Practise!

'All the notes I play have a vibrato effect'

❑   Is there another track with data for the same channel on it? Perhaps that's sending modulation (CC1) messages?

❑   Did you record a modulation sweep earlier for this channel and stop the sequencer recording before zeroing the modulation wheel? Or perhaps you accidentally removed the reset event. Enter the zero modulation event (CC1:0) in the right place. Or move the modulation wheel to reset the channel.

❑   Did you just play back a section of the file containing a modulation sweep and stop the sequencer halfway through? Move the modulation wheel to reset the channel. Make sure Chase Events is activated if you have it.

'The tone-generator won't respond to a program change message'

❏ Check that program changes aren't being filtered out by your sequencer or MIDI-controller.

❏ Are you sending a program change number higher than your tone-generator can respond to?

❏ Have you just changed to a bank that has no sound for this patch?

❏ Are you sending the program change on the channel you meant to?

'It won't respond to a bank select command'

❏ Are you sure the device *has* other banks of sounds?

❏ Is it set to *receive* bank select commands?

❏ Are you sending the correct control-changes? In the correct order and on separate ticks?

❏ Are you sending the bank select controllers on the channel you meant to?

❏ Check you're not sending a higher bank number than the tone generator can respond to.

❏ Have you tried sending a program-change? Usually the bank won't be seen to change until the program-change command is received.

❏ Is your device recent enough to have the MIDI Bank Select command implemented? (Post-August 1992.)

'The sequencer isn't recording anything'

❏ Check the MIDI connections.

❏ Have you selected a track (and channel if necessary) to record onto?

❏ Are you in *Record* mode?

❏ Have you specified a start and end position for the part you want to record? Check you haven't specified an illogical one (such as recording from bar 11 to bar 5).

❑ Check the input/output filters on the sequencer – perhaps all note data is being filtered out!

❑ Have you checked in *Edit*? Perhaps it *is* recording and you actually have a monitoring problem.

❑ See if it will go into *Play* mode – if not, it's probably waiting for sync messages from another device – turn off *External Sync*.

❑ For PC software sequencers: if it will play back a file but not record (and all the MIDI connections are okay) it could be that the interrupt (IRQ) setting of your MIDI interface is wrong.

'The sequencer isn't recording System Exclusive messages'

❑ Are you sure SysEx is really being sent?

❑ Does the unit require *handshaking*? This is a method of transferring data by two-way communication, a sort of 'Let me know when you've got it'/'I've got it, send the next bit' conversation.

❑ Is SysEx being filtered out by your sequencer's input/output filters?

❑ Are you in the correct mode for SysEx recording? Some sequencers have a specific 'area' for gathering SysEx rather than including it in the *List Editor*.

▓ Playback

There will obviously be a lot of crossover between the problems that can occur while recording and monitoring and those that happen when you play back the result. If you can't find the answer under this heading, take a look at the **Monitoring and Recording** topic.

If your sequencer has a facility to set playback parameters such as delay, compression, transpose and so on for individual tracks, search for the answer there first. These parameters usually don't affect the data you see in *Edit* mode, or have any effect on incoming data when you're recording, so they can be almost invisible!

'The sequencer won't play'

❑ Check you haven't set the sequencer to respond to sync messages from another device.

'I can see the sequencer is playing, but there's no sound'

❑ Is the master-volume knob turned up on your tone-generator?

❑ Have you specified the correct output port from the sequencer?

❑ Check output filters on the sequencer; receive filters on the tone-generator; any track or playback parameter settings you might have accidentally made on the sequencer.

❑ For PC software-sequencer users, check that the base-address setting of your MIDI interface is correct. It may also be that another application has 'stolen' control of the interface (even an application that you closed). Try restarting the computer.

❑ Did you temporarily unplug any MIDI cables during playback? If the sequencer transmits under Running Status the receiving device may now be 'confused'. Stop the sequencer, and restart from the beginning of the file.

❑ Has an empty track been accidentally set to *Solo*?

'One of the tracks won't play back'

❑ Check for CC7s and CC11s set to zero in the song header (or prior to the section you're playing).

❑ If this file doesn't have a *Reset* at the start, did you just play a file that had an un-reset fadeout at the end?

❑ Is the track muted? Or is another track soloed?

❑ Has its volume or expression been set to zero as a playback parameter?

❑ Have you accidentally muted that channel on your tone-generator?

❑ Does the track contain just System Exclusive, for example, that's being filtered out on playback?

❑ Is there data for the same channel on a different track that could be silencing this one?

'Notes keep disappearing suddenly or not playing at all'

❑ You might be trying to use more voices than the tone-generator can play. See **Polyphony Problems** on page 112.

❑ This might be an effect of retriggering – perhaps you've accidentally made a copy of the track (or part of it) on the same channel, or you may have some overlapping notes of the same pitch on that channel.

❑ Check you haven't set a *note-range* for the track or channel in any device – perhaps the track includes notes that fall outside the range.

'It keeps playing the same bit over and over'

❑ Sounds like you've turned on *Loop* or *Cycle* mode. Try turning it off again.

'Various types of data seem to be missing or occurring late'

❑ Assuming you can actually see them in the editor, check any output filters on the sequencers, and receive filters on the tone-generator.

❑ Check that no delay or volume/expression setting has been made as a playback parameter on any of the tracks.

❑ Are you using three or more tone-generators in a MIDI Thru chain? This can cause MIDI delays and data drop-out; this type of setup really needs a MIDI Splitter (see **Appendix One** on page 278).

'I'm getting hanging notes'

❑ Try using a different MIDI cable – an intermittent fault might prevent some *note-off* messages transmitting.

❑ Have you removed a *note-off* message while editing, or by splitting a pattern at a point where a note was sounding? Delete the *note-on*, reset the tone-generator, and step-enter a replacement.

❑ Perhaps your sequencer is transmitting under Running Status to a device that's not compatible – try disabling Running Status.

❑ Check for retriggering – if your sequencer has the facility, try to isolate all instances from that channel of the note that's hanging to see if any of them 'overlap'.

❑ Did you switch MIDI channels for the track during playback? If so, the *note-on* would be on one channel and the *note-off* on another so the note on the original channel wouldn't have been switched off.

❑ You might have left a sustain-pedal *on* message (CC64:127) for that channel somewhere.

❑ Has a rogue sostenuto pedal (CC66:127) crept into the file?

'Playback seems erratic but there's no identifiable pattern to it'

❑ Try disabling Running Status if your sequencer uses it.

❑ Try a different MIDI cable – it could be an intermittent fault.

❑ Do you have more than three receiving devices in the chain? Too many – you need a MIDI splitter!

'My reverb/chorus/pan (etc.) setting is having no effect'

❑ Did you step-enter the control-change? Check you've entered the *right* one!

❑ Is the setting being over-ridden by a playback parameters setting?

❑ Is the control-change event being transmitted on the correct channel?

❑ Are you sure your tone-generator supports this controller?

'All the sounds are wrong'

❑ Have you selected the wrong bank, or sent a Bank Select command by mistake?

❑ Check whether your sequencer uses the 0–127 or 1–128 patch-numbering system – maybe you've just copied the patch numbers from a patch-list and your sequencer's method requires you to subtract one from each number.

'The continuous controllers sound jerky'

❑ Have you accidentally quantized controller or pitch-bend data? A few sequencers allow this. Have a look at the data in *Edit* mode – you may still be able to *undo* the quantization.

❑ Did you record the data at a faster tempo than you're now playing it back? This will highlight any irregularities in your use of the wheel or fader.

'One of the tracks is out of tune'

❑ Check there's no 'hanging' pitch-bend event at the beginning.

❑ Did you just playback a section of the file containing a pitch-bend sweep and stop the sequencer halfway through? Move the pitch-bend lever to reset the channel. Make sure Chase Events is activated if you have it.

❑ Check you haven't activated a transpose function on any device in your setup, or as a playback parameter.

❑ If this file doesn't have a *Reset* at the start, did you just play a file that had an un-reset bend at the end?

❑ Check you haven't used RPN #1 or #2 (fine or coarse tuning) somewhere on that track.

'I've just listened to the file I saved as a SMF and things are going wrong'

❑ Did the original have any muted tracks in it? Some sequencers include that data; most don't.

❑ Did the original have settings made on the playback parameters section? On some sequencers you have to specify that these settings should be included in the saved SMF.

❑ Did you convert your ghost patterns to normal patterns first, if your sequencer requires it?

❑ Check the original for retriggering – sometimes this doesn't show up until you save as a SMF.

❑ Check for two conflicting events on the same tick (or consecutive ticks) such as CC7:0 and CC7:100 – unnecessary or daft data can occasionally slip through the editing net and not cause a problem, but the SMF conversion process can occasionally change positions of events as can *Mixdown*.

❑ If you're hearing a flanging or doubling effect from a track, check the original to make sure that you didn't accidentally copy a pattern over the top of itself, or change a track's channel to one already in use. Check the *Local Control* setting of your synth – for sequencer playback of a file *Local Control* should be off to prevent creating a loop through the sequencer's MIDI Thru making the synth play the notes twice.

'There are timing glitches in the file'

❑ Have you used program change commands during the song-body? These may be occurring too close to note-data on the same channel – program changes may take a few ticks (and sometimes a good deal longer) to 'kick in'.

❑ Is the music heavily quantized? This could be causing heavy MIDI traffic and delays. Try manually moving notes so there are fewer events on the first tick of each beat. See the **Time-Shifting** heading on page 105.

❑ Does the file contain a lot of continuous controller data? Try using *Thin* or *Reduce Continuous Controllers*.

'The System Exclusive messages aren't working'

❑ Are you sure they're correct? Check the device number and checksum especially.

❑ Have you altered the *value* section of the message and not changed the checksum (if your device uses one)?

❑ Check the transmit filter to make sure SysEx messages aren't being filtered out.

❑ Check that the receiving device is set to receive SysEx messages.

Editing

'I can't see the data I just recorded even though it plays okay'

❑ Have you turned on a visual-editing filter (or *mask*) that stops you seeing particular types of event?

❑ Are you trying to look at it in the wrong *Editor*?

'When I use Paste, nothing happens'

❑ Have you *Copied* or *Cut* something first? Try copying the data again.

❑ Have you specified the correct position for the pasted data? Perhaps it's putting it somewhere out of view!

❑ Have you *masked* the particular event type in the editor since you copied or cut?

'When I turned up all the velocities on a track, I lost the dynamic variation'

❑ Did you check the available headroom? If some of the notes were already on 120 and you turned everything up 20, these notes will only go up 7 and then stop, so the balance between these and quieter notes will change.

'I can't enter a negative delay on a track'

❏ A negative delay (moving all the notes so they occur earlier) will only work if there's somewhere to move them to. If the first note occurs on 1.1.0 it can't happen earlier.

❏ Do you have a header-bar or count-in bar? Don't include these in the delay setup.

'When I quantized a track, some of the notes moved the wrong way'

❏ Did you select the correct note-value for the quantization? Your eighth-note may have been dead on the eighth-note beat, but if you specified a quarter-note quantize value it'll move onto (or towards) a quarter-note beat.

❏ If your timing was particularly iffy, the nearest beat which is 'pulling' the note may not be the beat you were aiming for. It pays to look at note-position in *Edit* before you quantize. Too much bad timing can make it tough to work out what went where afterwards!

'When I quantized a track, the lengths of the notes changed too'

❏ Consult your sequencer's manual on this one. You probably have two similar types of quantize which both move the *note-on* onto the beat, but one will move the *note-off* position by the same amount and the other, as in this case, will leave it where it is.

'When I quantized a track, the notes hardly moved'

❏ If you're using a *Partial Quantize*, the strength is probably set to too low a percentage.

❏ Perhaps the notes are already so close to the beat that *Partial Quantize* can't have much effect.

❏ Are the notes already fully quantized?

'When I quantized a track, the whole feel changed'

❏ Check to see if you had a *Swing* percentage other than 50% entered in the quantize settings.

❑ Did you accidentally select a tripletized note-value instead of a straight one, or vice-versa?

❑ Did you accidentally select *Groove* quantize?

'I've just turned up all the volume controllers in the header and the balance is wrong'

❑ Did you just turn them all up to 127? If they weren't all the same to begin with, then making them all the same will change the relative balance of all the instruments. See the *Raise The Volumes* heading on page 88.

'The Unmute command doesn't work'

❑ On some sequencers you can enter *Mute* events into a track to silence it for a while. If you put the *Unmute* events on the same track it can't possibly work because the track is now muted. Keep these events on a separate track.

'The tempo changes aren't having any effect'

❑ Make sure you've actually activated the tempo track (or *Conductor/Mastertrack*), or it's not been muted.

'The tempo changes have moved!'

❑ Have you just entered a change of time-signature at a position earlier than some or all of the tempo events?

❑ Have you used a global cut/remove or insert to shove a few extra bars in somewhere? Usually you'll want the tempo-events to move in this situation, but it is an explanation!

'I just transposed the song and the drum-track's gone wrong!'

❑ Sounds like you transposed the drum-track too so that all the notes are now playing on different kit-instruments. Transpose this track back again!

▓ How Do I . . . ?

'How do I clean up a track full of retriggering?'

❑ If it's a drum-track, shorten all the note-lengths to about 4 ticks (this is always worth doing anyway – prevention is better, etc!).

❑ Use a visual-editing filter or mask to select notes one by one and work your way through to see if any of them overlap (bearing in mind that a single tick's overlap does as much damage as a whole beat!).

❑ If the track consisted of a lot of copied/pasted patterns, number all the different patterns and make a list of the order and/or position they occur on the track. Delete doubles so that you're left with one of each, and once they're tidied up you can string the track back together again.

> NB – you probably discovered the retriggering after saving as a SMF, playing the file back and hearing staccato blips where once were long legato notes. Always use the original (sequencer-song format) file unless you're happy to go through the SMF lengthening all the 'blip' notes as well!

'How can I hear the sound I'm recording as I play the part?'

❑ Set up the required channel of your tone-generator with the right sound, and pick a sequencer track to record on. Then rechannelise the track to match the channel you just set up on your tone-generator, make sure your sequencer's MIDI Thru (or MIDI Echo) is on, and play.

'How can I stop the sequencer recording aftertouch / pitch-bend (etc.) data?

❑ Most sequencers have some form of event filter system to let you choose which types of event should be ignored either on input, output or both.

❑ Alternatively, prevent your MIDI-controller sending a particular data-type – it may have a similar filter.

❑ Stop mucking about with the pitch-bend lever.

'How do I make a Standard MIDI File?'

❑ To start with, your sequencer must support Standard MIDI File format. If it does, select *Export MIDI* or *Save.MID* or something similar. You might be asked whether you want to save as a type 0 or a type 1 file: you usually want to save as a type 1 unless you intend to playback the file from a hardware MIDI-file player or a keyboard with a built-in disk-drive. If you save as both type 0 and type 1, make sure you give them slightly different names to prevent the second save overwriting the first!

'How can I input a pan-sweep when I've only got a volume-slider?'

❏ You need to do a spot of controller-remapping. You call it a 'volume-slider' because it sends out CC7 data by default, but it can probably be set to send out different controller-data. You could check out your keyboard's manual to see if it can be made to transmit a different controller (CC10 in this case). Alternatively, your sequencer will probably have a similar feature and it's often much easier to locate and alter. In this case, before recording and echoing data to its soft-thru, the sequencer will convert all incoming CC7 events to CC10 (or whatever you choose).

❏ If you find yourself in the unusual position of having neither of these options, just record a 'volume-sweep' instead, and then change all the recorded CC7 events to CC10s. Your sequencer should have a facility to do this for you automatically – if it doesn't do this either, you really do need a new sequencer!

'How do I switch off hanging notes?'

❏ Hit your sequencer or synth's *Panic* button if it has one.

❏ Play the offending note on your MIDI-controller then let go, thus sending it the *note-off* it's waiting for.

❏ If you can't tell which note it is, play as many notes as you can at once and let them go: you might strike lucky and find the right one (as in the point above) or, failing that, you might use up all of the tone-generator's polyphony so that it has to 'steal' the voice being used by the hanging-note.

❏ Turn your tone-generator off and then on again (noting any settings you'll need later, of course).

❏ Try pressing and releasing the sustain pedal (or sending a CC64:000) in case this is the cause, and check for sustain-pedal *On* messages left 'hanging'.

❏ Try the same thing for the sostenuto pedal (CC66).

'How can I find out if a certain note or controller occurs anywhere on a track?'

❏ If your sequencer has a visual-editing filter or mask facility, step-write the required event at the start of the file and then mask it so that only this event type is visible – if there are any more, you'll see them. (Don't forget to delete the 'test' event afterwards!)

❏ If your sequencer has a mathematical editor such as Cubase's *Logical Edit* or Notator's *Transform*, make a copy of the track and use this editor to delete all data that doesn't fit the description. (Once you know, remember to delete the unnecessary track.)

'How do I get my drum-machine to run in time with my sequencer?'

❏ Set your sequencer to transmit MIDI Clock (or *Internal Sync*) and your drum-machine to receive MIDI Clock (or *External Sync*), connect your sequencer's MIDI Out to your drum-machine's MIDI In and set your drum-machine to *Play* mode. When you start your sequencer, the drum-machine should start too (and keep time!). Keep an eye out for Running Status problems – if playback seems erratic turn off Running Status on the sequencer.

'How can I use my drum-machine as a tone-generator?'

❏ Find out which MIDI Note Numbers are mapped to each drum-sound in your drum-machine (and keep a list of these). Set your drum machine to receive on channel 10, and mute channel 10 on any other receiving devices in the chain. Then construct your drum-parts in your sequencer on channel 10 as usual, but watch out for possible Running Status problems.

> NB – (1) If your drum-machine lets you, it would be wise to remap all its internal sounds to the General MIDI map (see page 62) so that you can also playback GM files with it if you wish to.
> (2) Many older drum-machines are missing that useful ingredient, the MIDI Thru socket, which means they have to be placed at the end of your chain of devices (never a good place for drum-sounds). If this is the setup you want to use, consider investing in a MIDI splitter (see page 279).

'How do I get rid of MIDI delay and note-glitching?'

❏ Ease the MIDI traffic on the first tick of bars and beats by moving notes slightly backward or forward. If you have a few fully quantized tracks, try moving one back 2 ticks and another forward 2 ticks. Or use playback parameters to apply a 2 tick delay to one and a *negative* 2 tick delay to another.

❑ Ease MIDI traffic by using *Reduce* or *Thin Continuous Controllers* – continuous data clogs up the system and is never needed in quite the quantities that get recorded.

❑ Check the positions of any Program Change commands within the song body – if they occur too close to a note on the same channel there may be an apparent timing glitch.

❑ If there are more than three receiving devices in your chain, this could cause severe data-transmission problems. Invest in a MIDI splitter straight away!

'How do I record a lead-solo on a MIDI guitar?'

❑ Set your MIDI-guitar to Mode 4 (see **MIDI Modes**, page 40). Pick 6 channels on your tone-generator (or one for each string you'll use) and set them up with the same sound, volume, etc., and (usually) a pitch-bend range of ± 12 semitones. Select and configure *Multitrack Record* on your sequencer to record each channel onto a separate track, set your guitar to transmit each string on the chosen channel and start recording. If your sequencer doesn't have *Multitrack Record*, just record it all to one track (set rechannelize to *Off* or *Any*) and use *Remix* or *Split By Channel* to separate the data afterwards.

> NB – watch out for the unnecessary pitch-bend data MIDI-guitars chuck out. This can usually be seen in a Graphic Editor as almost continuous low-value events. These should be deleted to reduce the MIDI traffic, or you could just filter out pitch-bend messages if you don't need any at all.

'How can my buddy and I record ourselves playing live?'

❑ To start with, you need a MIDI Merger to combine the two signals and send them to the same device without any data corruption. Set your MIDI-controllers to transmit on different MIDI channels, and set up the two channels as you want them on the tone-generator. Select and configure *Multitrack Record* (see previous entry) and start recording.

'How can I use two devices without MIDI Thru sockets in my system?'

❑ If you have a single device with no MIDI Thru, this must obviously be the last device in the 'chain'. To connect two such devices to your system, you'll need a MIDI Splitter to send a signal to at least one of the devices directly. Many older drum-machines tend to be missing the Thru socket – to prevent the possibility of data delays and glitching it's a good idea to avoid placing a drum-machine at the end of a chain, and a splitter is a worthwhile acquisition. Many of the original MIDI-equipped effect and vocal-harmony devices were also lacking in the Thru socket department.

'How do I get more volume out of a particular channel?'

❑ Assuming you've got the note-on velocities maximised, CC7 at value 127 in the song-header, and CC11 running at value 127 (apart from occasional fades, etc.), the simplest thing to do is reduce the CC7 values for all the other channels. Adding chorus to a sound, or giving it a more extreme pan-position can make it more noticeable which may be as good as a volume-rise. Another possibility is to try double-tracking the sound (see page 129).

Detours

➡ For more hints and tips take a look at the next section, **The Big Idea**.

9

The Big Idea

Once in a while, we all come across a situation where we think How can I make it do that? or There must be a better way to do this, or maybe we're just looking for something a bit different. This section provides a 'quick-search' reference for tips, suggestions and ideas by gathering together a few points mentioned in some of the topics and adding a bunch of new ones. The section is loosely organised so that the functional stuff comes first, gradually giving way to the useful, the interesting, and the unashamedly wacky.

For ideas gathered from earlier topics just a brief description and a page reference is given. All the extra bits and pieces not previously covered are explained in full. Remember to take a look at section 4: **Tricks and Effects** on page 124 for more ideas.

■ Practical

❑ Make a point of learning computer-keyboard shortcuts or hot-keys on the synth-keyboard (page 87) as a massive time-saver.

❑ Use a repeated drum-pattern as a metronome – even a fully quantized 8s pattern gives you a better feel to work from than a 'straight-4' metronome click. Try saving a few useful one-bar drum-patterns for this purpose.

❑ If your sequencer has a *Notepad* or *Text Insert* option, use it to save information about the file similar to that mentioned in the Written Notes? heading on page 91. Remember this will be saved only in sequencer-song format though.

❑ If you're using a non-General MIDI device that doesn't have a SysEx reset (or you don't know what it is), use a collection of resetting controllers to do the same job for each channel. To cover all bases, use CC120:0, CC121:0, CC1:0, CC64:0, CC65:0, pitch-bend 0:64 (centre) in addition to the usual controllers included in the header-bar. To save the hassle of entering these every time, save this as a sequencer songfile (or as part of your Preferences file) to load up every time you start work.

❑ Try recording a melody-track early on or create empty patterns named after sections of the song (see page 85) to act as a guide to your position in the song as you move around it.

❑ Avoid the occasional problem of poor sample scaling across the instrument's range by using pitch-bend or coarse-tuning (see p. 171).

❑ Stamp personal details on a file: since drum-instrument lengths don't matter, use the lengths to enter your phone number (using 10 to replace 0) or your name (using 1–26). Pick a regular point in every file to do this, for example the 23rd drum note onwards. This can act as a useful method of identifying a file as your own work in case of argument. (Of course, to make this unnoticeable to others, you'll have to 'randomize' *all* the lengths.)

❑ Keep a library of useful programming effects and tricks (such as pitch-bend slides, crossfades, drumrolls, etc.) to import to a song whenever you need them.

❑ Use a 5-letter + 3-number naming/numbering system for files to prevent later files having the same name, and to keep track of the order in which you programmed them (p. 90).

❑ If your header-bars always seem to be chock full of controllers, NRPNs and short SysEx strings, try making all these settings in the tone-generator(s) directly and then performing a bulk dump to the sequencer to replace the standard song-header (see pp. 112 and 228).

❏ If you're struggling along with a low-resolution sequencer (i.e., 24, 48 or 96 tpq), the timing can sound a bit stilted at slow tempi. Try recording the song at double tempo, effectively doubling your sequencer's timebase. Editing becomes a little harder (one bar will now be split across two), but this can be eased a little by doubling the time-signature to 8/4 instead of 4/4. This way, one beat is split across two, but bar-numbers are still accurate.

❏ Make sure your speaker placement lets you hear a representative mix (see p. 73).

❏ Remember that you can use your MIDI file to control external effects, lighting, harmonisers, etc. (see p. 283), and to change your Local Control setting if your live setup uses synth and modules (p. 186).

❏ Start the sequencer recording at least a bar before you need to play in order to maximise the feel and prevent timing glitches (see p. 106).

❏ Try piecing together a tricky section of music by recording and keeping several takes and using parts from each to create the finished article. Try ignoring elements such as continuous controllers and overdubbing them later (see the 'Tough Stuff' heading on p. 83).

❏ When recording fast, technically challenging lines, try simplifying the notes you play to something more manageable – in this way you can get the right feel into the recording and then edit the notes themselves.

❏ Avoid using Program Changes in the song-body (see pp. 199–200).

❏ Try using a cheap set of drum-pads to enter your rhythm parts with more typical feel and velocity variations. This can also make rolls and flams easier to program (with a little practice!).

❏ Save your file with different names (such as 001, 002) while experimenting with different ideas so that you can return to a previous version any time you want to.

❏ Make sure you've always got some formatted floppy-disks handy if you're not using a hard-drive system!

❏ If your sequencer's metronome has a pre-roll option, it's worth using: it gives a less irritating countdown than a metronome click and helps you to start playing with suitable feel and dynamics.

❑ Use ghost patterns (p. 86) when working with double-tracking, delays, layers and echoes to make sure that the tracks containing the effect stay identical to the main track. You can usually use playback parameters to change their time-positions, velocities, etc.

❑ Consider whether you (or your end-user) will be playing the file back in stereo; if not, pan settings and effects will be lost. Will that make a big difference to the file? Try playing it in mono to see what result this has.

❑ If you're using a MIDI-guitar to enter your data (especially rhythm-guitar parts), filter out pitch-bend messages either from the guitar or the sequencer end.

❑ If you've got a drum-machine in your setup, try to make sure it's the first device in the chain: if any MIDI delays or timing glitches occur, they'll be more noticeable on the drum-parts than anything else.

❑ If you use a pattern-based sequencer, try to save a finished version of the song with the patterns still intact before you mix down any tracks – it makes any later re-editing much easier.

❑ Always carry type 0 Standard MIDI File format backups of your files for live work, whatever type of file player or MIDI setup you use (see the '*MIDI File Player*' heading on page 283).

❑ If there are any SysEx strings or NRPN settings you use regularly in your files, try saving them on a separate (muted) track in your preferences file. You can then just copy and paste the ones you need rather than entering the events from scratch.

❑ Make sure your left and right audio connections from tone-generator to amplifier and speakers are correct: if they're not, your pan-positions and effects will be reversed.

❑ Remember that track-names in a type 1 file don't have to be instruments. You could enter your name, a copyright marking, a good (if short) recipe, anything. Some file-players and keyboards display the name of track 1 when they play a file, so you could name track 1 with the song's title.

❑ Try setting up the tone-generator (by setting up the song-header and then playing it) before you start recording, at least to get the correct patch for each channel, and name each track so that you know what's where. It sometimes helps to make an educated guess at the

effect and pan settings too before recording on a new channel so that
you can hear a reasonably mixed sound as you play.

❑   Make sure you keep your safety copies and backups in different
places, and always keep them write-protected and well away from
magnets, speakers, mobile phones, thieves, etc. (see p. 91).

❑   If you're thwarted by having only two different conga sounds, or
only one clave, try using pitch-bend to re-pitch some of the hits
higher or lower. Bear in mind that pitch-bend will affect the *whole*
drums channel though – to get around this you'll have to move the
necessary hits a couple of ticks away from other notes to allow room
to insert the pitch-bend events before and after them.

❑   Remember that no other events should be transmitted at the same
time as SysEx. For short strings this can just be a case of ensuring
there are no other events occurring *on that tick*, but for longer strings
and bulk dumps you'll have to leave the way clear. Nothing
disastrous happens of course, but much of the channel data sent will
be ignored (note data usually glitches outrageously) and some of the
SysEx elements may also be ignored or misunderstood.

❑   Some devices are more forgiving than others in their handling of
data: if your file begins with a hefty SysEx bulk-dump and time
matters to you (for example in live performance) try setting a faster
tempo for the period this data is being transmitted to reduce the
time-span between each string. Check that everything is being
received correctly before committing yourself to this method, and
keep an eye on the receiving device's screen for error messages
during transmission.

❑   Select a different time-signature for a header consisting of a SysEx
bulk-dump: if the SysEx is spread over 9 beats set the time-signature
for the first bar to 9/4 so that your count-in can take place
immediately afterwards rather than having to wait until the start of
the next 4/4 bar.

❑   Avoid using a SysEx bulk-dump wherever possible: apart from
containing a host of settings you've probably left at their defaults, the
dump will also contain settings for all 16 channels when your song
might use only 8 – all this adds unnecessary length and time to the
header. Try to track down the SysEx strings you really need, and use
them in combination with channel messages (which are, after all,
much easier to edit if you change your mind about a particular
setting).

■ Effective

❏ Instead of copying identical short phrases one after the other, try one of the methods on pages 101 and 102 to give a more spontaneous effect.

❏ If you're limited to the General MIDI sound-set and kit, create an electronic kit by doubling kick, snare and toms with the synth-drum patch (#119). For best effect the pitch of the notes will have to span three or four octaves. This can give great results on 'round-the-kit' tom fills, especially if you give each synth-drum its own pan position and spread them out widely.

❏ To get more 'bite' or brightness into a sound but still keep it quiet, maximise its note-velocities and use CC11 (or CC7 in the song-header) to balance it.

❏ Try using a slap-bass patch just for the slap effects (p. 165).

❏ To get a greater range of velocities from a particular sound, try the idea on page 186 using a mixture of double-tracking and compression/expansion techniques.

❏ Instead of adding to the volume or velocities of a slightly quiet sound, try giving the channel a more extreme pan position or adding chorus to it (or both).

❏ Synth- and slap-bass patches can often make good general synth sounds when played a few octaves higher than usual, particularly in chorded parts.

❏ Experiment with cutoff frequency as a real-time controller (by setting up the correct NRPN 99 and 98 values and remapping a fader or wheel to CC6 Data Entry). This can give a great wah-guitar effect, and you can create types of gate-effect that change the tone instead of the volume.

❏ Try using pitch-bend on congas or toms to create a tabla or 'talking-drum' sound (see p. 171).

❏ Use RPN #1 (fine-tuning) for a detuned or chorused effect. This can be good with double or triple tracking, and makes a far more believable 'home-made' string or brass ensemble .

❏ Use CC11 Expression as a type of on-going swell-pedal in sustained sounds such as strings, pads, choirs and organ (see p. 214).

❑ When the file is finished, try adding about 30% to all the pan positions, widening the field, and see what you think.

❑ Try experimenting with some of the effect parameters other than depth: the default settings are okay, but they can't possibly be the best settings for every style of music. Take a look at pages 217–21.

❑ Moving the whole drum and bass tracks forward a tick or two can do wonders for a file that's supposed to drive but doesn't (see p. 125).

❑ Thicken a drum-part by moving other kit-instruments away from the snare hits: handclap works well placed two ticks earlier, tambourine 2 ticks later, hi-hat one tick later. All these work best if you first move the snare forward a tick or so.

❑ Try using small step-entered spikes of pitch-bend to create changes of pitch of individual drum and cymbal hits, or to imitate vibrato and tremolo in tuned instruments more effectively than by using modulation (pp. 147 and 167).

❑ Watch out for slow attack sounds: if they start on the first tick of the bar they can give a dragging feel (p. 127).

Unusual

❑ Try using synth sound-effects instead of (or as well as) drum hits (p. 170).

❑ Instead of spending time setting the exact note-lengths for smooth rhythm-guitar parts, try just shortening all the notes to a manageable size (e.g., 4 ticks) and inserting CC64 sustain-pedal events. This can actually give an even smoother result though it might tend to swallow a little extra polyphony and damage your street-cred as a programmer if anyone looks!

❑ Try adding a pitch-bend or coarse-tuning event to the drum-kit to move it up or down in pitch a little: you can get some great industrial sounds by bending it down 24 semitones.

❑ When applying echoes to a single-line part, try transposing them into arpeggiated steps. For example, an E3 (in a C major chord) could echo to G3, C4, E4, etc. Or set them to alternating octaves (E4, E3, E4 . . .).

❑ If your line is slow enough to let you fit in more than half a dozen echoes, try detuning each one (using RPN #1) so that the echoes gradually fall in pitch, similar to a siren effect.

❑ If you can use two drumkits (or your single kit isn't already in action), try copying a trumpet or brass line and assigning it to the drumkit channel (with the velocities reduced) as a layer effect. Since your trumpet line will be fairly high-pitched, this should trigger various latin-percussion instruments in time with your horn-line giving a fun 'festival' sound.

❑ Set up a sound that has a fairly long release phase, and hit a loud chord with CC11 at a low setting and fade it up as the chord dies away. Losing the attack phase of a percussive sound can give unexpected results – try it with an acoustic or electric piano patch. Combining this with pitch-bend can be eerie.

❑ Fade a long-release or sustained sound in or out rhythmically, similar to a gate-effect – see p. 134.

❑ Try applying tonguing techniques (p. 162) to instruments that don't quite deserve it. Good candidates are calliope, voice 'doo' sounds, and breathier synth sounds. Treating these like real acoustic instruments can give amusing and brain-teasing results.

❑ Another teaser is to 'strum' a percussive sound such as xylophone, harp or pizzicato strings in the style of a rhythm-guitar.

❑ Double-track a rhythmic (but not too chorded) guitar or keyboards part, pan the two tracks hard left and right and harmonise the notes of one with the other. At a slow or medium tempo with parts based around eighth-notes, this can give beautiful results.

❑ Create a 'wide' keyboard or guitar spanning the entire stereo field (if you've got sufficient reserves of channels and patience) – see p. 212.

❑ Try using various types of percussive patch instead of bass-guitar on softer ballad or new-age styles: pizzicato, vibes and voice doos are a few effective examples.

❑ To get more oomph out of the kick-drum, layer it with short, low-pitched notes using a sine-wave patch. If your tone-generator doesn't have a sine-wave, choose a clear sound like piccolo or whistle and edit out any vibrato and harmonic elements.

❑ Try setting up echoes and delays to play on different patches from the original part. Or use CC74 Brightness or cutoff frequency/resonance (usually via NRPNs) to change the tonal characteristics of the patch so that as the note echoes and dies away, each hit is brighter than the last.

❑ Create pan-positions to match the pitch of a single-line melody: copy all the notes and convert them to pan (CC10) events keeping the values the same as the note numbers. (Remember to move these events forward a tick or two so that they occur before the notes each time.) This works best with fast moving, meandering melodies, though you could manually widen the pan range covered.

❑ The above idea can produce strange results if you use CC1 Modulation instead of Pan so that as the melody rises the modulation increases.

Experimental

❑ Try moving a drum-track forward by a quarter-note; heard against a steady rhythmic backing a drum rhythm can sound completely different if you move its accents like this, and might give you a few ideas for new drum patterns and rhythms. This is especially worth trying with 'add-on' percussion parts such as conga patterns.

❑ Transpose all the notes in a drum-track up a semitone and see what the same rhythm sounds like played on different kit-instruments. Or try transposing it up an octave or two to hear the rhythm played at the latin-percussion end of the kit.

❑ When using echoes, try experimenting with rhythms: for example, if you have a 16th-note brass stab at the beginning of the beat, echo it with three 16th-notes followed by three 8th-note triplets and then two 8th notes, so the echoes are gradually getting further apart.

❑ An odd way of creating 'rhythms' is to use CC1 Modulation like a gate-effect instead of Expression – see p. 208.

❑ Try double-tracking (and panning hard left and right) bass and drums parts. This obviously requires two identical drumkits, and the sound will need a fair bit of filling out in the centre, usually with rhythmic keyboards or guitar and pad.

❑ Try transposing a hi-hat line to play on toms. For example, change open-hats to high-tom, closed-hats to mid-tom and pedal-hats to low. If the hats contained wide enough velocity differences this can sound superb. For more usable results, transpose them to mute and open triangles or congas. Deleting hits here and there can lead you to effective percussion rhythms to lay over the top of the existing hats part.

❑ Try doubling or halving the tempo of rhythm tracks, especially drums and bass. (Some sequencers have an automatic facility to do this for you.) This gives a song a whole new feel, and you'll probably hate it, but it could give you some ideas for a different song.

❑ Many sequencers have a *randomize* function which can be applied to velocities, timing, lengths, MIDI note-numbers and so on. Unless you can set particular ranges or parameters for it, it can be very random indeed but it can still be useful for creating effects – we humans find it very difficult to randomize things deliberately!

❑ If you're able to set up two drumkits, double-track your drum-part and try one of these: Transpose one of the parts to make it play different instruments (perhaps in the latin-percussion section of the drumkit patch). Try applying pitch-bend or coarse-tuning (RPN #2) to the parts to raise the pitch of one and lower the other. Finally, time-shift one of the parts by a tick to get a constantly 'thicker' sound from the drums. (Watch out for the cymbals when you do this – you're likely to get a flanging effect when you double up the kits – see p. 130.)

❑ Some sequencers have a *Reverse* function (sometimes called 'Retrograde') which is pretty much custom-built for experimentation: it takes all the selected events and puts them in reverse order. For melodic parts this can lead you to new melody ideas, but it's the rhythmic parts (especially drums and short percussive patches) that can really lead to new discoveries. It's a useful tool to apply to controller fades and sweeps as well. As far as notes are concerned, it usually gives best results when applied to short sections of up to about 4 bars.

❑ If your sequencer has a mathematical editor (such as *Cubase's* Logical Edit or *Notator's* Transform) try using the *multiply* and *divide* functions. Once again, these are really included as experimental devices but they can produce interesting results when applied to note-numbers or pan sweeps. If you use *multiply*, choose your multiplier carefully to avoid 'going off the end' of the 0–127 scale. *Divide* can be useful to compress note-velocities or continuous controllers' values, and *multiply* will expand them.

❑ Try using CC10 pan in the same way as a gate-effect to create rhythmic jerky movements of a sustained sound around the stereo field (if you have Dynamic Panning – see p. 212).

❑ Treating drumkits in the same way as other instruments can produce some strange results. If your tone-generator has a range of drumkits, try assigning your drum-part to two different kits (effectively creating a layered effect as you might with a tuned lead-line). Similarly you could apply various crossfade techniques (see p. 135) between the different kits. Another effective trick is the 'kit in the concert hall' – use two identical kits for this and pan one slightly left at normal volume. Apply a delay of perhaps 5 or 6 ticks (depending on tempo) to the other, reduce its volume drastically and pan it hard right.

▨ Biblical

Scattered throughout the book is a variety of dos and don'ts, points to note and exhortations of care. These may be for your own good as a programmer, the benefit of users of your files or the promotion of MIDI generally. This topic gathers the most important of them together in one place as a kind of 'bottom-line'. Of course, these rules are not carved in stone. But some of them probably should be.

The Ten Commandments

1 MIDI files are music created *with* a computer, not *by* a computer. Even many professional programmers fail to spot the distinction.

2 Judge results by *sound* not *sight*. No-one wants to sit down with a glass of wine and look at your list-editor.

3 Don't use global commands such as 100% quantize, or fix velocities. Unless you're sure you want a synthetic effect it's far better to use smaller percentages (several times if you have to), or edit the worst offenders manually – however ragged a phrase seems, it's usually caused by just a few notes ganging up to give that impression.

4 Don't just save regularly – save often! Save to at least two disks each time and keep at least one copy of each earlier save for as long as you can.

5 Edit as you record. As soon as you know you've recorded a phrase well enough, tidy it, balance it, mix it and listen to it in context before you record the next.

6 You don't have to use it! Whatever it is, it's there as an option not an obligation.

7 Make your programming-time easier. Keep your gear within easy reach and view, learn hotkey-combinations for useful facilities, find out what everything in your studio has to offer and how to use it.

8 Use the minimum of data to produce the effect you want. Making a sound jump back and forth between speakers, for example, can be done just as effectively by step-entering a few pan-events as by recording dozens of them in real-time.

9 Compare your own files with those of other programmers. Try to learn from your mistakes and (more enjoyably) learn from theirs.

10 When you think it's finished, listen to it. Are you proud of it? If not, it's not finished.

The Seven Deadly Sins

1 **Uniformity**　A rule of thumb in programming: *similarity breeds contempt.* Wide variations in velocity, pan position, effect depth and so on will create a far better effect.

2 **Repetition**　Don't copy and chain identical patterns or phrases one after another. Does anybody *play* that way?

3 **Familiarity**　Don't over-use your favourite tricks, effects and sounds. They'll soon become dull and then become irritating to listeners and users.

4 **Carelessness**　Always remove unnecessary data: something like 50% of continuous-controller data in your file is probably superfluous.

5 **Laziness**　It won't sound like an acoustic-guitar just because the patch is called Acoustic Guitar. That's *your* job.

6   Inaccuracy   If the record you're covering uses a string section, one hand on a Strings patch just won't cut it. If there's a tricky guitar-line that uses bends and slides, the easy option is to leave them out. Or is it? How, as a programmer, would you justify it if questioned?

7   Apathy   Read the first six again!

10

Appendices

This section covers a variety of MIDI-related topics that don't quite fit in elsewhere, but should still be of interest and use to MIDI-users. These topics are in no way intended to be exhaustive references, merely brief introductions to whet your appetite for some deeper investigations or maybe a spot of studio expansion!

■ Appendix 1 **Interfaces and Disk Formats**

The basic hardware connections for various types of studio setup have already been covered in the **MIDI Setup Diagrams** on page 33, but of course, it's often more complicated than that, particularly if you have several tone-generators in your system, or you want to record several MIDI signals at once; and different computers implement their MIDI compatibility in various ways.

MIDI Merger

The MIDI Merger is used to mix two streams of MIDI data together and send them into a single tone-generator. The primary function of this is when recording a live performance via MIDI, for example playing a keyboard part at the same time as a percussion part from drum-pads. A merger is also needed if you're recording to a sequencer at the same time as sending sync messages to it. For this reason, it's important to make sure that the merger supports MIDI Time Code.

MIDI Splitter

Also known as a 'Thru Box', the splitter gets around the problem of data corruption when chaining several MIDI devices together. It also removes the dilemma faced when you want to use two devices without MIDI Thru sockets. The splitter usually has a single MIDI In connected to your sequencer's MIDI Out, and several MIDI Thrus, each of which can be connected to a tone-generator. The splitter should be a powered unit which can amplify the signal to prevent deterioration.

MIDI Switcher

A MIDI switcher is a device that lets you change the way devices are connected together without having to unplug and replug cables. For example, your tone-generator is usually connected to your sequencer's MIDI Out, with your master-keyboard connected to the sequencer's MIDI In. To dump SysEx from tone-generator to sequencer would normally require changing the cable connections. With a switcher, everything can be inter-connected and the required link can be activated by simply flicking a switch.

MIDI Computer Interfaces

A MIDI interface is what allows a computer to 'understand' MIDI data. A few computers contain built-in MIDI interfaces together with MIDI In and Out sockets, leaving you the relatively easy task of plugging in the cable. Other computers require an interface to be fitted, either by attaching it to a spare port (a connector used to attach printers etc.) or by fitting an interface card to a card-slot inside the computer.

A basic interface will have one MIDI In and one MIDI Out socket, but interfaces vary greatly both in price and features. An interface with several MIDI Ins can replace an external merger box (outlined above); an interface with several MIDI Outs will allow you access to 16 channels per output, provided your sequencer can support multiple output ports. Let's take a look at the MIDI interfacing requirements of the three main computer platforms.

PC

The usual interface choice on *MS-DOS/Windows* computers is the MPU card which slots inside the computer and provides one MIDI In and one MIDI Out. The MPU has been around for years and is compatible with just about everything, but the single In/Out makes it rather restricted by today's standards, and its implementation of FSK sync is limited. Manufacturers are now beginning to produce MPU-compatible cards containing more ports which are worth a look; failing that, you can access 32 MIDI channels by installing two interface cards. As the MPU tends to be the 'standard' PC interface, it's worth making sure that at least one of the cards has MPU compatibility – one day you're sure to need it !

To make the computer 'speak' to the interface, a driver file is required which comes packaged with the hardware. Finding sequencing software that's compatible with particular interfaces can be fraught with problems if you don't go for the trusty MPU, so it's vital to check which interfaces are supported before parting with the cash. Microsoft have recently standardised the MIDI handling of *Windows* with Multimedia Extensions (MME). Gradually, MME drivers are becoming available for all interface-types and software-writers are including MME compatibility, so if you want more than the basic In/Out MPU card, and your sequencer supports Multimedia Extensions, look around for an interface packaged with a MME driver.

The configuration of interfaces can be a bit of a nightmare: each hardware element added to a PC requires a base address setting and an IRQ. For an MPU-type interface, the default settings are usually base address 330, IRQ 2. The settings for the card must be identical to those you specify in the sequencing software – one of the most frequent hitches is that the sequencer can transmit data but fails to respond to any incoming messages: this almost always means that the base address setting is okay but the IRQ is wrong. More import-antly, the settings must also be unique – if the same settings are used by other hardware on the system you could wind up with no mouse control (or worse) until you change them. Fortunately, most interfaces come with a software routine to identify available settings. Sometimes it's necessary to reconfigure the card itself, so try to get a card with DIP switches – some others need a bit of intimate poking with a soldering iron.

Apple-Macintosh

On the Mac, the MIDI interface is an external hardware which connects to one of the two serial ports, either printer or modem. And, of course, you can connect an interface to both to access more than 16 channels. In fact, some advanced interfaces actually contain 8 or more pairs of Ins and Outs. Make sure first that your sequencing software supports whatever configuration you want to use though.

Of course, this means that either your printer port or your modem port (or both) is full of MIDI interface! To be able to use a printer and modem as well, you'll need an interface that provides a Thru socket for serial devices.

The only other setting that matters in a Mac interface is the *Interface Clock Rate*. In recent interfaces, this has been fixed at 1 Mhz, but earlier interfaces were switchable between 0.5, 1 and 2 Mhz. For MIDI to work, the setting must be the same for both the card and the sequencing software.

Atari

The popular Atari models (ST, STe, TT and Falcon) are beautifully easy when it comes to MIDI – they all contain built-in interfaces and MIDI In/Out ports. This doesn't necessarily make them more suited to MIDI sequencing than other platforms, but it does mean that there are no configuration worries. The oddity of the Atari models is that they include a MIDI Thru port hidden inside the MIDI Out by connecting pins 1 and 3 which the MIDI specification leaves unconnected. As long as you use thoroughbred MIDI cables you're fine, but connect an ordinary 5-pin DIN cable and it's Trouble City.

Atari computers can be expanded to 32 channels by attaching an interface to the MIDI Out. Most of the major manufacturers of MIDI software for the Atari produce an interface, but each interface is sequencer-specific, so you need to be sure you're happy with their software before you splash the cash.

Disk Formats and File Transferral

As we've already mentioned, the obvious file-format for transferring files between sequencers is the Standard MIDI File – most hardware and software sequencers and MIDI file-players can read and write the SMF format, so if you give a SMF to a friend she should be able to play it without any trouble. But a second point to consider is how to transfer the file from one computer or hardware system to another. The standard medium is the floppy disk, but there's a bit more to it than that (isn't there always?): will your friend's system read your **disk-format**?

Most computers can read PC *MS-DOS*-formatted disks and this is the usual format to go for. PCs obviously read and write to this format automatically, either on a double-density or a high-density disk. Few other systems can read a high-density disk so the double-density is the one to use (usually abbreviated to DSDD).

Atari computers can read a DOS-formatted disk and can write files to it, but they can't actually create that format for a disk without help. Atari-users need a public-domain file utility (such as *Fastcopy*) to make an *MS-DOS* formatted disk. This little gem can also create custom-formats and significantly cuts down the formatting time.

Recent Apple-Macs are PC-compatible and can read, write and format an *MS-DOS* disk without working up much of a sweat. Older Macs once again need a file utility such as *Access PC* to do the job. A peculiarity of the Mac is that the files need a File Type; the computer needs to know that a file with the DOS-extension .MID is a MIDI file. Mac-users will know all about this as the file-typing has to be done at their end.

Some hardware-sequencers and workstations (though not many) use their own disk-format which makes it impossible to transfer the files by floppy-disk. The usual (though slightly messy) way of getting around this problem is to transfer the file in real-time by playing it from one system and recording it into the other. This requires use of the MIDI clock to synchronise the two devices, and the most successful method is to make the recording device the master (*Transmit MIDI Clock*) and the playing device the slave (*Receive* or *External MIDI Clock*). To do this, you need two MIDI cables to connect the In and Out of one device to the Out and In (respectively) of the other.

■ Appendix 2 **MIDI Add-Ons**

In earlier topics we looked at MIDI-studio setups and the types of hardware/software required for MIDI programming, supplemented by the previous appendix on the hardware needed for an expanded studio. This topic takes a look at the four additional pieces of hardware you might sling onto the back of the van when you trundle off to your sequence-based gig.

MIDI File Player

Although it's within the realms of possibility that you might use a laptop computer to play your files live, the job is usually done by a dedicated MIDI file player. At its most basic, this is a small box housing a disk-drive with controls to select, start and stop files. Of the devices that play Standard MIDI Files, most will only read a type 0. Some, however, use their own disk- and file-format, which means that you have to play the file across to the player in real-time to be recorded. These formats almost always take up more disk-space than SMFs, resulting in more frequent stops to change disks.

The features contained in file-players can vary considerably; a few useful ones to look out for are rewind and fast-forward controls, tempo control, screen-display of filename and size, and playlist. The last of these is especially useful in a live situation, and may have the added bonus of cueing up the next file while playing the first. Some players have a *Send All Files* function which can be used in the same way by retitling files alpha-numerically.

A point to consider whilst on the subject of file-players: always carry backups! Disks fail, and they rarely give a warning that they're about to do so. If your file-player uses its own format, carry SMF type 0 backups as well – if you ever need a replacement file-player at short notice you don't want to be restricted to one particular make and model.

MIDI Lighting

This is an effective addition to a live show, and is usually as easy to program as a single hi-hat part. The entire rig responds to a single MIDI channel with each light usually controlled by its own MIDI note number, the velocity of the note controlling its brightness. Some lighting rigs also include a desktop 'monitoring rig' allowing you to see the results of your programming without setting up the whole system. Using MIDI lighting, you can perfectly tailor the lighting to the speed of each song, highlight drum-fills and brass stabs in exact synchronisation and so on.

Hints

➡ Don't forget to turn some lights on after that final dramatic fade-to-black, or you'll be taking your applause and trying to change disks in pitch darkness!

➡ Don't forget to mute the lighting-channel's output on your tone-generator.

MIDI Effects

For guitarists and vocalists, controlling your effects via MIDI saves a lot of hassle. Once again, all the settings can be included on an unused channel in your files so guitarists can change from rhythm to lead and back again without tap-dancing on the pedals; vocalists can pre-program different effects for verses and choruses, or add extra effect-depth for high-notes. Some effects units also allow setting of delay and echo times to be triggered by MIDI Clock pulses for precise control. Effects are usually selected by Program Change commands, but other parameters such as mix or reverb decay might be controllable via MIDI note numbers, velocities or controllers. Bear in mind that many effects processors are less forgiving than tone-generators when program changes are received – very often, the current effect will be immediately cut off and the new effect will take a little time to 'kick in', so the positioning of the commands will take some care.

Hint

➡ Remember to turn vocal effects off at the end of each file or you'll be swathed in bright-plate with voice-doubler as you say Thankyou.

Vocal Harmonizer

Vocal-harmony devices are probably the most commonly used MIDI add-on around. They combine a note or chord feed from the MIDI file with a microphone signal to create vocal harmonies, often in a variety of modes. The most frequent methods of use are either to program a fully quantized and legato chord sequence at the points where the harmonies should occur and use a program change to select the harmony-type, or to create the harmony line itself. It's becoming an accepted rule that harmony parts should be on channel 5 for commercial files; it's certainly wise to stick to the same channel for each file to avoid having to reset the harmonizer for each song. And remember to mute that channel on your tone-generator too!

Appendix 3 Sampling

Sampling is a two-headed beast: firstly there's the act of recording and editing an analogue audio signal – the methods and results have a lot in common with creating new patches from scratch in synthesizers. The second aspect of sampling is the playback of sampled sounds and, since samplers are MIDI-equipped (though a few only include MIDI compatibility as an upgrade option), the use of samplers as tone-generators in MIDI-programming.

What Is Sampling?

Sampling has actually been around since the late 1970s, but only started to become affordable to the home-user in the late 80s when dedicated hardware samplers arrived. Around the same time, synth manufacturers began using samples as the basis for the preset sounds in their instruments; today, almost all tone-generators use samples to emulate acoustic instruments, accounting for the huge advances in sound-quality since the days of synthesis.

The essence of sampling is to provide full digital control over analogue sounds for recording, live and MIDI-programming uses. The sampler converts an analogue signal into a sequence of numbers using an *analogue-to-digital converter* (ADC) similar to the converters used to MIDI-up guitars, drum-kits and wind-instruments (see page 29). This makes it possible to view the data either graphically or numerically, allowing the sampled sounds to be edited in various ways and saved to disk for future use. The sampler's multi-timbrality means that it can also be used as a tone-generator to playback several samples at once, with 32-voice polyphony a standard specification.

Recording and Editing

The actual recording of a sound into a sampler is almost as simple an affair as recording to an analogue tape-recorder, requiring an audio input and the setting of record-levels. The additional setting is *frequency* – the higher the selected sample-rate, the higher the sound-quality (and the greater the memory required for storage).

Editing facilities vary from one device to another, but sampled sounds can usually be retuned, re-enveloped, cut, looped, and filtered to alter their tonal characteristics. Most samplers include some form of on-board effects-processor together with facilities to join together or layer two different samples to create a new one.

Looping is a vital part of the sampling process: a one-second flute sample might be very nice but not much use if you want a longer note. Looping is a matter of setting points in the sample between which the sound will cycle endlessly as long as the sample is being triggered. A popular use of looping is in drum-and-bass driven styles such as rave and rap where a single one-bar drum sample can be looped to form the entire basis of a record's rhythmic backing.

Samplers In Use

For performing and programming purposes, the sampler can be treated in the same way as the module or soundcard: by connecting a master-keyboard, the sounds can be triggered and the notes recorded to a sequencer in usual MIDI fashion. Also like preset tone-generators, samplers are multi-timbral: samples can usually be mapped to different MIDI note-numbers, or keyboard-zoning (splitting) can assign each sound its own 'area' of the keyboard so that several sounds can be triggered at once from a single keyboard. Alternatively, samples can be allotted their own MIDI channel and used for multi-channel recording in the same way as preset tone-generators.

Sample Libraries

Although most stand-alone samplers provide extensive recording and editing facilities, achieving workable results from scratch requires sizeable portions of knowledge and patience. As a result, most home-users tend to use their samplers simply as playback devices for the huge number of commercial samples available, rather like having an infinitely-expandable preset tone-generator.

Some manufacturers supply their own in-house samples on floppy-disk or CD-ROM, and at least one allows users to delve into their archives for free. In addition there are countless sample CDs available commercially, although since samplers (like sequencers) save files in their own formats and there's little in the way of compatibility between the different devices, it's vital to check the sample-format before buying.

The wide availability of 'off-the-shelf' samples, together with their ease of use, makes the sampler a very useful piece of kit for programmers not working to the constraints of protocols such as General MIDI. With a potential library of several thousand sounds for the most popular formats, plus copious editing facilities, the only likely limitation is that of polyphony.

Appendix 4   **Hard-Disk Recording**

Hard-disk recording (HDR) has a lot in common with sampling, in that an analogue audio signal is converted to a digital sequence and saved to memory. The essential difference is that samples are recorded to RAM which is an expensive form of memory best suited to holding small quantities of data (CD-quality stereo sound uses 10Mb of memory per minute of recording). Hard-disks are a far more cost-effective medium when it comes to recording an entire song which could easily require over 100Mb.

What's It All About?

The standard medium for recording a sizeable quantity of analogue sound is tape; indeed, until recently, it's been the *only* medium. The need to combine analogue sound with digitally recorded sound resulted in the arrival of synchronisation standards such as MTC and

SMPTE (see page 232). Useful though tape-sync facilities are, the gradual deterioration of analogue tape and the difficulties of producing a squeaky-clean recording make them less than perfect. HDR provides an alternative to tape along with the potential for cleaning and editing the results to a far greater extent than tape-recording can offer. The closest rivals to HDR are systems based around digital tape, which can compete on sound-quality but not in flexibility or editing terms.

Along similar lines to sampling, the analogue audio signal is converted to binary code and saved to hard-disk in file-formats such as .WAV (for the PC) and SD2 (Macintosh). As with MIDI data, once in the digital domain these audio signals can be edited in a variety of ways or stored long-term with no reduction in sound-quality.

Benefits Of HDR

One of the primary benefits of HDR is the ability to edit the recorded sound. Vocal recordings, for example, tend to produce unwanted noises and pitch irregularities which can be removed or cleaned up. Another hefty advantage is the ability to cut, split, copy and move parts of the recording in much the same way as blocks of MIDI data. Many HDR systems also have facilities to add digital effects such as echo and reverb to the sound, and to carry out more complex functions such as reversing sections of the recording.

Another huge benefit of HDR is its ability to run alongside MIDI recordings from within the same computer-software program, allowing full control of both analogue sound and MIDI data with all the editing and mixing facilities you need to create a complete recording.

HDR Systems

Like MIDI sequencers, HDR systems come in two flavours: the computer-based software version and the stand-alone system. The capabilities of the two are very similar in terms of editing, storage and expandability. The chief advantage of the software variety is the ability to use the same piece of sequencing software to control both audio and MIDI data in a familiar environment.

On the other hand, HDR requires a powerful computer with a fast disk-drive mechanism, together with add-on hardware to handle synchronisation, digital input/output and playback which are not necessarily bundled with the software package. The possible compatibility problems of the different hard- and softwares, together with the computer's workload in running all these elements, can cause some spectacular system crashes too.

The stand-alone HDR system, being an integrated unit, is far more reliable from this point of view, though some lack the features and editing flexibility of their software counterparts. Most integrated HDR systems can still be controlled from the computer via MIDI without the same risk of crashing.

Mid-range HDR software systems can usually record eight or sixteen tracks of audio together with their standard MIDI capabilities, but not all are easily or cheaply expandable, some requiring a far more powerful computer and additional hardware. Most stand-alone systems can handle either four or eight tracks.

And More Expense . . .

A further point to consider about HDR is the vast amount of hard-disk memory required to record a useful quantity of audio – for example, a song or an album. Apart from the disk-space required while actually making the album, some form of storage medium is going to be needed to free up disk-space ready for the next one when you're done (not to mention safety copies of the data you're working on!).

Digital audio tape (DAT) is an excellent medium for this, but adds greatly to the end-cost of an HDR system. It pays to be sure that HDR really is a road down which you want to go before you start putting on your boots.

Appendix 5 **Protocol Conversion**

If you're using General MIDI-compatible equipment, you should find that most of the files you play sound pretty much as they should: almost all the files available for sale or for download from the Internet, and all the files included with *The MIDI Files*, are constructed according to the GM sound set (see page 61), this being the lowest common denominator. Of course, there are dozens of GM tone-generators on the market in various shapes and forms which all sound slightly different, so some tweaking of volumes and effect-settings and perhaps even individual note-velocities may still be needed to produce the best results.

If you're using non-General MIDI compatible equipment however, you'll find that many of the third-party files you play don't sound as they should. To get around this, you'll need to remap the patches and possibly the drumkit instruments. This brief topic explains how to go about it.

Patch Remapping

This is the easy bit. In *Edit* mode, look at the program change commands for each channel and simply 'translate' them to the numbers which produce the same instrument in your own device, using your tone-generator's patch list and the 'General MIDI Maps' on page 61. For example, if you find PC #68 in a file, you need to change this to the number that calls up a Baritone Sax in your own tone-generator. But make sure you know how your sequencer displays program-changes: most devices number them 1–128 (i.e., the same as the patch numbers), but your sequencer may number them from 0–127, in which case PC #68 would refer to an Oboe.

Even with the correct patches, you might find that some mixing and editing is still needed before the file sounds right. For example, the bass-part may need to be transposed an octave higher or lower, or you may need to adjust the CC7 Main Volume settings (see below).

Controller Remapping

This shouldn't be necessary because General MIDI responds to a very limited range of control-changes, all of which should be the same in your own tone-generator. If remapping is needed, once again use your manual and the GM maps to translate them. Pay particular attention to RPN settings, and whether your device can respond to them. You should also delete the GM Reset System Exclusive, but you may wish to replace it with another SysEx string to reset your device (if there is one), or with a collection of 'safety' controllers such as 123:0, 121:0, 64:0, and pitch-bend zero to make sure everything is reset.

Watch out for CC7 Main Volume controls during the song-body: turning up the CC7 in the song-header won't do any good if the track contains more volume controls. In this case, use the CC11 Expression event in the header of each track to balance the sounds instead.

Drum Remapping

This is less easy – you may be unlucky enough to have a drum-kit in which few or none of the sounds are mapped to the same MIDI Note Numbers as their GM counterparts, in which case every note will have to be changed. The simplest way to do this is to construct a General MIDI drum-map in your sequencer and change each instrument one by one, once again referring between your own map and the GM maps. Your sequencer may even transpose all the instruments from one map to another automatically.

If your sequencer doesn't have facility to create user-drum maps, the process is more long-winded: you need to isolate each kit-instrument on a track of its own, and then transpose each track to the correct MIDI note number. This involves making quite a few copies of the original drum track and deleting all but one of the note-numbers from each, which takes a bit of organisation to make sure you don't miss any! Don't delete that original track until you're sure you've got the lot. The actual note-deletion part should be a simple case of selecting the note you want to keep in one of your copied tracks and telling the sequencer to delete everything but that note-number.

A third method is to use a 'mathematical' editor (such as *Cubase's* Logical Edit) to select and transpose each kit-instrument one at a time. This takes a lot of advance planning though, for example, if you remap all F#1s to C2s you must make sure you've already remapped the C2s to wherever they were supposed to go or all your F#1s and C2s will end up triggering the same instrument!

And In Reverse . . .

Of course you can remap non-GM files for General MIDI devices by doing all the same things in reverse. To do this, you'll need to know what sounds the program-changes and kits were supposed to call up, either from documentation accompanying the file or perhaps from the track-names in a type 1 SMF. Without this information, you'll have to rely on experimentation, intuition and a bit of luck!

Appendix 6   **Xpecting Xmidi**

As we've pointed out in previous topics, MIDI has in-built expansion possibilities. These come largely from using high-resolution controller pairs such as Bank Select and NRPNs to provide many more than the previous maximum of 128 'slots'. Further advancements in the shape of MIDI Time Code, Machine Control and Show Control, among others, are allowing full real-time control of external musical and non-musical devices. So it looks like Mr MIDI has got the job. But what of the future?

Over the last few years, the MIDI specification has grown slowly, adding the occasional new element. In the meantime, the market, the requirements and the possibilities for the use of computer-controlled music have grown fast. Suddenly, plans are afoot to create a 'replacement' in the shape of Xmidi. So what is Xmidi, and is Mr MIDI going to like working with this new guy?

What Is Xmidi?

Xmidi (eXtended MIDI) is ostensibly an extension of the current MIDI specification, using similar types of message to control similar parameters through ordinary MIDI cables. The basic difference is in the way the data is structured behind the scenes. Xmidi converts part of the message data into ternary (base 3) code as opposed to binary (base 2) which provides an immense increase in the range of figures that can be transmitted in a single byte. MIDI can transmit figures up to 255 in a single byte, compared to Xmidi's 13,122. This means that much more information can be packed into the same size and length of message, which is the equivalent of an increase in speed.

As a result of the denser Xmidi message, a program change command can select one of 4,374 patches from a single 2-byte message. For MIDI to access patch number 4374 requires the 6-byte Bank Select plus the program change, a total of 8 bytes. True, this 8-byte message does allow you to reach over 2 million patches, but can you really envisage a day when a device actually has 2 million patches? (And would you be able to lift the patch-list?)

A further difference is that Xmidi is bidirectional within a single cable – this allows easy and automated setting-up, acknowledgement and troubleshooting during data dumps and so on.

Son Of 'The Compatibility Question'

And so the old compatibility question comes back to haunt us. It may be similar, and it may be billed as an extension, but to make use of Xmidi calls for studio expansion to the tune of new hardware and software. The good news is that your existing tone-generators won't become defunct overnight – Xmidi allows MIDI devices to function in exactly the same way that they do now.

The Tasty Stuff!

Let's take a look at some of the major enhancements of the proposed system:

- ❏ **324 Channels.** The present 16 channels may seem just about adequate for music-programming purposes, but as you'll have gathered from the earlier topic about **MIDI Add-Ons**, once you start sacrificing channels for MIDI lighting rigs, harmoniser and effects-unit control, you can be down to 10 channels before you've inserted a note! With 324 channels you could program the traffic-lights for a small town to flash in time with Beethoven's 5th.

- ❏ **510 Linear Values.** Where MIDI can express a range of values from 0–127 for parameters such as velocity, expression, pan and so forth, Xmidi gives almost four times the resolution.

- ❏ **4374 Non-Linear Values.** A vast increase in the number of control-change and program change numbers available from a single 2-byte message. This also gives 4,374 MIDI Note Numbers allowing much more flexibility in the arrangement of drumkits among other things.

The Future Of Midi?

Do we need Xmidi? For programmers, the benefits are more expression and fewer restrictions in return for some investment in new hardware and software, and trust that manufacturers will support the advance by adding more sounds, effects and control-change accessible editing parameters. For commercial file programmers, there has also to be the expectation that the majority of MIDI-users will consider Xmidi a worthwhile investment too.

And on a more practical point, while an increased number of available channels is sorely needed, MIDI technology has only just reached the point of allowing 64-voice polyphony from a single device. But a couple of these devices can handle the most channel-intensive musical requirements imaginable, and still leave channels free for additional hardware such as lighting, by the simple expedient of using multiple output ports (current, affordable technology).

So is Xmidi really the future of MIDI? At the time of writing, this is unclear. Xmidi has been the subject of a patent application since early 1993 and efforts are being made to produce the first commercial Xmidi product.

■ Appendix 7 **MIDI On The Internet**

MIDI users who are already keenly 'surfing the 'Net' will know what it is, what it has to offer, and how much it increases your 'phone-bill. To the un-Netted, sadly this is not the place to begin explaining it all. Suffice to say that it provides access to an entire world of information and human experience. Some of the information of course pertains to music and MIDI. And some of the human experience pertains to actually looking for it – often a frustrating and expensive business so here is a list of useful sites which, between them, give fairly comprehensive coverage of all things MIDI.

World-Wide Web sites – General

http://www.PrimeNet.Com:80/~midifrm
'The MIDI Farm': links to software houses Emagic, Steinberg, Opcode, Twelve Tone Systems and more. Links to hardware manufacturers Roland, Yamaha, Kurzweil, Korg, Alesis and others.

http://www.music.indiana.edu/music_resources.html
Every musical link you could wish for is here ... Artists, Record Labels, Publishers, Magazines, Software Houses.

http://www.eeb.ele.tue.nl/midi
'The MIDI Home Page': Links to Steinberg, Emagic, Yamaha, Roland, Akai, Ensoniq, Korg. Patches, magazines, MIDI documentation, GM and GS Standard MIDI Files.

http://www.cs.ruu.nl/pub/MIDI
A useful collection of links relating to SMFs and commercial hardware and software.

http:///www.magicnet/rz/world_of_audio/midi_pg.html
'World Of Audio': MIDI and General MIDI documentation; links to software houses; links to PC and Mac archives.
Software sequencers and patch-editors/librarians for download.

http://coyote.accessnv.com/dhanley/m3/m3.html
'Macintosh MIDI Music': Archives of Standard MIDI Files, plus patches, samples and utilities for Apple-Mac computers.

http://www.eeb.ele.tue.nl/midi/midiweb/
Utilities, technical info, shareware/freeware programs and demos.

http://harmony-central.mit.edu/
Links to software, patches, product reviews, Standard MIDI Files.

http://ally.ios.com/~midilink
'MIDILink Musicians' Network': Excellent site for MIDI information across all platforms. Plus General MIDI SMFs, patches, software.

World-Wide Web sites – Standard Midi Files

http://www.prs.net/midi.html
The Classical MIDI Archives: over 17megabytes of Classical SMFs!

http://www.primenet.com/~alex
Mainstream pop and rock SMFs.

http://199.227.124.2/BEST/BEST.HTM
'Best Of The Best': These are billed as the best SMFs on the 'Net. See what you think!

http://www.mindspring.com/~s-allen/picks.html
'MIDI Composers' Exchange': A pretty neat idea: submit your own compositions in SMF format for possible inclusion on the page, and download other programmers' work to see how you measure up!

FTP sites – Standard Midi Files

Remember that all directories are case-sensitive – make sure you type accurately.

ftp.mcc.ac.uk/pub/MIDImisc/SMF
Huge collection of mainstream SMFs in General MIDI and Roland GS formats.

ftp.cs.ruu.nl/pub/MIDI/SONGS
Eleven directories of SMFs from Classical and Christian to Pop and Rock.

ftp.ibp.fr/pub2/midi/SONGS
Vast directories containing hundreds of SMFs from Classical to Pop and drum-patterns.

ftp.rc.tudelft.nl/pub/midi
Large directory of original compositions in SMF format.

ftp.ragtimers.org/pub/ragtimers/midi_files
Huge collection of Ragtime SMFs.

ftp.monash.edu.au/pub/midi/SONGS
Large directory of *Cakewalk*.WRK format files, plus directories of Standard MIDI Files including General MIDI, Classical, Christmas, Jazz and Pop.

wuarchive.wustl.edu/systems/ibmpc/ultrasound/sound/midi/files
A large collection of files, some specifically intended for the *Gravis Ultrasound* soundcard.

ftp.ucsd.edu/midi/scores
Directories of Bach and Classical SMFs, and *Cakewalk* .WRK files.

kilroy.jpl.nasa.gov/pub/D70/Midi
Directories of Classical, Contemporary, Jazz, Misc, Nostalgia, Originals in SMF format.

internexus.net/pub/sound/midi
A collection of .zip (compressed) files listed alphabetically, containing up to several dozen SMFs each. Plus a few classical solo-piano files.

FTP sites – Software and Documents

ftp.ibp.fr/pub2/midi/DOC
The most comprehensive collection of MIDI-related documents imaginable! Hardware and software information and specifications, format and protocol details, you name it! Plus patches for several popular synths and modules.

ftp.ibp.fr/pub2/midi/PROGRAMS
Shareware editions and demos of software programs including sequencers, editors/librarians, MIDI jukeboxes.

ftp.cica.indiana.edu/ ~ ftp/pub/pc/win3/sounds
A very useful MIDI site – musical and MIDI utilities, sequencers, patch editors and librarians, .WAV files, improvisation software.

dir.mcc.ac.uk/pub/cubase
Save-disabled demos of Steinberg's *Cubase* and *MusicStation* for PC, together with documents, software updates and new versions.

mort.isvr.soton.ac.uk/pub/pc/cakewalk
Save-disabled demos of Twelve Tone Systems' *Cakewalk.*

musie.phlab.missouri.edu/pub/korg
Patch editors/librarians and replacement sounds for Korg tone-generators.

wuarchive.wustl.edu/systems/ibmpc/ultrasound/sound/midi/util
A collection of useful MIDI utilities including sequencers, patch editors, file format-converters, jukeboxes.

ftp.mcc.ac.uk/pub/MIDImisc
Another large collection of documents, MIDI utilities and PC interface drivers.

Software Downloads

A few points to keep in mind when downloading software and Standard MIDI Files by FTP:

- ❑ Remember to select Binary mode transfer for data (as opposed to text) files.

- ❑ Always run a virus-check after downloading any form of file.

- ❑ Most of the software available for download will be either save-disabled or shareware, or a combination of the two.

- ❑ Remember to grab any documents or text-files accompanying the software: these usually contain installation procedures and details of where and how to register the program.

- ❑ Bear in mind that downloaded SMFs may require some tweaking to perform best on your MIDI setup: many of the files are General MIDI compatible, but GM tone-generators vary widely, so changes to the relative volumes of the channels may be necessary. If you're not using a GM-compatible tone-generator, use the **General MIDI Maps** on page 61 and **Protocol Conversion** on page 289 to 'translate' the program change numbers to the correct patches for your device.

❑ There are several directories of *Cakewalk* .WRK files available on the 'Net. This is a file format specific to Twelve Tone Systems' *Cakewalk* sequencer. To use these files, download the save-disabled *Cakewalk* demo from dir.mcc.ac.uk. Alternatively, grab the *Cakewalk*-to-SMF file converter from wuarchive.wustl.edu (both listed above).

❑ When first visiting sites containing larger collections of SMFs, programs or documents, download the INDEX file contained in most directories to read off-line instead of scanning through the whole directory – it's friendlier to the host computer, and avoids running up your phone bill. Make sure each index file contains the exact address and path to the directory so you can get back there easily if you find something you want.

MIDI On CompuServe

CompuServe users can GO MIDIFORUM for similar collections of Standard MIDI Files, documents, software and utilities. There is also on-line support from a multitude of MIDI hardware and software manufacturers in the four MIDI vendor forums, GO MIDIAVEN, MIDIBVEN, MIDICVEN and MIDIDVEN.

BTW . . .

Do you have any hints, tips, suggestions or MIDI-related topics that you feel should be included in subsequent editions of *The MIDI Files*? Do you have any MIDI-problems not covered here, or indeed any solutions or programming time-savers?

We want to hear from MIDI-users with any ideas or discoveries that other MIDI-philes would find useful or interesting. If you feel it will help to illustrate your idea more clearly, please include a Type 1 SMF. Submitted files will not be used for publication.

Please e-mail feedback to the author at: **rob.young@btinternet.com** with the subject-line **TMF**. Include your full name and city/state/country, together with details of what tone-generator(s) and sequencer(s) you're using. We can't promise a reply to all mail or guarantee to use every suggestion, but we will try to acknowledge all contributions we *do* use.

Glossary

A brief explanation of the terms used in this book. As everything in MIDI is inter-connected, **bold** text in an entry refers you to another Glossary entry. If the word or phrase you're looking for isn't listed here, or you want more in-depth info, use the Index (page 312) to find references within the text.

Active Sensing A type of non-stop error-checking process that MIDI devices carry out (several times a second in fact!) by sending a short code from the **MIDI Out**. If the receiving device doesn't get one (for example, if the MIDI lead has been pulled out), it automatically turns all notes off to counter the problem. It's hard to tell all this is going on, and maybe it isn't – not all devices use Active Sensing, and sequencers don't record it.

Aftertouch A form of **modulation** activated by varying pressure on a keyboard. Aftertouch isn't widely recognised or implemented by MIDI hardware and tends to be favoured more for live use than in MIDI programming.

Analogue Sound that you hear is a *wave* and the wave has a *frequency*. The higher the frequency, the higher the *pitch* of the note. Analogue recording creates an exact replica of the sound-wave onto tape or some similar medium – in other words replicates it in a form that can still be *heard* and that still can't be *seen*. Cf. **digital**.

Bank Select A **high-resolution** pair of controllers (CC0 and CC32) used to point to one of 16,384 banks of sounds in a tone-generator. The bank-select command is always followed by a **program-change** message to specify one of the 128 **patches** in the chosen bank.

CC An abbreviation for Control Change number, for example CC7 is Control Change 7 (Main Volume).

Channel Messages are MIDI messages containing a channel setting, to be responded to by one single MIDI channel, as distinct from System Messages which are directed at the deeper workings of the MIDI system. There are five types of Channel Message: Note On/Note Off, Controllers, Program Change, Pitch-Bend and Aftertouch.

Channel Priority A lot of tone-generators are designed to give priority to notes on certain MIDI channels at those times when **polyphony** is getting tight. Channel 10 – the drums channel – is usually given maximum priority, followed by the remaining channels in ascending order from channel 1, so channel 16 has minimum priority. This should be borne in mind when deciding which parts to assign to each channel.

Chase Events When you restart playback of a MIDI file at a different position from where you stopped, the *Chase* feature found on some sequencers scans back through the file and updates the controller-settings for the current position so that the chosen section plays back as you intended. The feature often lets you choose which data-types should be chased.

Controller There are two meanings for the word 'controller'. The most frequent use is as a sort of abbreviation for Control-Changes (one of the five types of **channel message**). Secondly, it is a sort of abbreviation for MIDI Controller – a piece of kit such as a master-keyboard or MIDI guitar whose sole purpose in life is to send the data you produce by playing to another device (such as a sequencer or tone-module) for processing. Luckily these dual meanings are different enough that it's usually easy to work out which is meant from the context.

Controller Remapping A sequencer facility which can change incoming controller events of one number into another as they're being recorded (and echoed to the **MIDI Thru**). This means that you can remap your keyboard's volume (CC7) slider to CC10 (pan) and use it to record a pan sweep. If your sequencer will let you save settings in a **Preferences**, Setup or Default autoload file, it's well worthwhile keeping CC7 mapped to CC11 (expression) to prevent CC7 events creeping into your files.

Delay The use of the word delay occurs in two different contexts: first as an effect applied to a track, or a section of one, forcing the events to play later than they were positioned to. A negative delay will make them play earlier, which can be useful for 'pushing' the beat when applied to a drum-track for instance. As a sequencer effect it's sometimes called slide. Secondly, MIDI-delay can be the undesirable result of heavy MIDI traffic (a lot of events being transmitted at the same time) causing timing glitches and data drop-out. So the first type of delay can be used as an ideal solution to the second!

Digital Digital sound in literal terms can't be heard, in the same way that you can't hear a phone number. You can however see the phone number and use it to make something happen, i.e., make someone's telephone ring. Sound waves can be turned into a digital signal consisting of 1s and 0s (binary code) and stored. In contrast with analogue sound, these numbers can therefore be displayed graphically or in lists on a screen and minutely edited, which is what your sequencer is for. The numbers can then be used to make something happen: they can make your tone-generator translate them back into sound that you can hear coming out of your speakers. Cf. **analogue**.

Dynamic Pan According to MIDI specification, once a note is sounding its pan position can't be changed: it isn't intended to be a continuous controller in the same way as Expression for example. Nevertheless, some manufacturers have corrected this egregious oversight so that a sustained chord can still be flung around the stereo field, and it's referred to as 'dynamic' panning. Try playing the file DYNAPAN.MID to find out whether your tone-generator supports it.

Event A single message of any sort – a note, a pitch-bend position, controller value, SysEx string, etc., which will fall on one **tick** and be displayed on a single line in your List Editor.

File Formats MIDI file is the generic name for any file created using MIDI data. Your sequencer may be able to save MIDI files in different formats with file-extenders such as .SNG, .ARR, .ALL, .WRK, etc. These are examples of specific file formats, which can be read only by the software which created them.

Your sequencer should also be able to read/write files in the universal Standard MIDI File (**SMF**) format, usually with the file-extender .MID. The SMF commonly comes in two flavours: Type 0 and Type 1. A type 0 file is created by mixing all recorded tracks down to just one track that has its output channel set to Off/No/Any thus ensuring all the data still goes off to its intended channels. A type 1 file saves multiple tracks and includes track-names. If you have an arrangement using 10 channels and 15 tracks your sequencer may save the file with all 15 tracks laid out as you had them, or it may mix down tracks with the same output channel to create a 10-track SMF.

Filters Many sequencers have facilities to let you cut out any unwanted event types (such as control-changes or System Exclusive) from incoming data before it's recorded and echoed to **MIDI Thru** – these are called filters. You may also have output or playback filters which let you hear what the file would sound like minus this data without actually deleting it, often called **Playback Parameters**.

GM Reset A short universal System Exclusive message which turns General MIDI mode on in GM-compatible devices and performs a basic clean-up operation by transmitting an All Notes Off message and resetting pitch-bend and controllers to zero or to their default value. The SysEx string is F0,7E,7F,09,01,F7.

GS Roland's extension to the General MIDI protocol containing extra instruments and more comprehensive editing and control facilities.

Hexadecimal (commonly abbreviated to hex.) A method of counting in base 16, used to construct System Exclusive messages. The figures used to count in hex (corresponding to our numbers 0-15) are 0,1,2,3,4,5,6,7,8,9,A,B,C,D,E,F. Numbers written in hex format have an 'H' suffix, such as 41H or 7EH, to distinguish them from decimal numbers. These two numbers translated to decimal would give us 65 and 126 respectively.

High Resolution and its counterpart Low Resolution describe the range and precision of some of the control messages. A Low Resolution controller, which we see most often, is a single **event** with a range of 0–127 (examples being the Program Change or CC91 Reverb Depth). A High Resolution message consists of two separate events (or two messages combined to form one event in the case of pitch-bend or polyphonic aftertouch). As each event has a range of 0–127, the message as a whole has a range of 0–16,383 (128 squared). Examples of high-res controller pairs are RPNS and NRPNS (CC101,100 and CC99, 98 respectively) and Bank Select (CC0 and 32).

LSB An abbreviation for Least Significant Byte. In a **high resolution MSB**/LSB pair of data-bytes, the LSB handles the fine-tuning of the value. The LSB controller always follows the MSB in these hi-res pairs.

Merge A sequencer facility very similar to **mixdown** with the exception that data is combined with an existing track.

MIDI is an acronym for Musical Instrument Digital Interface – a standard which enables electronic musical instruments to pass data to each other.

MIDI Implementation Chart This is a chart in a standardised layout which you'll find at the back of any MIDI equipment's user-manual. It lists all the various **System** and **Channel Messages**, with details on whether each can be transmitted and/or received, how they're implemented and what they'll do. The chart is entirely specific to that device, though many of the messages (if not all) will be part of the universal MIDI standard.

MIDI In One of the three types of MIDI socket found on devices capable of receiving MIDI data. **Controller** devices such as master-keyboards will not necessarily have an input socket. A MIDI cable connects the MIDI In with the **MIDI Out** or **MIDI Thru** of the sending device. Some devices have several MIDI Ins allowing input from more than one controlling device at a time, taking the place of a **MIDI Merger**.

MIDI Merger A small piece of hardware which takes incoming MIDI signals from two or more MIDI controllers and sends them into a single sequencer or tone-generator without the signals becoming confused.

MIDI Note Number or MNN. Notes, like patches, are numbered 0–127 from lowest pitch to highest. In the most commonly-used layout, the lowest pitched note is C-1 (MNN 0), 'middle' C3 is MNN 60, with G8 being the highest in pitch at MNN 127. A second popular system ranges from C1 to G9: in this case 'middle-C' is C4, but still MNN 60. Which system is used on a particular sequencer doesn't affect how another sequencer would play back the file.

MIDI Out One of the three types of MIDI socket found on devices capable of sending MIDI data, connected by a MIDI cable to the **MIDI In** of the receiving device. Some devices have more than one MIDI Out, enabling particular channels to be directed to certain devices and not others. This may also allow you to access separate sets of 16 channels from each output.

MIDI Splitter Box When chaining devices together by connecting the **MIDI Thru** of one to the **MIDI In** of another, the chain should consist of no more than three receiving devices. A way around this limitation is to use a splitter box. This is a small piece of powered hardware, usually consisting of one MIDI In and several MIDI Thrus which can amplify the signal to ensure that it reaches every device with unimpaired data-quality. Also known as a Thru Box.

MIDI Thru Most devices with a **MIDI In** also have a MIDI Thru socket which allows all the data received at the MIDI In to be copied back out to a second receiving device (see Fig. 5 on page 34.) Not all devices have a MIDI Thru (particularly older ones). Drum-machines seem to be particularly guilty of this crime which can be very irritating. When chaining several devices together, the device with no Thru socket has to be last in the chain and will suffer most from any MIDI delays that may occur which is about the last thing you want happening to your drum-parts ! In some **sequencers**, the MIDI Thru facility may be called MIDI Echo.

MIDI Thru Box – *see* **MIDI Splitter Box**.

Mixdown A sequencer facility that lets you combine the data from two or more tracks onto a single new track. The two primary uses of mixdown are to 'free-up' tracks for further recording (especially necessary on hardware sequencers) and to gather data for a single channel onto one track to make that channel's events easier to locate. Similar to **merge**.

Modulation A shorter term for Pitch Modulation, better known in 'live' music circles as vibrato. Usually controlled by a wheel or lever on a keyboard, or the mouthpiece of a wind-instrument, modulation is universally mapped to Control Change 1.

Module A smallish rack-mounted or desktop box which contains the workings of a synthesizer but without the keyboard. Also known as an expander.

Monophonic Able to play only one note (or sound) at a time. Attempting to play a second might produce no result, or may replace the first sound. A guitar string is a non-electronic example of monophony.

MSB An abbreviation for Most Significant Byte. In a **high-resolution** MSB/**LSB** pair of data-bytes, the MSB handles the coarse-tuning of the value. In low-resolution controllers, the MSB alone generates numbers up to 127.

Multi-timbral The sounds in your tone-generator are referred to as timbres. If a device is multi-timbral, it's able to play notes on two or more sounds at the same time (vital for programming!). An example of this would be '16-part multi-timbral' meaning that the tone-generator is capable of playing notes on 16 instruments at the same time, usually one instrument on each of MIDI's 16 channels. Compare this with **voices**.

Non-Registered Parameter Numbers NRPNs are a recent addition to the MIDI spec. The concept was to allow manufacturers to give access to specific functions of their devices via controllers 99 and 98, thereby reducing the need to muck about with SysEx quite so often. Oddly, the idea has not yet widely caught on, with Roland and Yamaha being among the very few manufacturers to implement NRPNs.

NRPN An abbreviation for **Non-Registered Parameter Number**.

Pad A type of synth-sound used to create a 'wash' or texture behind the other instruments in a song, padding it out. Pad sounds range from the bland to the exotic, and the more exotic they are the more **voices** they're likely to need. So that pad-sound you can barely hear may be swallowing truckloads of **polyphony**!

Partial Reserve In addition to **Channel Priority**, Roland use a system called Partial Reserve which allows you to allocate a number of **voices** (partials) for each channel. If you set a reserve of 4 on channel 16 for example, this should ensure that up to four notes will be able to sound on channel 16 despite it having the lowest channel priority. Yamaha uses a similar system, referring to the voices as elements.

Patch Another word for a preset or programmed sound stored within a **tone-generator** and accessible by using a **Program Change** command (or by pushing a button on the synth). Patches are usually numbered 1–128; the program-change commands that access them may be numbered in the same way or may use the 0–127 system, so GM Overdrive Gtr is patch number 30, but could be called up by program-change number 29 or 30 depending upon which system your sequencer uses. The word 'patch' is a roll-over from the days of the modular synth, where sounds were created by patching together different synth-circuits using patch-cables.

Pitch Bend A **channel message** that produces a change or slide in pitch of a note, accessed by a lever or wheel on a keyboard, or by bending a guitar-string. Pitch-bend is usually used as a continuous controller to create a smooth transition between pitches, but can be entered as calculated single events to produce an effect of 'stepping' from one pitch to another.

Pitch-to-MIDI converter A piece of hardware which converts an audio signal (such as a voice, a guitar or a saxophone) into a MIDI signal, usually a combination of **MIDI note numbers** and pitch-bend. Processing speed and accuracy of pitch-tracking have always been accident blackspots for pitch-to-MIDI-equipped instruments but there have been recent vast improvements in both.

Playback Parameters Many sequencers have a facility to let you enter particular settings for each track which alter or override the data the track contains. These can include delay, compression, program-change, **filters**, control-change settings and any number of useful things. These may also be called Track Parameters.

Polyphony/Polyphonic A polyphonic tone-generator is able to play two or more notes at the same time. '24-voice polyphonic' means the tone-generator is capable of 24 **voices** at once. Some manufacturers like to refer to their offspring as 24-note polyphonic which is usually stretching the truth: many sounds need 2 or more voices to create a note, so if you insist on using these sounds all the time, you are effectively cutting your polyphony by half.

Portamento An undisguised synth-effect that's been around since the early days of sound-synthesis, also known as Glide. When notes are played with the portamento pedal (CC65) switched on, the pitch slides from one note to the next. The time taken to reach the new pitch will depend equally upon the distance (i.e., difference in pitch) between the two notes and the setting of the Portamento Time controller, CC5.

Preferences Most software sequencers allow you to set various aspects of the program to suit your own working methods and then save this setup. These preferences will then be loaded into the program automatically each time you start it. It's well worth spending some time customising in this way – it's a pain to have to do it when inspiration strikes and you want to get recording. You may even be able to save different Preference files to suit different working methods or musical styles.

Pressure is another word for Aftertouch, giving rise to the terms channel-pressure and poly(phonic)-pressure.

Program Change A **channel message** used to select the sound to be used on a particular channel. The program change has a 128-point range allowing you to select one of 128 **patches**. Used in partnership with **Bank Select**, this figure tops the two million mark.

Quantization (also known occasionally as 'auto-correct'). A sequencer editing facility for automatically correcting timing errors. Tempting though it is to use, full quantization is the unconvicted killer of human feel in MIDI files. Fortunately, many sequencers now have wider quantizing facilities allowing you, for example, to move only those notes that fall outside a specified range from the beat you were aiming for.

Real-time recording is what you're doing when you set your sequencer's metronome ticking and record in time with it: for every beat that passes you're recording a beat of data. Cf. **Step-time**

Rechannelize When recording to a sequencer, your keyboard will usually send its data out on channel 1 (its default channel). The sequencer's rechannelize function lets you specify which channel you want the data recorded for quickly and easily without changing your keyboard's settings, and be able to hear the notes being played on that channel as you record and when you playback afterwards.

Registered Parameter Number(s) RPNs are a recent addition to the MIDI specification giving access to pitch-bend range and fine and coarse tuning via control-change commands 101 and 100. The value for CC101 is always 0; the value for CC100 is the number of the parameter to be addressed, those listed above being #0, #1 and #2 respectively.

Remap Controllers – *see* **Controller Remapping**.

Remix A frequently included sequencer facility that acts on a track containing data for two or more channels, creating a new track for each channel's events. This is a particularly handy feature to have if you ever need to load a type 0 file and edit it. Some sequencers use the more intuitive term 'Split By Channel'.

Resolution Another of those annoying words that crops up twice, once in connection with sequencers and again in the context of control-change messages. For the latter, see the **High Resolution** entry.

In sequencer terms, the resolution is the number of **ticks** per quarter-note beat. The higher the resolution, the greater the representation of human feel that will be possible, though a resolution of 384 tpq is more than adequate for most purposes; a resolution of 96 tpq will suffice for heavily **quantized** music like house and techno. Also known as the timebase.

Some sequencers work in only one resolution and therefore they save your MIDI file in that resolution. Loading the MIDI file into a sequencer that will work only at a different resolution may cause a few events to be shifted by the odd tick, but this shouldn't usually be noticeable. For this reason however, General MIDI specifies a resolution of 96 tpq which is really the lowest common denominator: most events will stay just where they were put in any sequencer-resolution of 96 or higher.

A few sequencers can actually recognise the resolution of the file being loaded and will change their internal resolution to accommodate it.

Retriggering The act of playing the same note twice at the same time on the same channel. Not usually possible in live playing, other than on a guitar, it's usually caused by careless editing or overdubbing. It can cause glitching from the tone-generator and unexpected clipping of the notes in the sequencer.

RPN An abbreviation for **Registered Parameter Number**.

Running Status A method of data compression. MIDI messages contain a status byte to tell the tone-generator what kind of message is coming next (such as 'This is a note'). Running Status removes status bytes from long series of similar messages so that the tone-generator goes on expecting notes until it receives a different status byte. Running Status should normally be on, but can be turned off if you have problems (particularly with an older device which may not support it).

Sequencer A hardware device or a piece of computer software that loads, saves, records and plays MIDI data. Almost all sequencers have facilities to edit this data, but what they are and how they're implemented varies greatly according to a whole host of variables. As a programmer, your sequencer is your most important tool and you need to enjoy using it: a vast array of advanced features is rarely a worthwhile substitute for a friendly and intuitive interface.

Slave A device such as a tone-module or soundcard that's being controlled by a separate device (see Fig. 4 on page 33.)

SMF An abbreviation for Standard MIDI File, a universally-used **file-format**.

Soft MIDI Thru A neat little feature of sequencers in which the **MIDI Out** socket combines the characteristics of the **MIDI Thru**, and then some! When in record or playback mode, data already recorded will be transmitted, along with incoming ('live') data. The clever trick is that the live data is first passed through any **filters** or **rechannelize** and **controller remapping** functions selected allowing you to monitor an accurate representation of what's being recorded.

Song Body Think of your MIDI file as three separate units: the **song-header** (usually a single bar containing all the required setup events for the channels used), the count-in (also normally one bar) and the song itself – this last unit is called the 'body' of the file.

Song Header The first bar (or possibly more) of a file containing all the settings your tone-generator needs to play back the file with the correct sounds, volumes, etc. These settings may consist of **channel messages**, SysEx data, or a mixture of the two.

Split By Channel – *see* **Remix**.

Step-time recording is recording within one of the Edit modes (or a dedicated Step-Record mode) of your sequencer while the music is stopped. In other words, you're entering data manually one event at a time. It sounds laborious, and you probably wouldn't want to create a whole song that way, but MIDI programming almost always requires a combination of both step and **real-time** recording.

System Messages are MIDI events which don't inherently contain a channel-number but are directed to your MIDI system as a whole. They may contain a manufacturer's code and device number (in the case of System Exclusive) to alter a parameter in a single piece of equipment, or they may contain a global message (System Common/Real Time) to synchronize timing of the component parts of the system, or allow remote-control of audio or non-audio hardware.

Tape Dump A few hardware sequencers have no built-in disk-drive, and instead provide a socket to let you dump the sequence-data to cassette-tape. This isn't usually a quick process and has the added shortcoming that tape isn't the most reliable storage medium. To play back a file, therefore, it first has to be loaded from tape, or you have to record it in **real-time** to a separate MIDI file-player's disk-drive. Most sequencers using dump-to-tape also have a Verify function whereby you replay the tape-data to the sequencer to let it check the accuracy, so we're talking minutes for the whole routine here as opposed to mere seconds for a disk-save, but to skimp on the Verify procedure is obviously self-defeating.

Tick A more common word for 'pulse', as in Pulses Per Quarter Note. A tick is the smallest possible division of a beat, the amount of ticks per beat being referred to as the **resolution**. A resolution of 96 **tpq** means that each quarter-note beat is divided into 96 ticks.

Timebase Another word for a sequencer's **resolution** – so it may be said that General MIDI specifies a timebase of 96.

Tone-generator For the purposes of this book, a tone-generator is any **polyphonic**, **multi-timbral** MIDI synth, module or soundcard. More generally, the term is used for any instrument of musical sound-synthesis.

tpq Ticks Per Quarter Note. 96 tpq is the General MIDI default resolution, giving 96 separate divisions, or *ticks* per quarter-note beat. Also referred to as 'ppq' (for pulses per quarter-note). A few died-in-the-wool abbreviation fans even go so far as to stick an n on the end of either of these to make sure the word 'note' gets fair coverage.

Track Parameters – *see* **Playback Parameters**.

Transmit Channel Most MIDI instruments and **controllers** can be set to send their data on any one of the 16 MIDI channels – this is referred to as the transmit channel. Most instruments default to channel 1; for most applications it's easier to **rechannelize** at the sequencer-end rather than change this setting.

Trig-to-MIDI converter A piece of hardware which converts an electrical pulse from a drum-pad into a MIDI note message. Speed of conversion is obviously a vital consideration here: a good converter should carry out this operation in around 3 or 4 milliseconds.

Type 0, Type 1 – *see* **File Formats**.

Update Events – *see* **Chase Events**.

Velocity How hard the note is struck, which will affect the volume of the sound you hear. MIDI Velocity ranges from 1 to 127. Some early synthesizers (and many comparatively recent drum-machines) were velocity-sensitive, but with as few as eight levels compared with MIDI's 127. Others had no velocity sensitivity at all so the volume remained the same whatever you hit them with.

Voices The real measure of a tone-generator's potential is in the number of voices it can produce at once. If you play a chord that uses all your tone-generators voices and then add one more note, one of the earlier notes will be silenced so that its voice can be reassigned. In order to make some of their sounds richer or more exotic, manufacturers sometimes blend two or more voices to make a single sound. So, for example, if you use just dual-voice sounds from a device that is 24-voice **polyphonic**, you'll be able to play only 12 notes at a time. Some recent devices can produce 64 simultaneous voices.

Voice allocation This is the tone-generator's system governing how the total number of **voices** will be shared amongst the instruments playing. The old system was called 'Fixed Voice Allocation' and required the user to decide in advance how many voices to allocate to each channel – if a channel then needed more voices it wouldn't get them, even if no other instruments were playing. The later system, 'Dynamic Voice Allocation' allows voices to go wherever they're needed but assigns a note-priority to each channel, with the drums (channel 10) and lower-numbered channels having maximum priority and high-numbered channels having least. A few systems, such as Roland's **partial reserve**, use Dynamic Allocation but add a new twist on the old system: the user can specify a fixed number of voices for particular channels, but these are minimum allocations (as opposed to the maximum allocations of the old system).

XG Yamaha's extension to the General MIDI protocol, launched as an answer to Roland's **GS**.

Index

Becoming a Prentice Hall Author

Getting published with Prentice Hall

1. Can I do it?

It is easy to think of the publishing process as a series of hurdles designed to weed out would-be authors. That may be true of some publishing houses, but not Prentice Hall.

- ❑ We do all we can to encourage new talent.

- ❑ We welcome unsolicited manuscripts.

- ❑ We carefully examine every proposal we receive, and we always write back to let the authors know what we think of it.

Although many of our authors have professional or educational experience, we look first for a passion for computing. Some of our most successful books are written by first-time authors. If you have built up expertise in any computing-related topic, please get in touch. You'll be surprised how easy it is to get through.

2. Is Prentice Hall a successful company?

Prentice Hall is a highly respected brand in technical and scientific publishing, a status reflected in our relationships with the book trade and various professional bodies. Our reputation has been made with classic computing titles such as Kernighan and Ritchie's *The C Programming Language* (over two million copies sold) and Bertrand Meyer's ground-breaking *Object Oriented Software Construction*.

We're part of Simon & Schuster, a $2 billion dollar global publishing company. Simon & Schuster is host to Macmillan Computer Publishing, home of renowned computer imprints such as Sams, Que, Waite

Group Press, Ziff-Davis Publishing, Hayden and New Riders Press (NRP). Simon & Schuster is itself owned by Viacom Inc, one of the world's largest entertainment and publishing companies. Viacom owns film and tv studios (Paramount Pictures), world-wide cable networks (MTV, Nickelodeon) and retail outlets (Blockbuster Video).

3. What sort of books does Prentice Hall publish?

The computing revolution in the office and home has prompted a massive and diverse market for computer books. That diversity is reflected in our approach. We are happy to consider book proposals on absolutely any computing topic.

Essentially, Prentice Hall publishes books for anyone whose job or hobby connects them to a computer. We are already familiar with your intended readership, whether your book is written for professionals, students, enthusiasts or beginners. Our progressive editorial policy encourages new authors and gives us the flexibility required in a rapidly changing technological environment. However, we do have a 'books wanted' list – contact the editorial department for the latest copy.

4. What are the rewards of writing a book?

Prentice Hall royalty rates are among the most competitive in the industry, and many of our authors earn considerable sums through royalties. Payments are calculated along industry-standard guidelines, i.e., the author receives a percentage of the publisher's net sales revenue. We always offer preferential royalty rates for senior figures within the computing industry, or for books on hot topics written by experts. For the right book at the right time, the financial reward to the author can be extremely generous. This is especially true of books aimed at professional software developers.

If you are a computer professional or an academic, your livelihood depends upon your professional reputation. Successful Prentice Hall authors enjoy a constant stream of business and employment opportunities as a direct result of being published. A book works like a business card, advertising the author's talent across a vast network of potential contacts.

5. How do I know my ideas are good enough to publish?

In assessing the market-readiness of book proposals or finished manuscripts, Prentice Hall editors draw upon a huge database of technical advisors. All of our reviewers are senior figures in modern computing, and their role is to offer free advice to potential authors, highlighting both the strengths and weaknesses of proposals and manuscripts. The aim of the review process is to add value to your ideas, rather than just approving or rejecting them.

We understand that errors are inevitable when writing books, but as a Prentice Hall author you need not worry about the quality of your finished work. Many of our authors have not written a book before, so we are there to help – we scrutinise all our manuscripts for grammatical accuracy and style.

6. How much control would I have over my book?

We understand that a book is a highly personal statement from the author, so we invite your participation at all stages of the publishing process, from the cover design through to the final marketing plans. A Prentice Hall book is a co-operative venture between author and publisher.

7. Will I get any help with the technical aspects of book production?

Our highly professional staff will ensure that the book you envisaged is the book that makes it to the shelves. Once you hand over your manuscript to us, we will take care of all the technical details of printing and binding. Beyond the advice and guidance from your own editor, our 64-page *Author Guide* is there to help you shape your manuscript into a first-class book. Our large and efficient production department is among the quickest in the industry. We are experts at turning raw manuscripts into polished books, irrespective of the technical complexity of your work. Technical queries can be answered by your production contact, assigned, where relevant, to you at contract stage. Our production staff fully understand the individual requirements of every project, and will work with you to produce a manuscript format that best complements your skills – hard copy manuscripts, electronic files or camera-ready copy.

8. How quickly can you turn my manuscript into a book?

The production department at Prentice Hall is widely acknowledged to be among the quickest in the industry. Our turnaround times vary according to the nature of the manuscript supplied to us, but the average is about four months for camera-ready copy, five for electronic file manuscript. For time-sensitive topics, we can occasionally turn out books in under twelve weeks!

9. Where would my book be sold?

Prentice Hall has one of the largest sales forces of any technical publisher. Our highly experienced sales staff have developed firm business partnerships with all the major retail bookstores in Europe, America, Asia, the Middle East and South Africa, ensuring that your book receives maximum retail exposure. Prentice Hall's marketing department is responsible for ensuring the widest possible review coverage in magazines and journals – vital to the sales of computing books.

Our books are usually present at major trade shows and exhibitions, either on our own stands or those belonging to major retail bookshops. Our presence at trade shows ensures that your work can be inspected by the most senior figures within any given field of computing. We also have a very successful corporate and institutional sales team, dedicated to selling our books into large companies, user groups, book clubs, training seminars and professional bodies.

Local language translations can provide not only a significant boost to an author's royalty income, but also will allow your research/findings to reach a wider audience, thus furthering your professional prospects. To maintain both the author's and Prentice Hall's reputation, we license foreign-language deals only with publishing houses of the highest repute.

10. I don't have time to write a book!

To enjoy all the advantages of being a published author, it is not always necessary for you to write an entire book. Prentice Hall welcomes books written by multiple authors. If you feel that your skills lie in a very specific area of computing, or that you do not have the time to write an entire book, please get in touch regardless. Prentice Hall may have a book in progress that would benefit from your ideas.

You may know individuals or teams in your field who could act as co-author(s). If not, Prentice Hall can probably put you in touch with the right people. Royalties for shared-author books are distributed according to respective participation.

11. Could my company benefit?

Many Prentice Hall authors use their book to lever their commercial interests, and we like to do all we can to help. If a well-written book is an excellent marketing tool for an author, then it can also be an excellent marketing tool for the author's company. A book is its own highly focused marketing channel, a respected medium that takes your company name to all the right people. Previous examples of marketing opportunities with our books include:

- ❑ free advertising in the back pages
- ❑ packaging in suitable corporate livery (book covers, flyers, etc.)
- ❑ mounting software demos in the back page on disk or CDROM.

Although Prentice Hall has to keep its publications free of undue corporate or institutional bias, in general the options for cross-marketing are varied and completely open to discussion.

12. I have an idea for a book. What next?

We invite you to submit a book proposal. We need proposals to be formatted in a specific way, so if you have not received our guidelines, please contact the Acquisition Editor at this address:

Jason Dunne
Professional and Consumer Computing
Prentice Hall
Campus 400, Maylands Avenue
Hemel Hempstead, Herts.
HP2 7EZ
England

Tel: +44 (0)1442 882246
Fax: +44 (0)1442 252544

e-mail: jason_dunne@prenhall.co.uk

MIX n' MATCH Lite - The Ultimate Rhythm Construction Software!

If you liked the MIDI files that came with this book, you will be pleased to know that the author is offering further examples of his programming abilities!

Some of the most popular items on a programmer's shopping list are programming aids: collections of drum patterns, bass riffs, guitar rhythms and so on. However, the standard of programming can vary enormously. Often you find that the quality of the files does not meet your standards, or maybe you find your programming skills do not quite match the quality of the files. On top of that, it's not easy to try out bass riffs from one collection against drum patterns from another - and then you have still got to add keyboard and guitar parts...

MIX' n MATCH Lite - Takes the strain out of rhythm-programming!

Rob Young's MIX' n MATCH Lite is a unique collection of files containing riffs, rhythms, patterns and fills for four instrument groups - Drums, Bass, Rhythm Guitar and Keyboards, with styles including Rock, Latin, Ballad & Shuffle. A total of over 200 separate Phrases! Each file contains up to 20 Phrases: just un-mute one Phrase for each instrument and listen. If you don't like the bass-line, mute it again and try a different one, and so on. The result is a complete rhythm template from one file, ready for you to cut, paste & edit as desired to create your song. You can even move Phrases from one file to another giving almost unlimited scope. Or just copy individual Phrases into the song you're working on. MIX 'n MATCH Lite is also an endless source of new arrangement and songwriting ideas. MIX' n MATCH Lite is fully GM/GS/XG compatible and includes comprehensive on-disk manuals. MIX' n MATCH Lite files are supplied in two formats to give you maximum flexibility:

. A collection of Type 1 Standard MIDI Files for sequencers that can give access to at least 20 tracks of MIDI data.

. A collection of Cubase Arrangement (.ARR) files for use with Steinberg's range of Cubase sequencers. These files are compatible with Cubase 2.0 or higher for Atari computers; any Apple Mac version of Cubase except 1.83; any version of Cubase for Windows.

Price: £14.95 + shipping (£3.00 per order in the UK), $22.50 + shipping ($7.50 for each order outside the UK)

ISBN   013-2808765 (to be quoted on all orders)
----
* Please charge my Access/American Express/Visa/Diners Club/Mastercard/Switch the sum of £/$.........

ACCOUNT NO: EXPIRY DATE
VALID FROM DATE: ISSUE NUMBER (IF ANY):

ADDRESS:

----
* CHEQUE I enclose a cheque for £/$............ (payable to International Book Distributors)

Please return this form direct to: Wendy Botwright, Prentice Hall, Campus 400, Maylands Avenue, Hemel Hempstead, Herts, HP2 7EZ, ENGLAND TEL +44 (1442) 881900   FAX: +44 (1442) 257115

Designed and Programmed by Rob Young.